The Book of Destiny

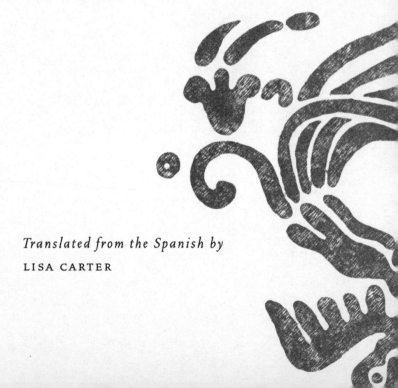

Translated from the Spanish by
LISA CARTER

CARLOS BARRIOS

The Book of Destiny

UNLOCKING THE SECRETS
of the Ancient Mayans and the Prophecy of 2012

HarperOne
An Imprint of HarperCollinsPublishers

HarperOne

Designed by Janet M. Evans

ISBN 978–0–06–157414–6

It is certainly interesting to know that we come from the stars, but even more interesting is the realization that we're part of the cosmos. Although we might only be a speck in the immensity of the universe, we are the Great Father's children, and our destiny is linked to that of creation. Every being has a role to play, a destiny to fulfill, and so every bit of existence is transcendent.

—DON ISIDRO,
Mayan sage

CONTENTS

INTRODUCTION

There is a place in the world where the meaning of creation remains intact. The magnificence of being, the essence and awareness of existence, and the knowledge of our life purpose are the roots of this safe haven. Alienation and aimlessness have been kept at bay. We can still feel the energies that traverse the infinite cosmos and those from the eternal fire in the heart of Mother Earth. Here we teach our children to respect everything that exists because our Grandfathers knew that nothing on this Earth belongs to us. Everything was planted by the Great Father and the Great Mother, and there is a Natural Order that governs us.

Our ancestors, the great sages, lit the sacred fire thousands of years ago, and it has never been extinguished. It is our light, the warmth of our spirit. It is the flame that connects us to the Heart of Sky. These wise men handed down the science of the cosmos and led us down the path of life, the Spiral of Creation, the cycles of *najt*, or space-time, where reality becomes manifest. This knowledge is the legacy they received from the first Fathers. This awareness of life, reality, and their connection to the cosmos allowed them to develop a guide, a way to behave as influenced by the energy of each day, and this guide affects every one of us. Their cosmo-vision—that is, their view of time and space based on a philosophy of harmonious coexistence with nature—is the truth behind creation, the truth regarding human existence. It teaches us to live in harmony with nature and to respect every life form, beginning with ourselves.

For the Maya, the famous date of December 21, 2012, marks the beginning of the fifth cycle of 5,200 years called *Job Ajaw*, or the Fifth Sun. This potentially apocalyptic date is the beginning of a change in consciousness, a time when a new socioeconomic order will arise in harmony with Mother Earth.

Just as the world did not end in the year 2000 at the start of the new millennium, it won't end with the advent of *Job Ajaw* in 2012. An unfounded fear was created before the new millennium by religious leaders who based their theories on misguided interpretations of ancient religious texts and predictions made by famous prophets. The same fear is rising again. The true guardians of our tradition have never been consulted about this date, but we are here to say: *December 21, 2012, will not be the end of the world or the end of humanity.* In fact, it will be the start of a period in which harmony, understanding, peace, and wisdom can reign. The prophecy says that during *Job Ajaw* we will move toward a harmonious

Natural Order so that both the Earth and humanity can attain the next stage of evolution.

We are reaching a transcendent period as predicted by many of the world's great traditions and visionaries. Now we have the opportunity to ascend spiritually together with Mother Earth. The Maya speak of such prophetic times when either this transcendence will be possible or we will self-destruct.

Mayan prophecies of events during this period have been astonishingly exact. The prophecies regarding the war in Iraq, the attack on the Twin Towers, conflicts such as those between India and Pakistan and between Israel and Palestine, the tsunamis, earthquakes, and floods are just a few examples. The predictions that have not yet come to pass are even more catastrophic—*but there is time to change the outcome!* Our Grandfathers warn of calamities and the possible destruction of a large part of humankind so that we can change such events. The Mayan Elders want to caution us that we must live in harmony, become aware, stop polluting, and safeguard our natural resources. The damage we have already done to Mother Earth is more than obvious.

Very little attention has been paid to the importance of earlier cycles, particularly the end of this one, *Kajib Ajaw*, or the Fourth Sun. It is during this period—right now—when we run the greatest risk of large-scale conflicts and natural disasters. The catastrophic side of the prophecy has unfortunately been misinterpreted as an inexorable, apocalyptic event. It is within our power, however, to prevent this from happening. We may be facing the self-destruction of much of humanity, but an ever-increasing number of us are also aware of the damage we have caused to the environment and what we must do to change this.

Somewhere along the way, Western society began to assume that human beings have the right to dominate plants, animals, even each other. The result of this materialist outlook is an economic, ecological, social, and moral crisis that has caused the downfall of other cultures.

Humankind has achieved a level of technological development that has enslaved us instead of helping us. This has led to our lack of awareness and tendency to value a person for his or her material possessions. We have forgotten what is most important—our life purpose. We have distanced ourselves from nature. We no longer make time for ourselves but seek distractions, in an effort to avoid looking inward, preventing us from evolving as human beings. Alienation has taken hold, and our actions are based on illusions.

Wars are breaking out as a result of intolerance and religious fundamentalism. We continue to exploit countries and natural resources for financial and political gains, blaming our aggressiveness on potential nuclear conflict. Even more alarming, thousands of people still die every day as a result of war, hunger, and disease while governments and we as individuals simply look the other way. How can there be so many murders and rapes and so much gang violence? How can we as humans exploit one another to such an extent? How do entire countries spin into chaos? How can we enlist children to be soldiers in wars they do not understand, to fight battles that are not theirs to fight? Why are so many of our seniors and mentally ill homeless? Why do we need to take prescription or illegal drugs just to get through the day? We are confused and directionless, and our political and religious leaders have no answers because they are lost as well.

It is no wonder that a drugged and alienated existence has become the norm. Unless we can find a balance between materialism and spirituality, we are doomed to be the victims of our own destiny! Could this be the reason for our fatalistic lifestyle, the reason why we wait impassively for humanity's disastrous end? Is this why we would rather envision the end of the world than take responsibility for our future?

At the rate we are going, a large part of humanity will disappear. This will not happen in 2012 but in the years leading up to this date as one cycle ends and another begins. This period is when we are in the most danger.

Although the Maya have known for centuries what our future holds, the Elders have felt that the world is not ready to use the information in a positive way and have kept much of their knowledge secret. Our Mayan Grandfathers' main objective in authorizing this book is to clarify these prophecies and thereby orient humanity.

Another purpose of this book is to introduce readers to Mayan spirituality, cosmo-vision, and teachings. I have used my own experiences and the stories told by my beloved masters, Don Pascual Mendoza and Don Isidro Akabal, to explain their view of the world and these prophetic times. Mayan philosophy is not looking for followers; ours is a tradition, not a religion. We are not a sect but a sector, and we simply present our cosmo-vision while respecting all other traditions. One of the first things I learned along the Mayan path was not to judge or compete, much less impose. We believe in respect.

Katun

Finally, the book includes an introduction to the sacred *Cholq'ij* calendar, around which the Mayan world revolves. An extraordinary legacy to humanity, it synthesizes the ancient Maya's wisdom while also serving as a useful, transcendent instrument that anyone can use. This sacred calendar presents the order of the energies that affect each day and, more specifically, the energy we were born under, which serves as a guide for our life purpose. The *Cholq'ij* is the key to becoming fully realized. If we use it, we can find our place in the world, understand our strengths and weaknesses, and shape our lives in order to reach our full potential and fulfill our reason for being.

This reference to our past enables us to forecast our destiny as individuals and as a people. I present this tradition here as it was told to me; some of it is based solely on the oral tradition, so some scholars may call it a myth or legend. Still, it is our tradition, and we believe it is an important part of human history.

By presenting this story without sources to back it, I realize that academics will doubt its credibility. My response is that we have the best reference of all: this is a tale told by an ancient people who have maintained their historical memory in various ways and have no interest in competing with anyone. Reality is the story our Grandfathers have passed down for thousands of generations during which, quite amazingly, not one word has ever been added or deleted.

MAYAN TRUTHS

The greatest truths, the simplest and loveliest things, are free. All the money in the world cannot buy the enchantment of mist-shrouded trees, the sun setting in the distance, and the varied hues reflecting on the soft, rippling waters of a magical lake. We see the world through the magnificence of creation, and thousands of such majestic realities exist, from the smile on a child's face to a butterfly on a stalk of grass. This is the way to experience life! When we take the time to feel, to absorb, this is when we start down the path of self-discovery, exploring our inner space in harmony with all existence. This is where we embark on the journey to become one with the immensity of creation.

The present-day Maya have witnessed their ancestors' prophecies come true. Western religions have forgotten their essence and become embroiled in the struggle for power and material wealth. Their followers are now lost in an endless labyrinth, desperate to rid their lives of dogma and to find a new direction.

Using both cosmic and terrestrial influences, the Maya find a path that follows the Natural Order based on a respect for Mother Nature. Such respect can be summarized in a single word: harmony.

Our first Grandfathers acquired this knowledge in the mythical Tulán—the Mayans' mother civilization—and spoke of reality as a manifestation on three levels: the underworld, the world, and the overworld. All of these, in turn, are manifest in *najt*, or space-time.

The ancient Maya sent emissaries into the world to share this knowledge—the key to development as both individuals and a community—in order to shape this new being. All Maya, as well as all those with a true desire to grow and evolve in harmony, are the rightful heirs to such knowledge.

The sacred *Cholq'ij* calendar is the key to this understanding and growth. It offers us the opportunity to become self-realized according to our individual capabilities, to increase our understanding of ourselves, and to relate to the energies that manifest each day.

A more enlightened humanity is anxious to achieve real, conscious growth. The Mayan tradition offers genuine answers to this need for active evolution. Today's Maya can guide this new humanity on a course to a more harmonious world that respects the Earth. The imminent arrival of the new prophetic cycle, *Job Ajaw*, a period of 5,200 years beginning on December 21, 2012, will bring future generations their rightful legacy: a return to a state of awareness.

DON ISIDRO AND DON PASCUAL

While I was at the university, the opportunity arose to do some fieldwork in Todos Santos Cuchumatanes in the highlands of Guatemala. The work was being led by a professor of sociology who was studying the indigenous people and I thought it would be a good opportunity to meet the descendants of the Maya *in situ*. I had always been interested in the ancestral cultures and was curious to see to what extent they had preserved the grandeur and wisdom of their illustrious forefathers. In that paradise I met my mentor and guide, Don Pascual, leader of the Eagle Clan, one of the most important clans to survive from time immemorial. Along with Jaguar Men and Coyote Knights, these three clans have preserved the science, calendars, and spirituality of the Maya.

In the traditional Mayan world, there are three ways to become an *Ajq'ij*, or spiritual guide. The first is through inheritance within the family line; second, the skill can be developed according to one's birth sign; or third, the Grandfathers may see specific indications that a person should develop these talents. Don Pascual was a wise heir of the purest tradition, and when I was just seventeen years old, he agreed to take me under his wing. A relationship grew between us based on mutual curiosity that would later become an extremely close friendship between master and disciple.

We first met early one cold, foggy morning when it was impossible to see more than a few feet away. Wandering aimlessly, I suddenly came upon a man carrying some candles. At first I thought he was using them to light his way through the fog, although that seemed ridiculous. As I got closer, I realized that he was speaking in his native language to a monolithic stone representing a Mayan figure that was half-human and half-jaguar. I was completely taken aback, and my initial reaction was to ask mockingly whether the rock would answer his prayers.

His simple, clear reply reflected a dignity and understanding that can only be acquired through experience and a life lived to the fullest. "Young man," he said to me, "I don't criticize the way you dress, your long hair, or your upbringing, so carry on and let me do the same."

"I'm sorry," I managed to say. "I didn't mean to offend you. I'm just curious. Why are you worshiping that stone? As far as I know, there's only one God, and it's not exactly that rock."

He introduced himself as Don Pascual and then said, "See here, young man: no matter how great, powerful, and just the gods are, *they're of no use if they're far away*. Mine are here. This stone that you mock represents the god placed here on Earth to help us. I ask for his intervention to stop the wind or for good rains, and he has never let me down. He might not be the Supreme Being, but his energy helps and protects us. He's not a severe, punishing god.

He's like our father, our friend, our brother. Although we might not understand him if he spoke to us, he does answer our prayers and solve our problems. That is his power and his mystery. The Great Father put him here. He acts as his assistant. He's the authority, and he speaks with the Father."

What could I say to such a succinct reply based on a vision completely different from anything I had ever learned? I didn't know how to answer, but he had piqued my interest. I thanked him and introduced myself. "My name's Carlos," I said, "and I'm a student with the university group. I'm sorry if I offended you. I'd like to learn about the Maya."

Thus began a relationship that would last for many years. In time, Don Pascual confessed that he had been given a sign moments before I arrived. The fire spoke to him, and that was why he spoke to me the way he did; that was why he decided to draw me in with his vision. For many years I split my time between the university and the mountains, where I followed the Mayan tradition.

From a Western point of view, Don Pascual would be considered nearly illiterate—it would take him half an hour to read a page, let alone write one—and yet he was one of the wisest men I have ever known. Having inherited the wisdom of his ancestors and masters, he became chief of the Eagle Clan, which had approximately 1,500 members in the late 1970s. Don Pascual was a *Chi-Mam*, or Mayan priest, from the Mam tribe, one of the most ancient groups of Mayan people. A strict traditionalist, he knew how to manipulate fog, wind, water, and fire and was an incredible visionary. He was also known as a *pulsista*, or pulse-taker— someone who can describe a person's life by simply feeling the blood pulsing through his or her veins.

Don Pascual is the Grandfather who taught me divinatory techniques. He was a man of power, and he was my guide for many years, revealing the secrets and knowledge of his ancestors. His school has used the same teachings for hundreds of years. A jealously guarded tradition, only recently has it become more open to people of other races and nationalities. He was a man of iron discipline, a pacifist, and a conservationist; his kindness and service to his community earned him the respect of his people. His disciples acknowledge him as the greatest heir to Mayan knowledge.

I later established a relationship with Don Isidro, a friend of my father's. He was a professional in various disciplines and had one of the largest private libraries I have ever seen. He agreed to let me use it and to tutor me. This not only helped me with my studies but also gave me the opportunity to learn from another of the wisest men in the Mayan world.

Don Isidro was a scientist, an extraordinarily learned man who had a postgraduate degree in international law and had studied oil and gas law as well as geology, anthropology, and economics. He spoke twenty-six Mayan languages, several Romance and Germanic languages, and he even knew dead languages such as Latin, classical Greek, Aramaic, and Sanskrit. He also loved poetry.

Much more reserved and secretive than Don Pascual, in part because of his cultural background, it took me years to gain Don Isidro's confidence. At first we spoke only of intellectual matters. It was not until I had known him for fifteen years that he invited me to a ceremony for the first time and introduced me to the clan in which he was third in line of succession. His own master, Don Justiniano, was a great prophet and visionary.

Don Isidro's talks spanned the breadth of universal knowledge. This wise Maya was a great thinker, philosopher, and keeper of his tradition. An expert calendarist, he knew all twenty of the Mayan calendars, thirteen of them to perfection, including the sacred *Cholq'ij*, or *Tzolkin*, calendar. As an *Ajq'ij*, he dominated the disciplines of earth and fire and was one of the few who had inherited the knowledge to manipulate the energies of the pyramids. Don Isidro was also one of the last *Halach-Winic*, or Mayan rulers, descended from Q'eqchi royalty in Cahabón in northern Guatemala.

These two men were my guides: Don Pascual, with his pragmatic natural wisdom, and Don Isidro, who knew as much about the Maya as he did about Western civilization.

DON PASCUAL'S VISION

The Mayan cosmo-vision is an attitude, an approach to life; it is the way in which we learn to live with our perceptions of reality. Everything is integral; nothing is isolated from the sequence of life. Every action is connected to, and forms part of, the cosmic forces, the manifestation of nature and telluric energy. This convergence arises out of a state of universal consciousness. Existence is a continuum, and our insertion into reality is a mystery. It is the power of the Creator and Maker, the connection between the three levels of reality: the underworld, the world, and the overworld. Each of these manifests as energy and is associated with a direction, possessing properties that lead to specific tendencies. *This entire manifestation of creation occurs in* najt, *or space-time.*

Everything that exists is part of this tapestry, said Don Pascual. We are just one thread in this wonder we call existence. We inhabit a reality shaped and modeled after the cosmos, and we vibrate in tune with the movement of the stars. This reality exists only in *najt* and disappears the second we stop the wheel of *k'atunes*, or the spiral of time. Life-evolution is the journey along this infinite path, and when we interrupt this movement, we find the antithesis of existence. We find other dimensions by stopping time, and this is achieved in dreams or in absolute stillness.

The ceremonial centers built by our Grandfathers are convergence points between the underworld, the world, and the overworld, and these temples interrupt reality as we know it in different ways.

"When I was with my master," Don Pascual said, "I asked him where we got the figures that represent our numbers. 'From us,' he told me, and this will clarify a few things for you. The dot that represents one unit is a fingertip. When five of these are combined, it is the hand in a horizontal position or line. When the eye is closed, the same line is formed. This is very important. We blink every five seconds. This is the time it takes the mind to reconfigure the world. If we stop blinking for a while and 'see without seeing' or don't focus on anything, reality begins to fall apart. You have to have a great deal of power and strength to do this, of course, because a tremendous fear takes hold when reality starts to disappear. That's why we blink—so as not to lose contact with what's real. We must always remember that *reality is from the eyes inward and illusion is from the eyes outward.*"

WHO ARE THE MAYA?

This question has intrigued all of humanity, and scholars in particular, given the Maya's scientific and mathematical achievements, the perfection of their calendars, and now the dissemination of their prophecies and the Western world's discovery of their deep spirituality. What is known about this civilization comes from archaeological research and historical sources (mainly pre-Columbian documents and those from the early years of Spanish colonization), as well as from the oral tradition. The former are often mired in a series of speculations; the latter sheds the most light on the mystery of this magnificent civilization.

Sadly, most of what is widely known about the Maya is based on unverifiable stories told by Spanish chroniclers during the conquest. These documents were written by priests who had Mayan informants, but even though these Mayans helped the Spaniards, they never revealed the essence of their origins, much less their true knowledge.

Scholars, anthropologists, archaeologists, and historians have all formulated theories about the emergence of this civilization and have speculated on the dates of its evolution. Not one of these investigators, however, was a Mayan, nor have any of them ever asked the heirs to this tradition about their origins. Quite erroneously, researchers have believed that nothing more than ethnicity connects the Maya of today to such a complex, magnificent past.

Accurate accounts of the Maya's origin and arrival on this continent can be found, however, in what are known as the sacred books. These include the *Popol Vuh*, the *Annals of the Kaqchikeles* (also known as the *Memorial of Sololá*), the *Title of the Lords of Totonicapán*, and the *Books of Chilam Balam*, all of which survived the conquest. These stories were written by the Maya before the conquest and then transcribed into Latin script after the first Maya to be converted learned this writing system from the Spanish priests. The stories sound repetitive or confused at times, but we must remember that the language used at that time is difficult to translate for today's reader.

Staff, Standard of Teotihuacán

PROPHECIES

Humans have always been intrigued by visions of the future. Everyone, at one time or another, has wanted to know what was going to happen to them. Most see this as impossible today, while others may smile, but in the end we're all paying attention because deep down the memory of the future remains. No one can deny that there have been great visionaries throughout history; they're not isolated cases. We believe this is great knowledge, and whoever is born with this ability has a duty to develop it. Our prophets are learned, traditional people.

—DIONISIO YACOC,
Q'anjob'al *visionary*

On my spiritual quest, prophecies motivated me more than anything else. As I have said, after forays into various spiritual schools and traditions, I gained access to two Mayan sages who became my guides: Don Isidro, an extremely learned man, descended from one of the most important royal lines in the Q'eqchi world, and Don Pascual, a shaman from the Mam tribe, chief of the Eagle Clan, and heir to the purest Mayan tradition.

Both of these Grandfathers were known to have inherited Mayan knowledge—Don Pascual's came from tradition and his contact with the Natural Order, while Don Isidro was a scholar and heir of ancestral Mayan science and technology.

The late 1970s were a difficult time in Guatemala because a civil war was raging. Don Pascual, Don Isidro, and other visionary wise men would predict or warn of danger on a local level as well as of events in the rest of the world. I was

Mrs. Xoc of Yaxchilán before her vision

curious to know how the Maya prophesied and tried to find out everything about the prophetic act in an effort to rationalize and understand it, but these two guides usually evaded my questions.

It wasn't until many years later that I understood, when Don Isidro explained that the Spanish word *profeta*, meaning "prophet," comes from Latin and can be broken down into the constituent parts *pro*, which means "for" or "in favor of," and *fe*, which means "the act of believing in something divine or inexplicable." Thus, prophecy involves an act of belief in someone who sees what we cannot: the future.

The ability to project events yet to happen comes by studying the occult, something that is out of most people's reach. The main resource for projection is astrology, the science that focuses on the relationship between the stars, our planet, and its inhabitants. An age-old discipline, it has been practiced by all of the great civilizations. Each culture used different techniques according to its traditions, but they all centered on the cosmic-human relationship. Just a few of the many ways of seeing the future are seeing visions in crystal balls and revelations through dreams, trances, and visions in a cauldron.

In Europe, this knowledge had to be hidden, which led to the establishment of secret societies. In the dark days of the Inquisition, practicing the magic arts or trying to learn things beyond what the Church wanted to teach was considered an act of disobedience, disloyalty to the Holy Church, and therefore the work of the devil. This was the basis for a witch-hunt that left thousands dead and instilled such terror that these sciences were no longer taught in public and the subversive occult schools came about. A generalized sense of fear led to the creation of myths surrounding these disciplines and those who practiced them. However, there has been a resurgence of these sciences now that the thirst for true knowledge is no longer dormant in much of humanity, including a resurgence of the science of astrology in order to bring the mysteries of the future to light.

"In essence," Don Isidro told me, "the act of prophesying is the ability to access a memory of the future. It is a matter of being able to move in space and time."

During the ancestral Mayan Classic Period, all of the visionaries, fortune-tellers, and astrologers would gather every fifty-two years to conceive the path their people would take. They would determine whether the cosmic and telluric energies were favorable in the established ceremonial centers and cities; then they would share their discoveries. Prophecy and divination are inherent parts of the Mayan tradition.

The world's oldest traditions, particularly the Mayan, Chinese, and Hindu, all speak of repetitive cycles. A specific amount of time elapses before the constellations and stars return to their original position. As one would expect, in a cycle where conditions are the same again and again, the astrological and energy conditions influence the planet and human beings in similar ways each time.

A number of prophecies from various traditions mention the same dates for the times we are currently living in: the Great Pyramid of Giza in Egypt; the prophecies of Saint Malaquias; those of Nostradamus, the most famous visionary of all times; the modern prophet Edgar Cayce; and perhaps the most accurate visionary ever, the Argentine Benjamin Solari Parravicini. Though perhaps less well known, prophecies by the Hopi, Navajo, and Lakota people are all equally correct and coincidental.

Walking through the imposing forests of the Cuchumatanes Mountains, I once asked Don Pascual how one prophesies.

He replied, "The first way refers to a talent. There are those who are born with the gift of sight. They can channel their sensations and premonitions based on the feeling that something is going to happen and then turn to the sacred calendar in order to make a projection. Such people may have a dream about an event. They don't know the exact date; they just know what's going to happen. That's when they turn to the *Cholq'ij* to find possible days when an element related to the vision could cause harm."

For example, if the vision is of a plane crash, we look for days when there is more interference with the Air element and make a prediction using the Mayan Cross—the sign for a particular day, including its conception sign, destiny sign, left hemisphere, and right hemisphere. We then direct it at a specific place where there is more concentrated negative energy. It's a way of combining a person's ability with the technology contained in the sacred calendar.

The *Cholq'ij* contains 260 energies that are influenced by Fire, Earth, Air, and Water during specific periods. There may be combinations of energies depending on the day. For example, there are Water signs in which the energy means Air, such as *Imox*. There are two ways of doing this using the *Cholq'ij* to predict events. The first is the one we have just mentioned: a person who has a vision uses the calendar to analyze that vision. The other is by reviewing the past, looking at the conditions and dates when events similar to the predicted one occurred.

Some people born under the signs *Tz'ikin, Imox, Iq', and Kan* are extremely intuitive, visionaries who can see the exact date something will happen. People such as these simply use the calendar to corroborate their forecasts.

The second prophesying technique uses the sacred *tz'ite*, perhaps the most ancient form of divination used by humans, dating back over 200,000 years. The *Pixom Q'aq'al*, or Sacred Pouch, is worn by and symbolizes the *Ajq'ijab'* (spiritual guides). It contains objects required for divination and cures, such as pieces of obsidian, quartz, and other stones, as well as seeds from the *tz'ite*, or coral tree. In divination, the *tz'ite* combines the energies of the various objects. First, a handful of seeds are taken at random and divided into groups that are placed in rows. These are counted out with respect to the day's energies according to the sacred *Cholq'ij* calendar. This way the *Ajq'ij'* can clearly see what, when, where, and why a particular event is going to happen and can then use a specific technique to determine months, days, hours, or minutes. The *tz'ite* is incredibly precise.

The third way of prophesying is by seeing visions in a cauldron of water similar to the one Nostradamus used. A base is made from three different pieces of wood, and the cauldron  set on top is filled with pure water—collected from dew or a natural spring. This water alone has power, but certain elements are added in order to concentrate the vision. Whole pieces of mercury or quartz, or ground quartz, are sprinkled into the cauldron. Once the energies have combined, the visions begin to appear as if a movie were being shown.

This divinatory technique has been used by various cultures. Both the Celts and the Vikings used it for the same purpose. The difference in the Americas was the use of three different types of wood for the three sticks at the base of the cauldron.

Another technique parallel to this one is the reading of stones, most commonly quartz. The diviner's eyes make one clockwise rotation known as a *dexbogiro* and one counterclockwise rotation known as a *lexbogiro*. At this point, the diviner goes into a trance, and images begin to appear in the stone, narrating the story we want to know about.

Although it is generally thought that rough quartz is the best for this technique, our Grandfathers tend to use the most polished, transparent quartz that still has a special cloudiness inside, known as *fantasmita*, or "little ghost." Another very powerful stone is obsidian, which needs to be in the shape of a ball to be read.

Finally, there is the sacred *Cholq'ij* calendar, which provides answers on its own. We can analyze events that happened in the past and correlate them with events in the future. Since the universe is a macrospiral, the same energy returns every 20 days. Therefore, we know exactly what the energy was 20 or 52 years ago, since these are distinct cycles. The greatest manifestations of energy are every 13, 20, 73, 260, and 520 years. The big cycles bring powerful energy.

The *Books of Chilam Balam*, for example, use the *Ajaw* cycles. They begin on *Ajpu* or *Ajaw* days and keep a record of events. In this sacred book we see cycles of twenty years, or *k'atunes*, and the *k'atunes* determine what is going to happen. These books were kept in cities where energy was going to be present. Energy moves, and therefore every year different places are known as energy centers or epicenters, which results in a series of traditions. The epicenter is where the energy cycle opens up, and the larger it is, the greater the magnitude of events in a particular region. It is therefore extremely important to know precisely where the center is located. For the upcoming cycle in 2012, the energy center in Guatemala is Zaculeu and the Cuchumatanes mountain range in Huahuetenango. This tells us that the extent of the changes will not be as great there as in the rest of the world.

There are different energy centers in various parts of the world, each with a greater or lesser intensity. Our Grandfathers made their projections based on past cycles and, as a result, were able to determine where this energy center would be. Energy returns to the same place every 520 years, while events are repeated every 52 years.

Earth monster

The question of the Maya's whereabouts usually arises at this point. It is important to note that the Maya did not disappear. Every fifty-two years they would extinguish all of the fires during the period of the *Wayeb* (a period of five days during which Mayans look within in order to see what's ahead in the coming cycle.) and begin to fast and do penance, and the Grandfathers would have visions. They would eat the seven sacred plants in order to tune their spiritual connection, and when they relit the fire, they would cast a fortune using the seeds of the *tz'ite*.

During these ceremonies, it was decided whether the people would stay in that particular place or whether it was better to move elsewhere. If it was favorable to move, the Maya would emigrate and found new cities. The Aztecs searched for over two thousand years before they found Tenochtitlán, and the same happened with other tribes. The Maya who built Mayapán later moved and founded Tayasal. Those who inhabited Tikal left to found Kumarkaj and then divided. Those who were in Tula split, some heading north to Arizona with the Hopi Indians, while others moved to what is now Guatemala City and then later moved south into the Sierra Nevada de Santa Marta in what is now Colombia before going on to the Andes in Ecuador, Peru, and Bolivia.

The importance of Tikal lies in the fact that it was the meeting place for envoys from all Mayan settlements. The Grandfathers would meet there every fifty-two years and agree on what should be done. Each tribe would present the progress it had made over the past fifty-two years when the tribes had lived apart. Mathematicians would come from Copán and present their discoveries, analyses, and all they had come to understand during that period of time. The other Grandfathers would learn from them and also present what they had to contribute. At this meeting, topics such as trepanations for the use of brain hemispheres, art, and visions were discussed. It was where the Mayan tribes would share and prophesy. During that time they would also analyze the prophecies and carry out correlations of time. This, then, is the fourth form of prophesying, and the way in which a prophecy can be announced with certainty.

To summarize, prophecies that are intuited go through a process of corroboration: dates and energies are analyzed in the sacred calendar and submitted to the Grandfathers to determine their veracity. This is particularly true of predictions that will affect not just the Maya but all of humanity.

After absorbing this information, I wondered whether it was possible to change the course of a prophecy, and so I asked Don Pascual.

"That's an ambiguous question," he said, "and therefore hard to answer. We know that the impact of the event can be changed. It can be minimized, steps can be taken to prevent it from having a widespread effect, but the event itself can't be altered. Take a tsunami, for example. This is going to happen no matter what. However, if we know it's coming, people can move away from the area of greatest impact and thus minimize the damage, at least in terms of human loss. In addition, if everyone who recognizes his or her own power concentrates on consciously manipulating the energy, this could reduce the size of the wave."

It is important to stress that we all have the power to prophesy, but we need to be in tune with ourselves to do it. That's the difficult part, especially if we take into account that in the West we have been raised to believe that it's impossible for anyone to see the future.

Throughout human history, great civilizations such as the Egyptians, Assyro-Babylonians, and Hindus have used prophecies for the same purpose as the Maya. Assyro-Babylonian astrology could predict the tiniest details and events in a person's life. If a person is truly aware of a coming occurance and doesn't act, the consequences will be much greater than if he or she had paid attention and done something to mitigate the effects of the event.

It must also be noted that prophetic techniques are being used today, in the West, even for transcendent decisions that affect the course of civilization. World leaders often use this technique, but it's not something that is made public. In truth, almost anything that could be described as mystical is frowned upon in the West, whether it's used by those in power or by the common man. Magic has long had a certain stigma that makes it seem worthless, forbidden, even diabolical. And yet, who doesn't want to know what is going to happen, especially when it involves decisions that will affect large interests? Those in power know how, when, and where to act. They are aware of the great cycles of energy and use this to their advantage, but keep such knowledge a secret.

This censorship of information began hundreds of years ago with the Holy Inquisition, when the persecution and killing of witches, wise men, and fortune-tellers left Western society without spiritual direction. It's interesting to note that the Spanish word *bruja*, meaning "witch," comes from the word *brújula*, or compass: the function of both is to guide us.

Witches knew how to use plants medicinally; their magic potions formed the basis of today's pharmacopoeia. They were well versed in astrology and used oracular methods such as palmistry, cards, and candles to predict future events. They were famous for being visionaries and highly in tune with the energies. There were, of course, those who used this knowledge for negative purposes, but many used these positive energies and techniques to benefit their communities. During the Holy Inquisition, the methodical elimination of such people resulted in syncretism and, worse still, spiritual alienation based on fear. Those in power used such practices solely for their own benefit and to subjugate the people.

Years later, Don Pascual spoke to me about the prophetic act. "Delving into the future requires higher knowledge. It's not for everyone. There was a time when all humans could see long-range in both space and time. This was the vision of *najt*. Our Fathers in the Sky saw that men were like gods: they created miracles, their breath was like the wind, and nothing was hidden from their eyes. Great was their presence on the Earth, and great were their powers. At the same time, their pride grew and their downfall came when they forgot their Creator and Maker.

"'This isn't right,' our Fathers thought. 'We didn't create beings who only think of themselves.' And so they blew on their creatures' eyes and created a mist. 'Let them see,' the gods thought, 'but only a short distance. Let the future be their mystery, their need. But those who remember their creation, who remember their origin, who turn to their Creator and Maker, who have a just cause and purpose, will see again!' So said the Creator and Maker. This was their thought, and this is their mandate.

"There are two elements to seeing the future that necessarily go hand in hand. One of these is precision. As I've said before, the cycles repeat. There is duality in *najt*. It's like the wooden bars in a marimba: the sound of one can be similar to another, but one will be lower or deeper and the other higher or sharper. Even though they're not the same timbre, one will resonate like the other.

"My Grandfather described it as being like a coiled snake. At a certain point, the same body is in several rings, all of which are visible, in the same position, facing the same direction. In other words, at this point one body folds and is repeated two, three, or more times. This is how it is with every fold in time: there is a similarity between events.

"Those who understand the calendar counts and the *k'atunic* [twenty-year] and *tunic* [one-year] cycles, and who learn precision when adjusting the Long and Short Count calendars, will possess the most highly prized instrument for seeing and establishing events that are yet to come. They will be able to see the future.

"The other element of the future is through the vision of a sign. Everyone has a propensity for certain things, according to his or her sign. This comes from the *nawales* that protect and give a person his or her internal powers. Whoever has the gift of intuition, visions, or dreams has an obligation to develop that gift, but it requires training. The elder visionaries see to this, teaching the person this magical knowledge. Those who learn precision, when added to the vision of a sign, will in time become prophets.

"This is not the only form of divinatory knowledge. We also have our sacred *tz'ite*, the oldest form of finding answers to questions about the past or the future. This is our Sacred Pouch and consists of the mystery of divine stones, the shape of a lightning bolt or *chay* [kernels of corn] and seeds from the *tz'ite* [coral tree]. When *Ajq'ijab'* cast a fortune, we watch how the seeds of the coral tree fall, and this provides the answer to our questions.

"This is the most ancient form of divination known to man, and it is described in our sacred book, the *Popol Vuh*. Our first Grandparents, Ixmukane and Ixpiyakok, father twice over, mother twice over, cast the *tz'ite* to confirm how to make human beings, what material to use, how they would look and behave. This tradition has been maintained for thousands and thousands of years.

"You, my children, my disciples, will learn to use this Sacred Pouch, but it is not for your amusement. It is to allay the doubts and fears of the afflicted who will come to consult with you about their problems.

"There is also another, more mysterious way of prophesying only used by *Ajq'ijab'* who are favored by I'ki' B'alam, the power of Water, and that is the cauldron on a base of three sticks.

"'Cast a fortune with corn and *tz'ite*, and it will be done. "Will they turn out, will we carve them, look, will we chisel their mouths and faces out of wood?" So said the Creator and Maker to the diviners.

"'And then the fortune was cast, the being hailed, using their corn and *tz'ite*. So replied an Old Man and an Old Woman: Ixpiyakok, the old diviner of the *tz'ite*, and Ixmukane, the old fortune-teller of the Sun [*Popol Vuh*].'

"This technique has mostly been preserved deep in the jungle. The sticks that support or act as the cauldron's legs are from three different trees that have been cut with the blessing of Grandmother Moon. The purity of the water, taken with absolute respect from a natural source, is what allows us to have a vision. This water is poured into the cauldron, and the clearest images will be seen of both the past and the future. The cauldron will only reveal its secret to the purest souls; only they will be endowed with this wisdom."

These teachings from my beloved masters, as well as all of the other knowledge they have imparted to us, come from ancient wisdom passed down the family line, preserved unchanged over time.

Prophecy is an inherent part of the Mayan world. The cycles and our Elders' highly developed ability to envision the future have been fundamental to preserving our traditions. The coming of the Spaniards and the Holy Inquisition were the start of a new era, an age of destruction that the Grandfathers had foreseen. The survival of the Great Tradition was based on nonconfrontation. Those who made it through the Inquisition unnoticed made this possible.

Given the events that are occurring today—wars, epidemics, plagues, floods, earthquakes, hurricanes, storms, tsunamis, global warming, and many other imbalances—the Elders have decided that it is important to convey our prophecy, because the cycles that mark a negative period affect not only the Mayan people but all humankind.

6

THE PROPHECY OF KAOKAN

As told to Carlos Barrios by his
brother, Gerardo Kanek Barrios

During the first half of the twentieth century, there was a Mexican man who was a traveler on the spiritual path. He was the sort of person who preferred to drink from the original source of knowledge, and so he journeyed around the world. While in India, he found answers and new goals. What he wanted most was to learn how to use an ancient mantra known as the *Maha* mantra, and he focused his efforts on searching for a teacher. He moved on to Asia, to the so-called top of the world, the fabulous Tibet. After an exhaustive search, he arrived at an ancient monastery, where the oldest spiritual guides told him that the last guardian of this mantra had recently died. But, they told him, in an isolated place in a faraway country, he could find the wise men who had taught it to them. That country was Mexico.

Amazed that this knowledge had come from his own country, he decided to return. Once he found these teachers, he learned how to use the magic sounds that transcend physical space and

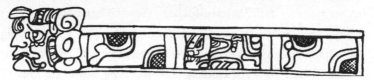

KINH-DIA, Time-Sun in its passage through Earth, Caban

time so that he could return to Tibet, where he was going to undertake a great mission. The exact details were not revealed; according to the sages, he would only be able to discover what it was upon his return.

After several years in Tibet without a single revelation, he thought his mission must be to teach the *Maha* mantra to the Tibetans again. He began to instruct a group of monks who wanted to learn the technique. Once he finished this marvelous task, he prepared to go back to Mexico. Then one night he had a strange dream. A woman appeared and told him she would help him accomplish his mission. She asked him to postpone his trip home, saying he would hear from her soon.

A few days later he met a woman who looked very much like the one in his dream. They quickly fell in love and married in the Tibetan tradition. She became pregnant. Again he had an unusual dream, and again the woman appeared. She told him he had already completed part of his task because he had helped to create her. She asked for his continued assistance. He and his wife needed to move to Mexico because that was where she had to be born. The family left Tibet, and Regina, the name they gave to this wonderful child, was born in Mexico.

After a time, they went back to Tibet, where Regina was to finish her training in order to fulfill her destiny. There, among other things, she learned to play the Tibetan bells. Once her training was complete and she returned to Mexico, she was told to move to a small town near the volcanoes Popocatepetl and Ixtazihuatl, outside of Mexico City, where she would prepare to fulfill the first of her great missions.

Before continuing this story, we need to look at the situation in Guatemala. Our great visionaries and sages Naq Puq Tun, Aj B'alam, Saqij Niqtee, Tecumanchu, and many others prophesied the coming of the Spanish conquistadors and prepared for this inevitable event. They sent their wise men to take shelter in the tropical jungle of Petén, and this was quite successful. According to chroniclers, the *Ajpop* (king) Kanek Itzaj was able to maintain his government until 1780, preserving the tradition intact until that date, including the sacred writing, or *Aq'ab' Tz'ib'*. The prophets had told them they were to take refuge and go unnoticed until this date, when no one would remember the Itzaj people any longer. Some surrendered, while others hid.

The rest of their plan was to send great sages into the Cuchumatanes mountain range in Huehuetenango, the sacred cradle of our civilization, our place of origin and matrix. A very isolated location even today, with no paved roads, telephones, or electricity, it is as if time has stood still in such a heavenly place. Some of the oldest Mayan communities are located in Huehuetenango, where the sacred practices have been maintained to the present day. Currently, five Mayan languages are spoken in these mountains: Qam, Chuj, Q'anjob'al, Popti', and Yucatec. Unlike other places in Guatemala, where people are mostly bilingual (speaking a Mayan language and Spanish), Spanish is not spoken here. The textiles, spiritual practices, and various calendars are still used, and there is great respect for the ancestral tradition, the *Tikutz'i'* (divine law), and the Law of Origin (common law). Here the true vision has been maintained in a way of life similar to the Classic Maya.

Our great Grandfathers also sent other sages through interdimensional gates of light to the parallel dimension of Paxil, where they are watching over the conservation of our tradition and the preservation of the purest lineage. According to the *Oxlajuj Tiku'* (Thirteen Heavens) prophetic calendar, they will return at the appointed time to help humanity take up its mission and follow the proper path. This is predicted to occur during these times, for we ended the gestation period of *Oxlajuj Tiku'* on August 16, 2001.

When I began my spiritual practices in Guatemala, I learned a little about the sacred Mayan calendars, and it awakened a great interest in me. I delved into studying the twenty calendars, each of which deals with a different energy and was created for a different purpose.

For over twenty years I have traveled to various communities, particularly to where the Mayan tradition has been preserved. It has been my great fortune to have the opportunity to speak with the *Laj Mam*, or great Elders, guardians of the sacred tradition, and to have been received in various *nimaja*, or great houses, where the lineage and knowledge are safeguarded. In my quest to learn about the calendars, I have also met Elders and guides in different villages in southern Mexico, Honduras, Belize, and El Salvador.

My travels have enabled me to accumulate many different forms of Mayan spiritual knowledge. I was honored to receive the *Atija*, the discipline to manipulate water and meditation, as well as the ability to control sacred fire as an *Ajq'ij'* (spiritual guide) and sun-worker. My mission has been to coordinate the twenty calendars that the Elders use—sacred, prophetic, human-terrestrial, cosmic, and divine—many of which the Elders feel it would be imprudent to bring to light at this time.

During this search, I returned to my birthplace in the Cuchumatanes, where I had an amazing experience, something I believe was transcendent not only for the Mayan people but for all native peoples and humanity as a whole.

Soloma is a village many miles from Huehuetenango. In ancient times this was the cradle of one of the most important tribes in the Mayan Mam domain and the glorious site of Zaculeu, or White Land, seat of the wise government of Kaib'il B'alam. There is a *bujil*, or pyramid, here that has the silhouette of the great Kukulkan, or quetzal, representing liberty. This bird, known as the Plumed Serpent, symbolizes the Mayan people. It cannot survive in captivity and is proudly carried by the great *Ajaw*, or lords.

The road to Soloma is unpaved, and in the rainy season it's a torturous undertaking. I finally arrived after traveling for several hours and met with some companions in the plaza. There were nine of us in total, and we were all wearing our *Pixom Q'aq'al*, or Sacred Pouch, which identified us as *Ajq'ij'.* We stocked up on flashlight batteries, candles, and other provisions and left for Santa Eulalia, where we met with some of our Q'anjob'al brothers. From there we set off to visit the *nimaja* in Jolom Konob', where we asked that our journey be blessed. It was the 1980s—the bloodiest period of the civil war that ravaged Guatemala for nearly forty years. It was difficult, if not impossible, to travel at night given the frequent attacks between the different sides. The many patrols through the conflict zones were always wary of ambush and therefore ready to shoot anything that moved.

One of our companions knew someone who lived along the way, but after walking for some time we realized that we wouldn't get there by nightfall. The temperature in this area regularly falls to freezing, so we took shelter as best we could. We decided to stop in a small hollow surrounded by hills that would protect us from the wind and make the cold a little more bearable. Another fellow traveler, Juan, had miraculously survived an attack on his village, which was burned to the ground. We all sensed that simply being in this area terrified him. We could only expect the worst if either the army or the guerrillas, known as *canchitos*, happened by. Fortunately, they did not, and we were on our way again at dawn. We walked all day and by evening had reached our destination, a small town deep in a valley. It appeared desolate, as did most communities in my country at that time. After resting for a while, we headed to the *nimaja*, one of the oldest and most traditional of the ceremonial houses. Because our *Pixom Q'aq'al* identified us as *Chi-Mam* (Mayan priests), a man came out to greet us.

He spoke Q'anjob'al and asked us what brought us there. Thankfully, our Q'anjob'al companions were able to interpret for the rest of us. After each of the others had explained his purpose, I told the guardian of the house that I wanted to meet an Elder who would teach me about the calendars. He went into the house without a word and came back with several candles and colored threads. He grouped the candles into bundles of two and tied each pair with a different color of string, lit them, and passed a pair over each of our heads. He then told us to wait while he consulted to see who would be allowed to enter. After a while, he came back out and allowed just four of us to pass. The situation became increasingly surreal because none of us who were chosen spoke the language, and we had to communicate through gestures.

I was taken into a room and, after a while, an Elder *Chi-Mam* came in. He was a small man, dressed in traditional clothing and wearing an enormous hat that made him look like an elf. After studying me for a moment, he indicated that I was to sit on the floor. He held out his *Pixom Q'aq'al* and, after arranging the sacred *tz'ite* seeds, signaled for me to hold out my Sacred Pouch. He took two of his seeds, put them with mine, and motioned for me to do the same. I realized this meant that we were now brothers: a part of each of us was with the other. I tried to explain why I was there, but it was impossible to communicate. He embraced me, and I got the impression that he had something important to tell me, but he made it clear I must come back another day. Seeing that he had ended our meeting, I withdrew after kissing his hand and thanking him for his blessing.

The others who had been left outside were feeling a little disheartened that they had not been received. I asked why this was, and one of my Q'anjob'al companions explained that that was just the way things were done there. When the guardian of the house passed the candles over our heads, he had tied them with the same color thread as the clothing each of us was wearing so that he would know who the candles belonged to. These were given to the most senior Elder, who looked into the flames and saw each of our intentions, as well as who would have to purify himself or his thoughts before he could come back and be received at that time.

I was eager to speak with the Elder again and returned at the first opportunity. This time I found a local boy who was about eight years old and spoke both languages. My interpreter would be allowed to accompany me because, in the Mayan world, a boy is considered pure until he reaches the age of puberty.

Once again going through the same procedure, I was given permission to speak with the Elder. He was happy to see me. Together we offered our candles to Ajaw, the Great Spirit, and the Great Father, and he invited me to talk. I began to explain, but he stopped me after a few words, indicating that there would be time enough for that. He had other matters on his mind, and he thanked Ajaw for bringing us together. He was sure I was the person meant for the mission he was about to give me.

Village Elders are great wise men who possess a power and knowledge rare in our world. However, even though they have the ability to transport themselves anywhere through their dreams, their knowledge of our culture is limited. They do not understand the divisions the Western world has created between nations.

The Elder told me that this mission was part of the knowledge his ancestors had left him, that it was a prophecy as well as a mandate; and it was urgent.

He said that several years earlier a group of Elders from another country had traveled and performed ceremonies in order to move the spiritual energy that was manifest in their homeland. Because of this energy movement and cosmic changes taking place, the magnetic centers of the world were coming to the North American continent.

As this current made its journey, it awoke energies that had been dormant for several centuries. Unfortunately, there was a blockage at some point that stalled its progress. The Elders saw, in their dreams, that man had created an artificial passage connecting two oceans and blocked the continuity of energies. The waters were overflowing and turning back, so it was urgent that a series of spiritual works be carried out in order to transfer that energy south. I assumed that he was speaking of the Panama Canal and that, given what I had learned on my trips to India, this was the region where it all started. I decided I would have to come back with a map so that he could explain what we needed to do. I left once again, thanking him for receiving me. I was very excited about what he had revealed to me.

Two months passed before I was able to return to see this dear, respected Elder. His obvious pleasure at seeing me was reward enough for the hardships involved in reaching the blessed place. After the usual rituals, we went into the room where he had revealed his secrets to me, and I spread out the map I had brought. He smiled. I don't think he had ever seen a map before, but he said, "Yes, that's it, that's the way it is. Look," he said, pointing to the Himalayas in Tibet. "This is where those people I told you about are from. This is where they're from, and here's where the energy went, over this mountain range." He indicated the path the energy had taken through China, up the eastern part of the former Soviet Union, then over to Alaska. From there he traced it down the Rocky Mountains, the Pacific Northwest of the United States, through Mexico, Guatemala, and the rest of Central America, until he stopped in Panama. "This is where they did their mischief," he said. "Here's where they cut Mother Earth.

That's why the energy couldn't continue. Now it's returning, causing pain and destruction. On the way down it brought about changes in the places it touched, but now it's wreaking havoc, bringing death, and it hasn't even gone all the way back yet. Certain ceremonies must be performed in order to rechannel the energy. As you can see," he continued, "we need to assemble a large group of spiritual people from different traditions. This is up to all of us."

"Your mission," he said, "is to call these people together. I don't know where you'll get the funds to do this, but we'll help you from here with our ceremonies. We need Elders from all over the Americas to come and touch various energy centers to redirect this energy south." He pointed to the Colombian Amazon on the map. "Then they'll have to move the energy here," he continued, this time pointing to the Andes Mountains in Peru and Bolivia. "To conclude this mission they'll have to work here as well," and he indicated southern Argentina.

He told me to keep him apprised of my progress. When I left what I now considered my home, that great *nimaja*, I was worried about the enormous responsibility this task entailed.

I couldn't stop thinking about his revelations. Images came to mind of the changes that had taken place in the world as the energy moved until it reached the Panama Canal. When it left India and Tibet and passed through China, the latter became a communist country, with many social and political changes and many deaths. Tibetan monks were exiled when the Chinese annexed their territory. In Russia, Stalin ruled and more than 50 million people were killed. It was the start of the Cold War.

In Canada the French province of Quebec sought independence. Passing through the United States, the Great Depression was a prelude to the many changes that would come. The civil rights movement began; confrontational personalities such as Malcolm X and pacifists such as Dr. Martin Luther King Jr. came on the scene. There was the Cuban Missile Crisis, John F. Kennedy was assassinated, and the Vietnam War raged on. The pacifist movement and hippies arrived offering a refreshing new vision. People began to take a critical look at materialism, governmental power, and war. Another consequence of the energy's journey through our part of the world at that time was the introduction and popularization of Hindu and Tibetan philosophies. This was the first call for humanity to rediscover true spirituality.

As the energy passed through Mexico, it unleashed a chain of events that had to do with Regina, the woman from my earlier story. Once she returned to Mexico with the secret knowledge, her next mission was to perform a ceremony at a full Mayan temple and ring the Tibetan bells in order to wake the Sleeping Woman. This is the name given to the mountain formation near the town where she was living, with the volcanoes of Popocatepetl and Ixtazihuatl being her breasts. Regina called upon several spiritual people and asked representatives from the various indigenous groups in Mexico to come as well. Knowing that self-sacrifice was her destiny, that her blood would have to be spilled at this place, she said good-bye to family and friends and walked toward her fate.

At the same time, a student protest was being held in the Mexican capital just before the 1968 Olympics. Because of the monumental amount of construction required to stage such an event, the cost of living had skyrocketed, and money had been diverted from other areas such as health care. Although it was assumed that no one would pay much attention to the demonstration, thousands of protesters were there. For the government, it became a source of embarrassment, something that could not be allowed in view of the upcoming opening ceremonies.

Regina headed to the plaza in Tlatelolco, a neighborhood of Mexico City where there was a pyramid that met the requirements for the rite she was to perform. It must have been quite a sight for the inhabitants of that area: a march by indigenous people in their typical dress and a large group of other men and women dressed in white was no everyday occurrence. Regina and her followers arrived at the pyramid and began their ceremony.

Meanwhile, the demonstration had grown violent. Some undesirables had infiltrated the march and were looting businesses and destroying vehicles along the way. The army was called in to break up the crowd, who by pure coincidence were heading to the plaza in Tlatelolco where Regina and her group were performing their ceremony. The protesters arrived at the square, and their mood calmed somewhat when they saw Regina and the indigenous people. Slowly they began to take part in the ceremony, giving it that much more strength and power. When Regina finished ringing her bells and the Elders completed their invocations to awaken the new energy, they realized that the plaza had been surrounded by thousands of soldiers. The situation was extremely tense. Someone in the crowd discharged a weapon, which caused the soldiers to react immediately and hundreds of people were massacred. Regina was among the dead, having spilled her virgin blood and thus fulfilled her destiny.

As this energy continued through Central America, the first Socialist regime came to power in Guatemala, and it started one of the longest and cruelest conflicts in Guatemalan history, resulting in the deaths of over 200,000 civilians. This conflict had nothing to do with our people; we were simply a "Cold War" battleground where superpowers contributed the weapons and we contributed the casualties. The civil war directly affected the Maya. Many of their traditional sites were destroyed, and entire villages were razed to the ground. A similar conflict occurred in El Salvador, where thousands died. The same fate befell Nicaragua as the energy continued south. Once it reached Panama and was blocked by the canal, the energy slowly began its journey back.

Passing through Nicaragua once again, the energy caused an earthquake that destroyed half the capital city as well as several small towns; then the dictator Anastasio Somoza died. A new regime came to power, the Sandinista guerrillas, and the country was mired in a prolonged crisis from which it still has not recovered. El Salvador had a huge earthquake, the biggest in that country's history, and the civil war intensified. On its way back through Guatemala, the energy caused one of the most devastating earthquakes humanity has ever seen. Entire villages were wiped off the map, with over 50,000 missing or dead. The civil war was also at its peak in the mid-1980s. The energy caused yet another earthquake in Mexico City, as well as the emergence of the Zapatista National Liberation Army.

The need to complete the transfer of energy is obvious, and several people have been instrumental in this work. Thanks to help from caring individuals, we were able to hold the first meeting in Guatemala in late 1995. Spiritual leaders from various Native American nations met for the first time and activated the energy centers in Tikal, Zaculeu, Kaminal Juyu', and Atitlán.

Peace was also sown in a transcendental ceremony on Baúl Hill in Quetzaltenango, Guatemala in which Elders from the Americas made an offering. Within the year, a peace treaty was signed, and the Guatemalan civil war came to an end. The ceremonial center of Tecpán in El Salvador was also touched, thus fulfilling the first part of our mandate. In 1996, all of the Elders were able to meet once again in Colombia, deep in the Amazon jungle, to plan the next step. Peru and Bolivia will be next, then finally Argentina, in order to redirect the energy to the south of the continent and thereby activate the energy centers in the Andes and further inland.

This prophetic mission requires the support of all those who understand the need for the energy to journey through South America. It will come about if we all put our minds to it. Once this is achieved, as our Grandfathers hope it will be, a period of harmony will begin in this new world.

7

THE CREATION MYTH

*I*t is extremely important to understand how the Mayan civilization arose and where the Maya came from. The following excerpt from the *Popol Vuh*, the sacred book of the Maya K'iche people, will bring us closer to such an understanding:

We shall put the old stories into writing, beginning when all things were made and their foundations established.

With what is said here, we shall provide a clear idea of how the universe was created, what is still hidden and what we can see in our world, how the Maker and Creator put his essential qualities into action and his mere word was enough to create everything.

One attribute was *Tz'aqol*: the divine will that manifests itself in nature, making it awake into action. Another was *B'itol*, which constitutes the formative power. Part of *Tz'aqol* acts in creation.

The next was *Alom*, the very power of emanation in his

presence, the seed of life, the word-action of the Great Father, the greatness or essence of which cannot be explained since we cannot comprehend it.

Finally, the fourth quality was *K'ajolom*, consisting of space, the Infinite Void, the matrix from which every Universe arose.

In times past, our knowledge was contained in an original book that was hidden many centuries ago. Its meaning is obscured from those who gaze or meditate upon it. It is the book of our Elders.

It told how Sky and Earth were created, quartered into equinoxes and solstices. Divided into four parts, the directions:

Red, the East;
Black, the West;
White, the North; and
Yellow, the South.

Each star was set in its place and the path established for each. Boundaries were fixed, distances measured by means of a string that was stretched into Earth and Sky, establishing height and depth.

It told how the Creator and Maker made the air we breathe, gave us the breath that brings life and existence. He keeps us, watches over and protects us. He grants us peace and clarity.

Here it is told how out of a watery void the Creators and Makers made and gave life to plants and animals.

Then the divine fathers created the first generation of men made out of mud, but they fell apart and returned to the earth.

The next race appeared, made out of wood, but they were idiotic, brainless. They did not remember their Creators and so they were destroyed by the gods and replaced.

Thus man was made out of flesh. But men became evil, filled with pride, and forgot their Creators. They were annihilated when black storm clouds formed and the earth was inundated by a great flood.

Finally, true humanity, we who populate the face of Mother Earth, was made out of corn.*

The history of the Mayan people may be one of the greatest controversies of recent times. Historians, archaeologists, and other scholars have been unable to agree on it, and research has not shed much light. The thick vegetation, geological formations, calcareous terrain, and constant rain and humidity of the tropics hamper the search for and preservation of remains that would allow us to establish a definite date for the birth of this extraordinary civilization. The original carbon dating was unreliable owing to the rate of decomposition in such a humid climate. Most Western scientists place Mayan emergence at a much later date than Mayan tradition suggests.

The Maya safeguarded their knowledge, which they recorded in their sacred books, on the stelae they erected, in their ceremonial centers, and through a long oral tradition. This legacy provides clarity, establishing locations and prophetic dates.

---

* We have chosen to use the Spanish translation of the *Popol Vuh* by the eminent scholar and historian Agustín Estrada Monroy, published by Editorial José de Pineda Ibarra in 1973. As one of the few researchers to approach the Elders and obtain their counsel on several occasions, he produced a translation that, in our opinion, is the best one to date.

8

MAYAN ORIGINS

According to stories told by Elders from the most traditional tribes, the Maya are descended from a mother civilization called Tula, or Tulán, which gave rise to all of the mysterious and powerful civilizations that populated Mesoamerica. This civilization is also the mother of tribes in northern Africa, India, Tibet, part of the Mediterranean, and the northern part of the Iberian Peninsula. It is the source of all our traditions. In many Mayan languages, "Tula" means "mother's breast"—the place where our forebears drank of knowledge. This original civilization was located on a continent, now gone, in the middle of the Atlantic.

The *Popol Vuh* gives the following account:

From there we came, from Tulán Zu. That is where our first fathers were created: B'alam K'itze', B'alam Aq'ab', Majukutaj, and I'ki' B'alam.

From there they came, from the East.... Many left, each with their families, multiplying there in the east. Still in darkness, before the sun had dawned and there was light, they were all together doing many things there in the east. Without knowledge of food, they lifted their faces to the sky and did not know how to leave it. There they were, there in that sweetness, white men and black men. There were many languages and two ears. From them the different generations in the world are descended. . . .

They did not have idols then, but all spoke the same language. They followed the mandate the Creator had given them, Heart of Sky, Heart of Earth, waiting for the Sun to rise.

From there we came, that is where we were given our names. There they came together to await the dawn, to wait and watch for the star that comes before the sun when it rises.

From there we came, that is where we divided, they said to one another. Thus they were sad and felt pain because they had no food or sustenance. Only the roots of sweet cane did they smell, and it was as if they were eating but in reality they were not.

Their passage over the sea when they came was clear, as if there were no sea at all. They crossed over on stones. They came here, and the stones were protruding in a row in the sand when they came. Stepping-stones they are called, pulled up out of the sand that path they used to cross the sea, which divided and they came here.

Here we will not see the dawn of the sun on the face of the earth, they said when they came. They left the path and surely fell asleep along the way. One of the tribes that woke up continued to watch the star that signaled the coming of the sun.

This was the sign they thought was the dawn when they came from the east. Their faces were one when they came from there, such a great distance away.

The *Memorial of Sololá*, also known as the *Annals of the Kaqchikeles*, tells a similar story:

> I shall write the stories of our first fathers and grandfathers, one of whom was called Jakawitz, the other Saqtekaw. In the stories they told, from across the sea we came from a place called Tulán, where we were begotten, where our mothers and fathers gave birth to us. Oh, our children! So said the fathers and grandfathers who were called Jakawitz and Saqtekaw, they who arrived in Tulán, the men who begot us, the Xajila'....
>
> When we arrived at the gates of Tulán, we went to receive a red staff, and thus we were given the name Kaqchikele.
>
> Oh, our children, said Jakawitz and Saqtekaw. Let us thrust the tips of our staffs into the sea, and soon we shall cross the sea on the sand, using the colored staffs we received in Tulán. And so we crossed over the row of sand when the bottom of the sea had parted. All rejoiced when they saw the sand in the sea.

Both documents speak of the Maya's arrival from a place called Tulán Zuiua, Tulán Zu, or Tulán, in the east, across the sea. Many historians and researchers have confused this mythical region of Tulán Zuiua, Tulán, Tula, Tulan Zu, or Tulán Ziu with the ceremonial center of Tula in Hidalgo, Mexico, where the famous Atlantes statues are found. The situation becomes even more confusing in light of the fact that the city and ceremonial center we now call Kaminal Juyu' (where Guatemala City is located today) was once called Tulan Siwan or Tulan Ziu.

The importance of these two stories lies in their clear assertion that the Maya came from across the sea, which parted as a result of the power and high magic possessed by the Tulanese sages. This location in the east and across the sea does not seem to coincide with present-day geography. Of any people in the world, however, the Maya would most certainly have known the east. Even today, their tradition is based on the movement of the sun. To them, the sun represents the Great Father, Heart of Sky. The sun is their connection to the Heart of Hearts, the Sun of Suns, the center and generator of the universe. For this reason, Tula of the North in Hidalgo, Mexico, can be ruled out as a possible place of origin, as well as because it was built much later.

With respect to their crossing over the sea and how it parted, this may be a Western influence on the story. After all, it was the Spanish friars who taught the indigenous people to transcribe the *Popol Vuh* and other books. In any event, it is unmistakably clear that we cannot simply make a pronouncement on the Mayan civilization's origin without more in-depth study.

Ancient Mayan texts also speak of a cataclysm that changed the planet and, according to legend, caused the mythical Tula to sink. The visionaries of that time warned that this would happen, and so they crossed the sea to this continent. This is certainly reminiscent of the mythical Atlantis, located in the east, in the Atlantic Ocean. It is also important to note that the word *atl* exists nowhere but in Mesoamerica and means "water." It is said that Atlantis means "land surrounded by water."

Neither the age nor the authenticity of the *Popol Vuh* or the *Annals of the Kaqchikeles* is disputed. Both books were written before the conquest and then rewritten in Latin script. They were kept secret until the seventeenth century, when the first was revealed, and the eighteenth century, when the second came to light. Realizing their inestimable value, researchers then began to study them and have them translated into other languages. Unfortunately, many other documents were acquired by private collectors and became inaccessible to scholars.

The academic world is uncertain of the Maya's origin, and theories have been discarded one after another. The most widely accepted hypothesis asserted that the Maya came from Asia and are descended from the Mongolian races that crossed the land bridge over the Bering Strait at the end of the last Ice Age, then traveled and settled in Mesoamerica. This idea has now been discredited, however, owing to the skeletal differences between these two people and the lack of a clearly proven genetic relationship. Similarly, although it has been shown that 100 percent of pure Maya have the blood type O, indicating that they descend from Cro-Magnon ancestors, recent discoveries have found a factor in this blood type that does not occur anywhere else.

Likewise, the theory of Polynesian emigration is no longer accepted. Although the two peoples have more cultural features in common, their physical differences are more obvious. It now seems that emigration may have been in the other direction—that is, from the continent to Polynesia. This is not surprising given that Native Americans had highly developed navigational systems that would have allowed them to travel that far. Finally, it's more likely that the Maya are linked to the Incan civilization.

Lugar
Quiriguá

13 B'aktun
0 Tun
0 Q'ij
8 Kumku

0 K'atun
0 Winaq
4 Ajaw

3 Piedras
fueron
colocadas

Sucedió en
la Tierra

El lugar de
las 3 Piedras

Estela C de la Creación en Quiriguá.
Con la fecha de la Creación o Año 0.
13.0.0.0.0 4 Ajaw 8 Kumku

Scientists have ruled out the possibility that the Maya originated in the Americas, and they have certainly not tried to research any possible descent from the mythical lost continents of Atlantis or Mu. And yet, in addition to some physical proof, the many stories of our Grandfathers' tradition point toward these origins. Suffice it to say that the pyramid of Tulum near Cancún in the state of Quintana Roo, Mexico, is recognized as being the earliest Mayan pyramid. It was built on the seashore facing the Bimini Islands, which are allegedly the tops of the highest mountain chain in mythical Atlantis. The location of Tulum is unique: there are no other Mayan pyramids beside the sea. Our Mam Grandfathers emigrated from there, and they are widely accepted as the earliest Mayan civilization.

9

EL MAYAB

When the first Maya arrived from the mythical Tulán across the ocean, they settled in Mesoamerica, extending from south-central Mexico through Guatemala, Belize, El Salvador, and northern Honduras. The oldest settlements are found in Mam territory, in the Cuchumatanes Mountains in western Guatemala.

El Mayab is the name the ancient Maya used to refer to the territory that encompassed their city-states, which developed around their ceremonial centers and bound their daily life, cosmo-vision, and spirituality to a single tradition. The city-states shared royal family lines that not only served as a common defense against other powers, such as the Toltecs and later the Aztecs, but also united them in conducting trade, managing their system of underground irrigation canals, and developing scientific and technological advances.

This ancient Mayan world spread over 200,000 square miles, and the population density during the height of the Classic Period was higher than it is now.

Although we do not agree with the dates historians have used to divide the Mayan civilization into periods, we do agree with their stages of development. The Pre-Classic Period was a time of settlement after a matriarchal period. Our civilization changed to a theocracy during the Classic Period, with society being governed by priest-rulers. Then came a period of intense fighting called the Post-Classic Period, when harmonious society was threatened by cultures from the north, particularly the Aztec-Mexica and the outlying Toltec people. The Toltec's influence was marked during this time because they settled in some of the Mayan cities that were abandoned when cosmic and terrestrial energies no longer converged there.

10

THE UNKNOWN STORY

The wisest beings were created at the dawn of this humanity. Their gaze encompassed the whole of Mother Earth. They had no language as such but transmitted their thoughts and visions by means of images. Their strength and power were limitless. Their thought and essence reached the presence of the Great Father, Heart of Sky. Nothing was unknown to them except death. Not since that time have such magnificent beings walked on the face of this beautiful Earth.

It is said that they were demigods because the Creator, the Maker, the Shaper, and the Giver of Life, the council of gods, agreed to make them. However, their descendants' hearts became filled with pride and vanity. They were so arrogant that they believed they had the right to make use of the rest of creation. Since they did not respect one another, what could our brothers the animals, the wise trees, and the water creatures expect from them? What's more, what could Mother Earth expect from them?

Pride made such beings believe that they were as great as their creators, and soon they forgot their makers. Thus, Heart of Sky called upon the Creator, the Maker, the Shaper, and the Giver of Life. After consulting, the gods decided to limit the power they had given these beings, since harmony with the Natural Order is what keeps creation alive. When harmony is not respected, a higher power will surely come and put everything in its place. The council of gods thus agreed to mist the eyes of human beings, and their sight today is limited. No more can they see the images with which the rest of creation speaks. The gods closed humans' ears so that they can only hear what is near. No longer can they hear the sound of the cosmos. They have lost their intuitive strength; their power is only material now. They do not see the purpose for which they were created. And now they know death, but they play at being eternal.

Once when I met with Don Pascual after I'd been living in the city for some time, he said that I looked like one of the first four Men-Gods, a *B'alameb'*, returning from the Pleiades. This strange greeting piqued my curiosity, and I immediately bombarded him with questions about what he meant. He had never brought up the Maya's relationship to the cosmos before, and as far as I was concerned, the Pleiades was nothing but a cluster of stars.

As always, Don Pascual's strategy was to spark one's interest by means of a completely unexpected remark or as a prelude to one of his fabulous tales. "No one can prove anything about the origin of humanity, about how we came to be in the position we're in, though myths and traditions help. It doesn't matter whether others pay attention to these or not. After all, it doesn't matter what you believe if you are unconscious of existence.

"I met an Elder once when I was young. Some called him the oldest of the old, and others described him as a man of few words. I was able to earn his trust, so he told me his truth. He said the universe, and therefore the world, arose because the Creator willed it. The Creator met with the Maker, and they made their will manifest, begetting reality. This came about in the magical form of *najt*, or space-time. Reality exists in a preordained place and is determined by the ability to give shape to the manifestations of energy, or unreality. We learn this once we lose the innocence we are born with. When this happens, our lives may become caught up in this unconsciousness, and that is when we become fragile. When this humanity was lost after the Great Father punished them for having become vain and forgetting their creator, he sent our first Grandfathers, the *B'alameb'*: B'alam K'itze', B'alam Aq'ab', Majukutaj, and I'ki' B'alam. They came from *Tzob' Uxe' Ch'umil*, or the Pleiades. These were great wise men, visionaries, and incredible wizards. Their homeland is our homeland, their tradition is our tradition, their legacy is our way of life. They taught us all of the arts and gave us knowledge because this place where our first Fathers came from is where reality occurs.

"Here begins the manifestation of everything, our Grandfathers said, and this is how we express it. When they came to our world, they were disoriented, as if lost outside their reality. They longed for their place of origin and their dignity, but they were sent by the Great Father to have descendants and populate the earth in order to remember their Creator and Maker."

This story changed my life. I suddenly understood that we have a shared origin, that our Grandfathers' divinity was a dignity bestowed by the Great Spirit, the Sun of Suns, and that knowledge can be found in both the stars and on the earth. This is where my journey began. This story was what awakened my desire to return to our Elders' tradition!

The extraordinary thing about these words was that, while they made me feel that I had always been distracted and disoriented, in time I was able to value the depth of Don Pascual's story. I was shocked when twenty years later I was reading about the latest scientific advances and learned that astronomers discovered an enormous wormhole, as they call it, just next to the Pleiades. This wormhole contains all of the galaxies and nebula, and there is nothing outside of it but an immeasurable void.

I now understand the power and fascination that the Pleiades holds over the Mayan world as the origin of everything that exists, the mythical Paxil and Kayala—parallel dimensions known as Mayan paradise—and I place more value in our Grandfathers' stories.

11

MAYAN CIVILIZATION

The Maya have operated continuously as a theocracy for thousands of years, with one of the most balanced forms of social organization. Throughout this time, both rulers and subjects lived according to the sacred *Cholq'ij* calendar: everyone assumed their role in society according to the sign or energy they were born under. This prevented conflict and allowed the Maya to develop in accordance with their abilities because everyone did what they were truly meant to do.

The agricultural cycle was of the utmost importance to the Maya. It was based on the sacred corn plant, *ixim*, as well as on beans, amaranth, chilies, fruits, and herbs. The agricultural cycle had a basic duration

TERRITORIO MAYA

of 260 days, with another 100 days dedicated to personal development, including the arts, architecture, and spirituality, while the remaining five days in a year were a period of introspection and self-discovery known as *wayeb*.

During the one-hundred-day period, almost the entire population spent their time building the monumental ceremonial and energy centers. Rulers, scientists, astronomers, and mathematicians directed construction based on celestial events such as equinoxes and solstices—movements of the sun that were significant for the agricultural cycle. Temples were oriented based on a meticulous, systematic observation of such cosmic phenomena and built to indicate key dates for planting, bending the stalks to allow the cobs to mature, and then harvesting the corn. The pyramids also had a religious and spiritual function—pointing out astral influences on terrestrial phenomena—and were thus built where cosmic and telluric energies converged.

As a society, the Maya were highly oriented toward community. Personal gratification was never their goal, and even today, in the remotest regions where tradition has endured and Western influence is minimal, the well-being of the whole is the Maya's highest priority. Everyone tends to the needs of the community before their own and leaders, or chiefs, are those who have demonstrated an ability to serve the people. Tribal leadership governs with close counsel from spiritual authorities who are held in high regard as the wise heirs to ancestral knowledge. They possess extraordinary powers, including the ability to access the different manifestations of divinity.

12

COSMIC AND TECHNICAL
KNOWLEDGE

The Maya were one of the most mysterious and amazing civilizations ever to have existed. They are one of only a few peoples to have endured for over twelve thousand years. This phenomenal civilization achieved greatness in a variety of disciplines of human knowledge.

Mayan scientific advances are not widely recognized, but the legacy the Maya left us is evident in everyday life. Their far-ranging endeavors were always in harmony with nature and respectful of all forms of life. They never hunted more than was necessary and never abused the land, planting only what was needed. Not even a tree was cut down without first conducting a ceremony in which the Maya asked the tree's spirit to live in a ritual object or become part of them.

One of the greatest Mayan contributions that has permeated every facet of our daily lives was their variety of crops. The Mayan diet based on corn, beans, and amaranth provides the body with all of the amino acids, carbohydrates, and proteins needed for proper development. After Mayan scientists domesticated and developed different varieties of corn by crossing various species, it became the most important nutritional substance on the continent. Besides the Native American populations, corn also sustained other peoples when it spread across the globe. Both corn and potatoes from the Americas saved Europe from famine because potatoes in particular adapted easily to the extremes of the European climate. Corn now forms part of the diet in Europe, Africa, and Asia and is also used as fodder for domestic animals. According to Agustín Estrada Monroy, given its protein and caloric content, it was the real gold that the Spanish should have been searching for deep in the jungles. Corn has many other purposes as well: as pulp for paper, as a substitute for oil derivatives, as an ingredient in cleaners and organic fuel. Mayan geneticists experimented with other crops by establishing an experimental field along the shores of Lake Atitlán, where they developed the seventy-nine varieties of avocado found in the world today.

The Maya's principal concern was living in harmony with nature. It is therefore no surprise that Japanese experts attributed the regular spacing of trees in the huge tropical forests of Guatemala, particularly those in the department of Petén, to a colossal work of forest engineering.

The Maya built subterranean irrigation canals that stretch for thousands of miles through Petén in Guatemala, Belize, Quintana Roo, and much of the Yucatán in Mexico. This astonishing network of canals was discovered in the 1960s using infrared satellite technology. Unfortunately, after the initial amazement and enthusiasm, information about the canals was kept from the public.

The Maya took the water for these canals from the Gulf of Mexico and desalinated it in large tanks, most of which have been lost or destroyed. The water evaporated and filtered through chambers containing large boulders. It then flowed into underground tunnels that were laid out in a grid pattern, with thousands of small branches conducting water throughout their vast territory. These canals brought water to the remotest corners of El Mayab for thousands of years. Combined with the technique of terraced agriculture—growing various food, medicinal, and other crops at different elevations—the Mayan irrigation system allowed millions of people to survive for thousands of years. The Maya's use of gravity and the sheer magnitude of this project make it one of the greatest engineering works ever carried out by humankind.

By developing such sophisticated engineering projects in harmony with nature, the Maya created a form of architecture in which the cosmic and the telluric acquired meaning: not only did they manage their agriculture and measure the cycles of time by coordinating their pyramids with celestial events, but the pyramids also took advantage of the convergence of cosmic and terrestrial energy. The Maya used the knowledge gained from placing their pyramids as energy receptors and catalysts as a guide for laying out their ceremonial cities to form energy belts. Thus, the sphere of influence of each form of energy was designated in the perception of both the subtlest and the most concrete levels that make up reality. These energy belts were outlined by roads that ran from east to west called *Saq B'e*, or the White Road, a name also used to refer to the Milky Way. The Maya would determine the meridian by noting the sun's position on the horizon at both sunrise and sunset during various times of the year. By aligning these points, they then determined the angles and bisectors to the north and south at a midpoint. This analysis allowed them to calculate the duration of the four seasons and the existence of what we know as the ecliptical plane, which they used to design their cities. This was the knowledge they used to erect their many temples, columns, stelae, and pyramids in line with one another to receive and distribute both physical and psychic energy.

Don Isidro had the following to say in this regard:

"Mayan architecture is closely related to the cosmic; temples were built with respect to cosmic events. Archaeo-astronomers are still taking measurements today and are astonished at the ingenuity with which the pyramids and entire cities were built. Their precise awareness of celestial events such as equinoxes, solstices, and sunrises was pragmatic, since these indicated the times for planting, bending the stalks to allow the cobs to mature, and then harvesting the corn. The pyramids still contain knowledge that has yet to be revealed and that shows the heights that Mayan engineering reached before anyone else in the world."

The Mayan achievements in the field of medicine were also extraordinary. Their surgical techniques were so precise that they were able to perform trepanations to relieve cranial pressure and thus allow for more highly developed brains. They amplified and restructured the cranium to decrease pressure on parts of the brain they wanted to expand. A particular area of the brain would be chosen based on a person's sign according to the sacred *Cholq'ij* calendar, whether he or she had a tendency toward any of the disciplines of human knowledge would be determined, and the appropriate part of the brain would then be decompressed. This knowledge of the hemispheres of the brain has never been lost.

Mayans were excellent dentists as well. They made dental amalgams, incrustations, and fillings whose superiority remains unrivaled to the present day. Unfortunately, however, this knowledge was lost.

Though Western tradition may not yet acknowledge it, natural Native American medicine has made important contributions to humanity, including a series of natural antibiotics. The Mayan expertise in administering plants and herbs to cure what in the West are called terminal illnesses is a good example of how much humanity could still benefit from that knowledge.

Mayan herbalists have yet to reveal all of their secrets, and we thus expect new advances in this regard. For example, using the liquid from certain roots, bonesetters can knit fractured bones in just a few weeks. The Maya also used to be able to soften and remold bone, but I am not sure whether this knowledge has been preserved.

Mayan mathematicians gave us the vigesimal, or base-twenty, positional system. Only three symbols are needed—a dot (equal to 1), a line (equal to 5), and an eye or a shell (equal to 0 or 20)—to represent any number. Numbers are written from bottom to top, rather than left to right as in the Western base-ten system.

The Maya made unprecedented breakthroughs in math. They created the concept of zero, and this miracle of abstract thinking was passed on to the Hindus, from whom the Arabs adopted the concept before finally passing it on to the West. This joining of mathematical precision and abstraction—resulting in the notion of zero as a value as opposed to nothing—is one of the most extraordinary achievements of human thought.

In turn, the concept of zero contributed to the development of the world's most precise calendars. Not only did the Maya establish a series of measurements and calendar systems for Venus, Mercury, and Jupiter, but most astonishing of all, they created calendars for our galaxy and those that make up our cluster of galaxies.

The simple fact that the Maya produced such perfect calendars indicates their proficiency in astronomy. North American astronomers, using an atomic clock, calculate that the tropical year is 365.242222 days long. In the year 2800 BCE, the Maya had already obtained the figure 365.24229956, which they corrected one thousand years ago to 365.242229999999. This difference between the modern and Mayan calculations is equal to just 0.8 seconds per year, or one extra day every 10,800 years.

The Maya also understood the concepts of latitude and longitude. They were great navigators and travelers, so maritime trade flourished between cities in the north and south. Navigators would use letters containing reference points and then simply corroborate the movement of celestial bodies through the zenith in order to establish their location. Mayan oral tradition, records, and legends even speak of going on journeys to other continents and taking their ancestral tradition and technology to faraway places.

Further, the Maya determined the exact equinoxes and solstices based on the positions of stars, the passing of the sun through its zenith, and the movement of the North Star. Mayan astronomers left us this legacy in the form of codices. Four Mayan codices are known: the Paris Codex, Madrid Codex, Dresden Codex, and Grolier Codex. The codices were sacred Mayan documents written on paper made from the *amatle* tree or on deerskin. The writing went from left to right on both sides of the sheet, and the pages were folded into an accordion-style book. Thousands of such codices were destroyed during the conquest, while a few were taken to Europe and still others were hidden.

The Dresden Codex shows that the Maya unerringly calculated lunar movements, solar and lunar eclipses, and the cycles of Venus, Mars, and other visible planets. One codex alone contains both lunar and solar eclipses perfectly calculated 3,500 years into the future. The Maya also knew the orbits of galaxy clusters, the alignment of those that were closest, and their influence on our galaxy. They were thousands of years ahead of the Western world.

In the *Popol Vuh*, for example, we read that millions of years ago Venus was one of Jupiter's moons. It fell out of orbit as a result of some kind of collision, possibly with a giant meteorite, and passed very close to the Earth, affecting our planet's axis and causing earthquakes, floods, and geographic changes.

Don Isidro tells us that this is the reason Venus is so important to our tradition. As our Elders remember it, Venus was responsible for the great cataclysms. Known as Vukuk Kakix, it thought it was as great as Heart of Sky. Its teeth made of gold shone when it smiled, reflecting brightly. It wanted to trick everyone by saying, "I am the Sun. I am the Moon." For a while Vukuk Kakix actually did appear bigger than both the sun and the moon. It had two children, Cabrakan and Zipakna. Zipakna would form big hills and mountains while his brother slept. When he was done, he would rest and his brother Cabrakan would shake the Earth and destroy the mountains, changing the course of rivers. These two were finally defeated by humans. Heart of Sky, hearing the pleas of human beings, rearranged the sky and left Vukuk Kakix in its current orbit, punishing its arrogance and forcing it to announce the coming of the Sun and the Moon.

In addition to ancient traditions in Tibet and among the inhabitants of the Nilgiri, or Blue, mountain range in India, the learned Russian astrologer Belikoskiv agrees with the theory that Venus was once Jupiter's moon.

The Maya's obsession with Venus led them to calculate its synodical phases and to develop a Venusian calendar that records the planet's movement across the face of the sun. They believe that the alignment of other stars and galaxies with respect to this phenomenon dictates what will happen in our solar system and specifically on Earth.

Undoubtedly the greatest legacy the Mayan sages left us was their method of handling energies. The technical ability to clearly see the convergence of cosmic and terrestrial currents is used by Elders and wise men. Each of us can find the right place in order to live a full, harmonious life by understanding and utilizing this skill. It is closely tied to the Mayan signs set out in the sacred *Cholq'ij* calendar and the key to well-rounded development.

The Catholic monks and priests who came with the conquistadors saw such wonders and thought they were the devil's work. They made it their mission to liberate the world from such dangerous information by destroying thousands of codices that contained invaluable information. Father Diego de Landa alone incinerated over ten thousand codices in a single day. Fortunately, several codices survived and will soon be brought to light.

The Maya's technological advances are so astonishing and relevant today because they span the full range of human activity.

Similarly, the Mayan cosmo-vision—the Maya philosophy of harmonious coexistence with nature—has much to impart to the Western world. All of the Maya's incredible developments were a means to enable them to live in harmony with Mother Earth.

13

MAYAN GODS

The ancient Maya had a vision of total connection between the cosmos and nature. The gods were representatives of the Supreme Being, Jun Ab Ku, or "that which contains everything." These deities were regents of the various levels and configurations of the universe, and they, in turn, had representatives in the underworld, the world, and the overworld. A series of deities is related to natural phenomena and the four basic elements, for in the Mayan cosmo-vision everything that exists has a spirit. Just as important are the deities that represent the energies of the sacred *Cholq'ij* calendar. Each of the twenty days, known as a *nawal*, is a manifestation of one of these deities.

The purest Mayan tradition says that we are intimately related to the cluster of stars known as the Pleiades, the origin of reality, the manifestation of life, and all knowledge. Our first guides, the *B'alameb'* B'alam K'itze', B'alam Aq'ab', Majukutaj, and I'ki' B'alam, lived on the Earth to settle and spread our tradition, and once they restored harmony to the planet, after a great punishment, they wrapped themselves in the *Pixom Q'aq'al*, or Sacred Cloak, and left for their fathers' homeland, Tulán, in the infinite space of the Pleiades. Further, according to the *Popol Vuh*, the deity Zipakna killed the Four Hundred Boys who rose up to the sky and became the stars in the Pleiades.

Unlike gods in other traditions, Mayan deities are incorporeal and have no common meeting place; their relationship with human beings stems from the petitions that humans make. This relationship is based on the priest's purity (through abstinence, fasting, and cleanliness of thought) and requires a ceremony in which the deities are remembered as our protectors. Very few Mayan gods take human form, and any such figures are anthropomorphic. For example, the representations for water and rain relate to powerful animals, such as the crocodile, that reign in the water. These manifestations come about to enable us to understand and come closer to the element that the god dominates. Ultimately the deity has no physical form at all. The gods are energy, and their representations are often viewed as assistants. Mayan gods possess the duality presupposed by this dimension: they are positive and negative, benevolent and malevolent. Each deity exists in quadruplicate—in the four corners of the world, the four cardinal points—and yet is a single entity.

The main Mayan deities are the first couple, the mother-fathers who gave birth to humanity: B'itol K'ajolom, the Maker or begetter, and Tz'aqol Alom, the Creator or conceiver. These withstood the conquest and are always present in Mayan thought and ceremonies.

There are also the great twins, our fathers Jun Ajpu and Ixb'alamke. These two demigods passed the tests of the underworld,

or Xib'alb'ay, defying death, and rose up to the sky. The first became the Sun, and the second became the Moon.

The individual moon deity is called Iq. The sun represents the sacred and is known by the name Kin. Kin is the Father, the Sun of Suns, the reigning energy, the one true, living god, the great Jun Ab Ku or unnameable one. *Jun* is "one," *Ab* means "diversity," and *Ku* stands for "heart"; thus, Jun Ab Ku is "unity in diversity with heart." This is the true Creator and Maker, and he has representatives throughout the universe, which is his concept. It is an energy that cannot be represented because it is incorporeal. Everything proceeds from it, and its presence and every idea govern all of the deities.

Kin, or Father Sun, and Kukulkan, or the Plumed Serpent, are the two most ubiquitous deities throughout Mayan territory. The great Kin is known variously as the giver of life, the power and mystery of the equinoxes and solstices. He is represented by Kolop and also known by the titles Chac Ahau, Lord Red, or Kin Chac Ahau, Lord Red of the Sun. Another manifestation of Lord Red is Kinich Ahau.

Jun Ab Ku in turn has a son called Hun Itzam Na, the famous Itzam Na, whose name is related to his father's. He is the image of his father, and his name means the same thing: the true or only one. He is perhaps the most important Mayan deity, with temples and cities dedicated solely to him, such as Izamal in the state of Yucatán, Mexico.

The goddess Ixchel, or Ix Chebel Yax, is the wife of the creator Itzam Na and is represented by Iguana Earth. She is the mother. Some tribes adore her as the Moon, wife of Kinich Ahau, the Sun God. She is worshiped everywhere as the mother goddess who taught us to weave, while Kinich Ahau is adored for having taught us to write.

Other living gods are the four *B'alameb'* mentioned earlier, from whom all Maya are descended. They are the divine beings who appeared at the end of the last Ice Age and regenerated life, teaching man about weaving, writing, architecture, astronomy, timekeeping, and many other things. Each one is the regent-owner of one of the four corners of the world and the elements associated with each:

B'ALAM K'ITZE' represents the *East*. His energy is Fire. He is manifested in light and clarity. He is the generator of life and associated with the color red.

B'ALAM AQ'AB' represents the *West*. His energy is Earth. He is manifested in the hidden, the internal, and the night and associated with the color black.

MAJUKUTAJ represents the North. *His* energy is Air. He is manifested in subtlety. He is the breath of life and the generator of ideas, and he is associated with the color white.

 I'KI' B'ALAM represents the *South*. His energy is Water. He is manifested in nature. The Earth's water and vegetation and giver of life, he is associated with the color yellow.

Chac, god of rain and accompanying frogs, with the glyphs of the four directions

The forces that make up the world, the Seven Deities, converge in the middle of this square. The Tree of Life represents the center of the universe. It is the *axis mundi*, the middle, the space where the underworld and overworld converge. (In humans, this is one's alter ego.) The Tree of Life is symbolized by the sacred ceiba tree. Its roots are nourished by the underworld, captor of telluric energy, while its trunk represents the reality of this world (a phallic symbol), and its canopy is the connection to the cosmic, the subtlety of the overworld.

The oldest story of Mayan cosmo-vision describes how reality is manifested in the three levels of the Tree of Life: the underworld, the world, and the overworld. The Nine Deities rule the underworld, while the Thirteen Deities rule the overworld. These deities are related to the great cycles: those of the underworld to the *B'olom Tiku'* prophetic period, nine cycles of fifty-two years each that are negative, and those of the overworld to the *Oxlajuj Tiku'* prophetic period, thirteen cycles of fifty-two years each that are positive.

It must be noted that attempts have been made to equate Xib'alb'ay, the underworld, with the Christian concept of hell, but Xib'alb'ay and hell are actually quite different. Xib'alb'ay is telluric energy and a real space within this dimension, a physical place where one form of humanity lived.

14

PRESENT-DAY MAYA

Mayan history does not end with the conquest. Present-day Maya are not simply the degenerate descendants of this fabulous civilization, as we are often led to believe.

At the time of the conquest, Spain was superstitious and greatly influenced by the Holy Inquisition. We must remember that while the rest of Europe was living in the Renaissance, Spain was still in the Middle Ages, lagging far behind its neighbors after eight centuries of Arab rule. Poverty was rampant, and the country was weakened by the instability of its small kingdoms. Given this state of affairs, a majority of the conquistadors were illiterate and lacked the culture needed to appreciate anything they found in the "New World." Their primary goal was to become rich by finding gold and precious stones.

As if that weren't enough, Catholic priests, most of whom were inquisitors, accompanied the conquistadors. These holy men saw the devil at every turn and strove to destroy all traces of the great Mayan culture. They murdered our Elders and *H-Menob'*, or Mayan priests, leaving our people devastated and deprived of their leaders. The Elders knew this period of darkness was coming because the prophecies had been very clear. Therefore, many of them had already moved deep into the jungle or hidden in the highlands, where they maintained their lineages, rulers, and cosmo-vision.

The conquistadors never managed to subjugate all of the Mayan tribes. For example, Tayasal on the shores of Lake Petén Itzá in the region of Petén, Guatemala, was never vanquished. The Maya continued to live there and lead a traditional life until the late nineteenth century, when they decided to move elsewhere. In Mexico, the Spaniards never made it past Mérida, Yucatán, a city the *H-Menob'* left to the conquistadors when they moved into the jungle and along the coasts of Yucatán and Quintana Roo. It was not until this century that the Maya began to assimilate into Western society. The same is true of the Ixiles in the highland departments of Quiché and Huehuetenango in Guatemala. The people there had little or no contact with European civilization until the 1940s, so the Mayan tradition and culture were sustained. The Chamula, Chortí, Chol, Dzensal, Tzotzil, and Lacandón people in the highlands of Chiapas, Mexico, are considered among the most classical preservers of the legacy. The culture also continued in the departments of San Marcos and Huehuetenango, cradle of the Mam civilization and the ancestral Q'anjob'al. In the department of Alta Verapaz, cradle of the Q'eqchi' civilization, nothing other than Q'eqchi' was spoken until approximately fifteen years ago, and their heritage has been preserved intact all this time. This honorable people beat the Spaniards in every battle and were never conquered. Their ruler at the time actually signed an armistice in Spain with the king himself, who declared the Q'eqchi' kingdom free and not tributary. This territory covered what are now the departments of Alta Verapaz, Baja Verapaz, Izabal, and southern Petén in Guatemala, as well as southern Belize. It was the Dominican priests, led by Friar Bartolomé de Las Casas, who annexed these people through sheer trickery. Once they established a presence in the region, the priests then allowed the fortune hunters and soldiers to come, and they murdered the Q'eqchi' leaders.

After five hundred years of slavery, exploitation, isolation, discrimination, and extreme poverty, it is no wonder that the Maya ceased building their pyramids and lost some of their impressive knowledge and abilities. Such is not the case with other aspects of the tradition. The Maya developed a way of life based on a theocracy, governed by kings who were also *Ajq'ijab'* (spiritual guides) representing Father Sun on Earth. Possessing vast knowledge that the Western world is only beginning to discover, they refined the arts and developed the highest form of spirituality. The great sages preserved this esoteric science, and our *Ajq'ij* Grandfathers and wise men still pass it down from generation to generation within the various clans. Magical mysticism sustains our cosmovision and forms the basis of a living tradition, perhaps the oldest in human memory.

Modern-day Maya, the millions of indigenous people in the highlands of Guatemala, southern Chiapas, northeastern Guatemala, and some areas of the Yucatán, are the heirs to the Great Tradition. There are Elders in Petén who still know how to read our ancestors' hieroglyphs. A number of secret codices are being held in the northeast and elsewhere, and we expect them to be brought to light soon. Given the incredible breadth of scientific, mathematical, and astronomical information in the four known codices, those still in safekeeping are sure to reveal even more wonders of ancient knowledge.

According to the prophecies, there has been a resurgence of deep Mayan spirituality during our present period. Over 60 percent of the population in Guatemala is of Mayan origin. Despite the introduction of other religions over the last half-century, most still follow their Grandfathers' traditions. More and more people around the world are beginning to recognize the potential of the unique and pragmatic simplicity of the Mayan tradition to lead us to a state of supreme awareness.

15

RI LAJ MAM AND MAXIMÓN:
A NATIVE AMERICAN SAINT

One day I stood with Don Manuel Mendoza, one of the greatest authorities on the Mayan Tzutujil tribe, on the shores of beautiful Lake Atitlán in the town of Santiago Atitlán in the heart of the Guatemalan highlands. I asked him to tell me the story of Ri Laj Mam.

"Long ago," he said, "there was a respectable old man, perhaps the oldest of the Elders, though no one knew his age for sure. He was an extraordinary man. After the conquest, the Spaniards divided up all of the land that used to be ours. They gave us their word and even brought documents from their king in Spain supposedly certifying that we legally owned small plots known as indigenous communal property. Since we had been forewarned of the grand design for this period, or *k'atun*, we didn't protest. However, the Spaniards' ambition was more powerful than their documents or their word. As increasing numbers of Spaniards came to live in our lands, the conquistadors decided to take back what little they had given us, raped our women, killed wantonly, and forced us to work constantly without any regard to age or condition. Our leaders had told us we must endure—it was our Grandfathers' prophecy—if we didn't want our entire people and tradition to disappear.

"This was the state of affairs when one of the greatest men to have survived the cruelty and killings decided to come out of hiding. This great *Chi-Mam* possessed superior knowledge and power and had the ability to counteract the worst spells and sorcery. He was famous among our people, though we hadn't seen him perform any wonders for a very long time. Ri Laj Mam, as he was known, was furious with the way things were and began encouraging people to rise up against their oppressors. In addition to all of the torture, suffering, and death, there were the Spanish priests and friars who came to teach their commandments and their truths in order to subjugate, persecute, and enslave us. What sort of future could we hope for under these conditions?

"Ri Laj Mam first went from house to house and then began coming to the town square. Incredulous, the Spaniards tried to arrest him, but he always managed to slip away through the crowd. Our people's spirits were lifting, so the Spaniards sent a large regiment to capture and imprison Ri Laj Mam the next time he came to the square. To their great surprise, however, he escaped and was out in the plaza the very next day stirring up the population with even more fervor. They took him again, this time handcuffing him and using heavy chains to hang him from a dungeon wall. But Ri Laj Mam was out in the main square again the next morning as if nothing had happened, inciting his fellow citizens to act. He was caught once again, handcuffed and bound, and this time guards were posted both inside and outside the cell. However, his guards fell asleep that night, and he escaped once more.

"The Spaniards couldn't believe it. Unable to keep him in custody, they asked some Tlaxcaltec sorcerers whom they had brought with them for help. Their combined strength was enough to counteract our Grandfather's power. The next time he was caught, these sorcerers were sent to guard him, and he was unable to escape. The Spanish authorities called the townspeople to a meeting, where they tried Ri Laj Mam as a subversive and a witch. He was decapitated, and they set his head on a pole that they placed in the middle of the square to illustrate their power and terrorize the indigenous people. Suddenly, this *Chi-Mam* appeared on the other side of the plaza. Whenever they rushed to grab him, he would turn up across the square. News later came that he appeared in several towns at once with that same ability to disappear right under the noses of the guards who were trying to catch him.

"Emotions were running high, and the people were organizing a revolt. The other Elders and *Chi-Mams* called a meeting, and the great Ri Laj Mam appeared as they were discussing matters. He asked them to combine all of their power and magic arts to vanquish the conquistadors once and for all. The Elders reminded him of our Grandfathers' prophecy and asked him to stop because his actions would only lead to the complete annihilation of the Great Tradition. They knew they had to accept the grand design and simply endure this period of darkness and death; the time would come when light and wisdom would return.

"This great *Chi-Mam* agreed to accept the grand design and the Elders' counsel. He then asked them and the entire clan to let him live with his people forever, where he could protect them from injustice and help them whenever they needed it. He therefore sent them to find a tree that would take his spirit. The Elders set out to search for such a tree, but none would accept the honor. They finally asked one of the oldest trees in the forest, and it told them to look for the *tz'ite*, or coral tree, that grew on the coast. They went and found one willing to accept this sacrifice. After various ceremonies, they cut down the tree and carried it back, never letting it touch the ground and without any women being present, as their tradition required.

"Before the ceremony that would allow Ri Laj Mam's spirit to become part of the tree, he asked the Elders to cut it into four pieces and send one to each of the four cardinal points, from which he would safeguard the tradition and ease his people's suffering."

The story does not end there. Evil returned to our lands after a very long time, toward the end of the century before last. A governor came to power who favored his compatriots, stripped us of what little land we had left, and took many of our children for forced labor. We were once again enslaved by a malevolent, cruel man.

At about the same time, the governor had been told to appoint the learned Don Francisco Zojbel as a judge in our town. The son of an influential Spanish father and a Mayan mother, Don Francisco had been born here and raised in our tradition by the Grandfathers, so he empathized with our suffering. He immediately began setting things right, revoking the privileges that the governor's friends had been given and curtailing their excesses. He also gave the land back to everyone who had been stripped of it, thus becoming our community's benefactor and protector.

All of this, of course, enraged the *kaxlanes*, or white men, and they plotted to have Don Francisco assassinated. First they hired a group of bandits who ambushed and shot at him several times, but none hit their mark. Then they tried to kill our beloved, powerful benefactor by planting a servant in his house who poisoned his food at the first opportunity. Don Francisco ate heartily of that meal but didn't get so much as a stomachache. Finally, at a loss for what to do next, they chased after him on horseback as he was returning to his village. When they rounded a corner at top speed, by some miracle his executioners' horses suddenly took fright. Several became mired in the mud, and quite a few were badly injured; the rest died.

Word of these events spread, and the people began to believe that Don Francisco was a powerful *Chi-Mam*, none other than the reincarnation of Ri Laj Mam come to protect them once again. This beloved Grandfather, judge, and mayor had a big mustache, liked to smoke cigars and stay out late drinking, and was a renowned ladies' man. The people affectionately called him Ximon. After Don Francisco died, effigies were made of him because they thought he was Ri Laj Mam, and the two names were combined: "Mam" from Ri Laj Mam and the term of endearment "Ximon" for Don Francisco resulted in the name Mamximon, or Maximón.

He is still revered today. We ask Maximón to intervene and perform miracles whenever we need help. This powerful figure is one of the most famous and most deeply respected saints for how quickly and effectively he provides assistance. His image can be found around the world. We drink a toast to his effigy and offer him one of the cigars he loved so much. Unlike others, Maximón is a very human saint who understands our nature, our weaknesses, and our needs.

16

NAJT, OR SPACE-TIME

Unlike the Western world's more linear vision, the Mayan perception of time is intertwined with space and frequency. Time in the West consists of limits in the form of schedules and agendas. This is perfectly summed up in the expression "time is money." Space is seen as a physical, territorial manifestation in the form of possession. This division is what has given rise to conflicts and confusion.

Stories from our Mayan Grandfathers, particularly in the oral tradition, say that everything exists within a giant macrospiral that arises right next to the Pleiades. This sole spiral contains everything that has a material form, what we call *teos*, or the universe. Anything without an essence exists outside of this spiral. Scientists did indeed find a wormhole next to the Pleiades.

Within this Mayan understanding, *najt* is defined as space-time with the addition of frequency. These three factors delineate what we know as reality, and matter exists within this reality. Everything that exists is energy, and everything has a frequency or vibration. This is what differentiates every living thing: a person's energy or vibration is faster than a stone's, for example, but both consist of energy. The difference between the two lies in frequency.

"Follow the light," we've been told, as if darkness were negative. However, when Mayan sages say to follow the light, they don't mean follow behind it, but get ahead of it. The idea is to move forward and exceed the speed of light. Light and dark are merely facets of reality. Once one achieves this, one's connection with reality is no longer linear.

If we are able to manipulate the light, it means that we're able to shatter constraints inside our spirit and consciousness and go beyond it. We blaze a new trail, and everything comes into focus. This is when we acquire a sense of being. We no longer struggle with demons. We are outside the limitations of space-time; frequency is our channel to transcendence, to exceeding such limits. When we are able to perceive the essence, we touch God.

In infinite space there is no visible light between one planet and another. All that can be seen are the planets reflecting the sun, highlighting the sun's importance. Everything is based on *Ajpu*, the Sun, and everything is relative to the center of the galaxy, which is a black hole. We are actually spinning in a revolution of the macrospiral. The borders of the macrospiral come into contact with one another, and that is when adjustments take place in the universe. The Maya were obsessed with breaking through these borders in order to travel in space-time. *Najt* is where we reside and what most people understand. More precisely, it is where most people are trapped, in what we call reality. It is also what leads us to what we call the past or future, both of which are abstractions. The past does not exist. It existed. Now it's only a memory. The future does not exist either; it's what will be. There is only this instant, this very moment, the eternal present.

Explosions in the universe can be compared to those that take place inside of each of us: one has to explode mentally in order to break free of the limitations of one's perceptions.

This then begs the question: are there other dimensions or realities? The answer is yes. There are other dimensions where space-time-frequency is measured or configured differently and is beyond our comprehension. We have potential access to thousands of other dimensions, while even more fall outside our perception. The Grandfathers call these unreal dimensions "unconfigured space."

The *Popol Vuh* speaks of parallel dimensions as paradise and calls them Paxil and Kayala. In Paxil our perceptions are different. Our senses sharpen, and we are surrounded by a tranquil, harmonious, peaceful energy. It's like going back to the matrix, the origin. *Najt* is manifested differently here. What happens in one day in Paxil takes a year in our world, while what happens in one year in Kayala takes a day here. The reference of space, time, and frequency is therefore not the same in other dimensions.

Light behaves differently in these parallel dimensions. There is no sun. The light is brighter, but not warmer. It's a clear, all-encompassing light. The most exquisite fruit and the most incredible stones can be found in Paxil, but most importantly, we are accepted unconditionally there—we are truly loved!

None of these wonders, not so much as an apple, can pass from one world to another. Therefore, those who cannot let them go are trapped. The importance of this is set out in the account in the *Popol Vuh* of a mouse and an ant being able to bring kernels of corn back from Paxil and Kayala to make human beings. This is the only reference to any transfer from one dimension to another.

Some six hundred years ago, when the ancient Maya knew that a period of destruction was coming, they sent entire populations to Paxil. According to the prophecies, these Maya are now returning in order to help humans and Mother Earth during this time of transition to *Job Ajaw*.

17

DON ISIDRO'S VISION

Sadly, humankind is divided by a different vision when inter-
preting the world, humanity, its reason for being, and its destiny. Western culture found its answer in the form of material
reasoning, while the Eastern world developed based on natural
thinking.

—DON ISIDRO,
Mayan sage

There are reasons we are in the state we're in," Don Isidro
said, "reasons we see, perceive, feel, behave, and act the way
we do, even reasons for how we conceive of 'thought.' This word
encompasses a vast complex of mental structures, ideas, and images that grew as the Western world evolved. Amazingly, these
have no order or rational classification," Don Isidro observed,
"even though thought is the matrix that guides and drives an eth-
nocentric culture. There is no comprehensive order to thought!"

Despite what modern logic says—the essence of which has
been reconstructed and influenced by phenomenology—not all
aspects of thought have been cataloged or divided into categories.

Few understand, or even realize, that thought, as differentiated from thinking, is the most varied concept to which Western humanity has access. The concept is much more diverse than the monotony of everyday "life," as we call our existence. We could even say that thought is more varied than death itself. If we perceive of our lives in the day-to-day sense, then only thought is unlimited: it is changeable, adaptable, big, small, comprehensive, even finite in its infiniteness.

The Western world views reality through the narrow lens of ideas based on reason. This is where it differs from what the Maya believe. Caught up in worshiping reason and ignoring abstraction, the West is adrift, adapting to historical events. The Maya believe, on the other hand, that reality is connected to the Natural Order, to the perception of energy. We see the heart!

One day I asked Don Isidro what the Maya's vision is. "To understand our vision," Don Isidro said, "first you need to know how we see you. That way you'll be able to understand the natural cycle, the cosmic plan we're a part of, and the teachings our Fathers and Grandfathers passed down to us. What I'm about to say isn't meant to offend or to impose my way of thinking. This is not a competition. Most of humanity is now at the mercy of the white man's way of thinking. The white man, or *kaxlan*, is in control, in this and in a material or financial sense. All that has happened in the past few centuries was written. Our prophets warned our Grandfathers about the coming of the conquistadors [Hernán Cortés in 1519] and told us there would be no way to stop their rule until the Great Night, a period of 468 years, had elapsed.

"There are two visions, two ways of thinking about existence. The Western world starts from a position of logical reasoning.

This is the result of the state of spiritual neglect they're living in. Materialism is nothing more than a palliative for having distanced themselves from nature. Big cities were built without incorporating nature; they even overrode it. There was this sick need for possessions, wealth, and power; the Western world began to think that humans own the earth. They created religious dogma that became a series of impositions designed to dominate the masses. Out of this Puritanism arose an even greater illusion, that of technology and materialism. The West is mired in a state of confusion, licentiousness, and a worship of consumerism. Now they play at being gods and use scientific reasoning to back them up. This has brought nothing but destruction to the planet because they believe it's their divine order to possess or destroy the minds and lives of others. The entire economic system is controlled by one group, and they only see people as numbers, as puppets with a productive life span. To keep people in such a position, they blind them to true existence, making them believe they're free when actually they live in police states, ruled by laws and regulations that benefit only those in power. The saddest thing of all is that they've forgotten to live, forgotten to respect the Great Father, and every day they pollute our earth a little more.

"As a misguided response to this manipulation, some have taken refuge in fearsome religious fundamentalism, creating even more stringent rules. Under this new illusion, they dream of a paradise where they'll live in peace and harmony. Unfortunately, no such kingdom exists in this life; they must wait for death. In the meantime, they must suffer stoically. In other words, there is a submissive population that accepts everything about this 'divine' mandate.

"Along the way, they've created concepts that, under the umbrella of materialism, abuse the use of reason. Hand in hand with science, they've attempted to classify and place a value on everything. Anything they can't understand is snubbed, denied, or destroyed. They've appointed themselves judges, dismissing other cultures' truths and imposing their vision for all these years.

"All of this disorder has brought us to a dangerous point. There seems to be no end to the ecological disaster resulting from insanity, ambition, greed, and irresponsibility. This is how we see the West. Many of our own people have adopted this vision and lost touch with our ancestors' tradition. We were taught to respect and live in harmony with nature. In our vision, we are a part of creation, and we are equals with every other being that inhabits the earth. The knowledge our Father left us was respect. Our vision is of a Natural Order.

"Since their religious tradition gave them dominion over all beings and the earth, they control the life and resources of our brothers the plants and animals. In the name of development, they've determined the destiny of all of us who are a part of creation.

"By isolating themselves from nature, fear became a part of their lives, and they created rules to contain it. These are a contradiction to the Natural Order. In our vision, humans are not the owners of Mother Earth; we belong to her."

18

NOSTRADAMUS AND
THE MAYAN PROPHECIES

There is a special story told by our Grandfathers regarding one of the most renowned prophets in history, none other than Michel de Notredame, better known as Nostradamus. Don Ramón Carbala, a Mayan sage, told the following to me after a fire ritual at the ceremonial center of Tikal.

With the Pleiades visible in the sky as night fell, Don Ramón suddenly asked me what I knew about Nostradamus. Before I could answer, he said something that surprised me.

"Did you know that Nostradamus knew Mayan astrology?"

"No," I replied. "How is that even possible?"

As he sat on the grass in Tikal's plaza, Don Ramón said, "You know, history has forgotten all about a particular man, a doctor. No one knows if he was from Spain or Germany because he would sometimes introduce himself as Ulrico de Maguncia and other times as Ulrich von Maguncen. This doctor came to the Americas with the conquistadors, and in battle he would tend to both the

Spaniards and the indigenous people. His superiors weren't pleased; they didn't want him treating the natives. After being questioned several times, de Maguncia replied that he had to be true to his Hippocratic oath. The Spanish captains argued that it hadn't yet been determined whether the aboriginals were human or not. De Maguncia declared that he would leave for Europe if he weren't allowed to treat all patients equally. Because he was the only doctor, the Spaniards were forced to accept his conditions. When the conquistadors arrived in Chichén Itzá, Mexico, the Mayan priests had already heard about de Maguncia's stance and invited him to exchange ideas. He accompanied them into the jungle and wasn't heard from for fourteen years. The Spaniards assumed he was dead. Actually, de Maguncia was studying the Mayan sciences—medicine, astronomy, and astrology in particular.

"When the plague hit Europe, the Mayan Elders were afraid that it would make its way to the Americas and cause even more deaths here. They told de Maguncia how to control the problem and asked him to go back.

"The Spanish civil and religious authorities in the city of Mérida, Mexico, were shocked when he appeared before them, his hair grown long, dressed in a white Mayan tunic. He asked for permission to return to Europe and was finally given the funds to finance his voyage. De Maguncia chose to go to France because that was where he had studied for the priesthood before becoming a doctor. Quite strangely, he renounced his vows the day he was ordained and turned to studying medicine.

"Back in the chaos that was Europe, Nostradamus was one of the first of the alchemists, doctors, and sorcerers whom de Maguncia recruited. To get rid of the scourge, he instructed them to boil the water, burn the deceased's clothing, and put calcium in the graves and on the walls of the houses.

"Once the plague was under control, seven people came to study what de Maguncia had been taught by the Mayan Elders. Nostradamus became his closest disciple and learned to divine using the cauldron. The Mayan technique, unlike the European, used powdered quartz and mercury to obtain more clarity in the images of the past, present, and future. Nostradamus also studied Mayan astrology and projection techniques. Many of the quatrains in his centuries can only be understood if you are familiar with Mayan astrology, and Mayan experts are still making projections about Nostradamus's centuries. All agree that December 21, 2012, is not the end of the world but a change in the state of humanity.

"Ulrico de Maguncia and Nostradamus formed a secret society in which they taught ancient alchemy, astrology, and magic techniques brought from Egypt, India, Greece, and the Mayan world. Nostradamus was put in charge of this group when de Maguncia returned to the Americas."

There ended the story that Don Ramón told me some ten years ago. When I spoke to him recently and asked for permission to include it here, he told me much more about the secret society, which he called "the Brotherhood," and how it has maintained contact with Mayan clans and tribes. When the time is right, I will be able to share this with the world.

19

THE *TIKU'* PROPHECY

This extraordinary prophetic time, as Don Pascual liked to call it, is one of those rare, historic moments in *najt*, or space-time, when several convergences occur. We are currently at the end of one calendar cycle and the beginning of another, and it is without a doubt the change in the *Tiku'* cycle that has the most influence on these times.

The *Tiku'* cycles have to do with positive and negative periods that affect the planet. These are laid out in a calendar called the *Cycle of the Tiku'* and based on periods of fifty-two years. This is a magical number because the *Ab'* and *Cholq'ij* calendars coincide every fifty-two years, and it is also the age at which a person is in the prime of life.

The *Tiku'* is divided into two cycles. *Oxlajuj Tiku'* is a cycle of thirteen periods of fifty-two years each (13 × 52 = 676 years), known in the West as the Thirteen Heavens, or the Thirteen Lights. *B'olom Tiku'* is a cycle of nine periods of fifty-two years

each (9 × 52 = 468 years), known in the West as the Nine Underworlds, or the Nine Hells.

Oxlajuj Tiku' is a positive cycle for humanity, a time when harmony and knowledge prevail. Throughout history, we can see advances in the arts, sciences, and knowledge when this cycle
reigned. *B'olom Tiku'*, on the other hand, is a negative cycle when
obscurantism prevails. It is governed by materialism, frivolity, a
worship of the ego, and the mechanization of human beings. The
biggest wars and greatest tribulations in human history have
taken place during these periods.

The last *B'olom Tiku'* began with the conquest of the Americas,
and Hernán Cortés was none other than the architect and driv-
ing force behind it. The Spaniards' cruelty when imposing their
beliefs is widely recognized, and Cortés became known as Lord of
the Great Dark Night.

Many wonder how such savagery
was possible, how six hundred men
could defeat powerful armies that
numbered in the thousands. However, our Grandfathers' prophecies
had been clear: there was to be no
confrontation. These men had come
to dominate; they were the tyrants
and regents of this disastrous pe-

riod. Our Grandfathers' texts and prophecies were unambiguous
in this regard: if there was resistance and the conquistadors were
defeated, even more would come, and they would completely
eradicate the guardians of the Great Tradition.

The so-called Curse of Kukulkan, or Quetzalcóatl, the mythical sorcerer and prophet, warned that certain Aztec or Mexica witchcraft practices and human sacrifices were to be abolished, or the cruelty that would manifest itself during this *B'olom Tiku'* would be unlike anything in recent history.

This period began on August 17, 1519, and ended on August 16, 1987. August 17, 1987, marked the beginning of the "transition," which would last for five years (a period called *Wayeb Tiku,* which lasted until August 16, 1992.) The transition is a period of adjustment to a new cycle when events that occur are a preamble to what the new phase will bring. During this particular transition, the Berlin Wall came down, the Soviet bloc fell, military regimes and dictatorships disappeared in the Americas, democracies began to take shape, and apartheid came to an end in South Africa.

August 17, 1992, was the beginning of a new *Oxlajuj Tiku'* cycle, an interval of peace and harmony, when reason would rule and there would be a return to the Natural Order. Before we entered this period, however, there was a lapse of nine years, the *Alanem,* or the "gestation." A comparison can be made between what occurs during the nine months of pregnancy and events that have happened to humanity during gestation times. This cycle ended on the night of August 16, 2001, a date that coincides with prophecies from other traditions such as Saint Malaquias, Nostradamus, the Great Pyramid, Edgar Cayce, and Parravicini.

We warned that at the end of this *Alanem,* or "gestation," several events would occur that would have an impact on humanity. If they happened during the first twenty days after the *Alanem* period, the cleansing would accelerate. In other words, the cataclysms and therefore purging of the human race woul d be on a large scale. If the events occurred during the second period of twenty days, however, humanity would be able to minimize the destruction. Fortunately, everything happened during the second group of twenty days, including the destruction of the Twin Towers and the confirmation of the effects of global warming on the polar ice caps.

All of the Mayan prophecies that were made public have come true on the predicted dates, as did projections for the war in Iraq, the tsunamis, and events that are occurring in Asia such as the economic booms in China, India, and Malaysia. We are also experiencing the counterpart to this material energy that is expressed through violence. As a result, the Maya and their knowledge are becoming the focus of more attention.

Just as a child isn't born knowing how to walk, neither does the *Oxlajuj Tiku'* develop immediately. In the Mayan world, those who turn thirteen have completed their training and are ready to begin their own personal development. There is a period of thirteen years before the *Oxlajuj Tiku'* takes root. Thus, this period of light, harmony, and love will begin in 2014. It is not, of course, like flicking a switch and the light comes on all at once, but rather the beginning of a slow progression.

These cycles are described in books such as the prophetic *Books of Chilam Balam.*

PROPHECIES FROM THE
BOOKS OF CHILAM BALAM

The *Books of Chilam Balam* refer to several Mayan stories or texts that tell of the prophecies for various *k'atunes* (twenty-year periods). These were found in different towns by Catholic priests and friars during the conquest and translated into Latin by Mayan scribes.

Such texts were named for the town where they were found and for the most famous prophet, Chilam Balam, or Jaguar Fortune-Teller Sorcerer, one of the greatest Mayan diviners. Unfortunately, all we know about this sorcerer-priest is that he was called Aj Zotz' Tz'i' Kan. Although the  *Book of Chilam Balam of Manik* and the *Book of Chilam Balam of Chumayel* are the best-known, we have used the text from Saq Kan Tiku' because this ceremonial center maintained its tradition until just two centuries ago and its prophets were of the highest prestige.

Those interested in studying the *Books of Chilam Balam* will find that the same prophecies are repeated in the different manuscripts. This indicates that the ancient prophets communicated with one another. We know they held large council meetings to deal with scientific matters, especially the calendars, and to discuss the guidelines issued by the Council of Elders and wise prophets. They would meet in the city that had been designated as the seat— the ceremonial center with the highest concentration of energy according to the reigning *k'atun*—and would issue their prophecies for that and subsequent twenty-year periods. These would determine the rules and strategies that all Maya were to follow.

The Maya, and particularly those who had the gift of sight, developed the act of prophesying, as we have noted, by studying the divinatory techniques. All of the prophecies in these books were very similar given that they all referred to the same people during the same period of time.

This period of twenty years began on April 5, 1993, and will end on December 20, 2012. The prophecy of 6 *Ajaw K'atun* was foretold in the *Books of Chilam Balam* as follows:

"Six *Ajaw K'atun* shall have its seat in Uxmal, which brings its own energy. Take note of its words and they will come true in time. Since this is the word and order that will be manifest in our ancient writing, the one in our folded books, the figures that speak to us, so shall it be in the times that are indicated and spoken of in the corresponding *k'atun*, *Kinich Kakmo*.

"This reign will be one of shameless looks and foolish talk;

lecherous will be these words, lies, illusion, and deceit. Life will be hypocritical, for deceit and the breakdown of truth will reign. So shall it be. The usurpers of the mat shall reign.* Arguments, violent disputes, hidden and deceitful disputes—there will be disputes among subjects and these will be hidden. So says 6 *Ajaw*. Trees will be consumed. There will be insufficient food; even stones will be sought. A great famine will occur if the damage is not corrected, if the impostor, he of the lecherous word, is not stopped. Death will sit on his mat. This will be his throne. The *Halach-Winic* [rulers] will be persecuted, the false ones who do not know their position or duty because they are not noble, for there is no limit to their ambition.

"Certain stars will bring violent disputes, hidden disputes on men and on their sons. There will be sadness in the sky given this violence among its subjects. Three times there will be famine. There will be no tortillas, only yam beans and breadnuts to eat. There will be depopulation and the destruction of peoples. There will be powerful men and princes only at the end, for at such time the day will soon come when the Mother will turn to see the sky, then turn again. Nothing will be beneficial. So shall the lies and lechery end.

"A somnolence will begin with the new reign of a new god, the one of the cross. All will fall under the lies told in flattering words and the subsequent hope of resuscitation that will come about with this new law, with this prophet, this one who allows no other stars in the sky. The lecherous word will make men drowsy. Few will be honest with this new *Ajpop* [Lord of the Mat]. He will

---

* *Translator's note*: In Mayan tradition, only gods, great lords or chiefs, were allowed to sit on the mat.

be a false *Halach-Winic*. His word will be twisted and his powers humbled. Nearly everyone will come to his palace.

"Foolish, lecherous words are the first burden of this *k'atun*. God the Father will come down to lay blame, to judge the falsity of the word. Thus the people will be servile. They will live half-asleep. So shall they eat and so shall they die. For this they will be judged.

"This is the burden of 6 *Ajaw K'atun*."

The prophecy in the *Book of Chilam Balam of Chumayel* is uncannily similar:

"Six *Ajaw K'atun* is the tenth that is told. Uxmal is the seat that focuses on itself. Ardent is the power on the face of its reign, which will lie with foolish, lecherous words. Thus God the Father will come down to lay blame and cut the throats of those who use false words. Then he will resuscitate and await the justice of Our God the Father so all subjects will come to the new but old religion of a fundamentalist God, a severe, punishing God. For everyone born on this Earth must go through this new but old conquest. This is the burden of 6 *Ajaw K'atun* established for this *k'atun*."

As you can see, not only are the two prophecies clear but they coincide. Although the first is more revealing, both speak of a lying, lecherous government and especially false prophets, those who dominate politics through lies and illusion.

These prophecies warn of events that are occurring now. The lecherous lies, the way in which we have allowed ourselves to be subjugated, and the false promises are glaringly obvious. We are being controlled by the system and manipulated by politicians offering false promises. There is economic chaos all over the planet. When you add in the wanton consumerism incited by mass media and the damage we've done to Mother Earth, the result is a state of absolute human recklessness. We are suffering the consequences of this on many levels: climate change, pollution, and, worse still, widespread racial hatred and intolerance that have resulted in wars and famine.

Globalization as a panacea for the world ultimately forces humanity to live under a single vision, one of consumerism. It disrespects the individual and annihilates traditions. Essentially, globalization is the basis for much of the world's conflict today. The wars in Iraq, Afghanistan, the former Yugoslavia, the Middle East, India, and Pakistan—we have become inured to all of them. The pain, violation, and destruction only serve to satisfy the whims of those who are drunk on power and believe they have been called upon to save the world. They impose their interests on other cultures, ignoring people's right to self-determination. We are only sixteen years into this period, but more conflicts are in store.

Further, the prophecies speak of a different religion, one brought by the conquistadors in the four-hundred-year cycle prior to 6 *Ajaw K'atun* and imposed on the Native American population under circumstances we are all well aware of. Another form of the same religion arises in our current cycle, that of fundamentalist sects whose vision is confrontational and dogmatic. These have already gained ground in Central America, converting nearly 40 percent of the population, thereby fulfilling this part of the prophecy. Without a doubt, the combination of lies and subjugation is changing their values, drawing them into a state of unconsciousness—all in the name of a religion that has lost its true purpose and must return to its beginnings and reclaim the true transcendence on which it was based.

"The Mother will turn to see the sky, then turn again." This means there will first be a warning about what could happen, and then a second period will arrive during which, if we haven't gained awareness or managed to find accord with Mother Earth, all of humanity will be cleansed.

Prophecies regarding the changes in store for humankind during the next *k'atun*, 4 *Ajaw*, are much more benign. According to the *Books of Chilam Balam*, the quetzal, or green bird, will arrive: hope, harmony, a fourth vomiting of blood or purification. This will be an era of unity and the reestablishment of humanity.

THE PROPHECY OF
THE CRYSTAL SKULLS

Crystal skulls are ancient carvings, in different kinds of quartz, of the human skull. It's said that they possess extraordinary powers. They are a complete mystery within the already enigmatic Mayan world. Neither their age nor their provenance has been determined, and we have found no references to them in historical documents. Most of the crystal skulls were found in Mayan temples in Guatemala, Belize, and the states of Yucatán and Quintana Roo in Mexico, but one was also found in Teotihuacán near Mexico City, one in South Africa, one in Greece, one in Albania, and three in Egypt. Those found in temples such as Grand Jaguar in Tikal and La Danta in El Mirador, both in the Petén region of Guatemala, together balanced the pyramidal energy and were aligned to create a vibratory space that stimulated humanity.

The Mayan Elders have three different stories about where they came from. What we do know—because it is the same in all three versions—is that the skulls appeared in Atlantis and Lemuria, also known as Mu, the two lost continents. In the most widely known account, told by Elders in Guatemala, the skulls were created by great scientists from the lost continent of Atlantis, although some link their origin to Lemuria.

In the Guatemalan highlands, they say the Maya come from the Pleiades, where they obtained all of their knowledge and technological ingenuity, including the crystal skulls. The second star in the Pleiades was even named Maia by the Greeks.

The rarest stories say that the greatest wise men live in parallel dimensions related to Kayala (paradise) and that this is where they sculpted the crystal skulls. They say that these skulls contain all historical and scientific information. The closest modern comparison I can make is to a super-computer—that is, something more advanced than anything we can imagine.

Each of the skulls has a specific property. Some predict the future, others align energy or purify the environment, still others can elevate one's level of consciousness or increase one's ability to visualize, while some even have the power to cure illnesses. Almost all of them can alter the perception of reality.

The best-known is the Mitchell-Hedges skull, found in Lubaantun, Belize. It was the first to attract attention because of its magical qualities. Staring at this skull, one begins to see waves; focusing the attention a little more, one can see images of events happening elsewhere or in the future. It is made of pure quartz, changes from azure blue to crystal clear, and is perfectly representative of a human, dolichocephalic skull. It was the first to be studied at university laboratories. Although the results were never made public, it is rumored that the computer manufacturer Hewlett-Packard obtained copies of them.

The skull found at the El Mirador site, known as Rosewood, is one of the most amazing. It projects two holograms of the sign *Ajpu* from the *Cholq'ij* calendar when a light is shone on its crown. This skull is made of rose quartz, as is another called Paulie. Rosewood is the only known skull to depict the human brain inside, complete with glands, veins, and cells! We are unable to explain how these skulls were made. The craftsmanship, beauty, and other wondrous qualities are unrivaled.

Many of these treasured objects are in museums or private collections. The Elders believe that the skulls possess living properties and that taking them from their rightful place and locking them away is tantamount to imprisonment.

It was Don Isidro who announced the prophecy of the crystal skulls. He said they were created to help Mother Earth and humanity during the transition from the Fourth to the Fifth Sun. The ancients created 520 skulls in the hopes that at least 52 would survive. These will be reunited at a lake on or around December 21, 2012. A person will walk across the water to a small island, pass under a waterfall, and enter a cave where the mother skull will be. When it is brought out of the cave, it will activate all of the other skulls encircling the lake with their respective guardians. As soon as these skulls are activated, we will have access to knowledge so profound that modern-day humanity can't even conceive of it. The guardians, sages, and scientists will be able to use this technology to regenerate the ecosystem and repair the hole in the ozone. They will also be able to activate the 52,000 pyramids and create an energy belt providing enough electricity for the entire world.

Some of our Mayan Elders traveled to a Native American reservation where one of the spiritual guides mentioned that their

Grandfathers had told them that they were descended from the Maya. Later they showed our Elders a codex that spoke of the Spaniards' arrival, Hitler's rise to power, the Cold War, the era of materialism that would destroy the environment, and the times we are living in now. They told the Maya that they refer to them as the Lords of Time and also said that they had forgotten when they were to return the Warrior's Bow. Once our Mayan Elders gave them dates to return the bow on a hill shaped like an ear, they told the Native American Elders that they were looking for the crystal skulls. One of the Native American Elders pulled out some maps that showed the lake where the skulls will be reunited and said that two of their great sages had safeguarded the knowledge needed to activate the skulls.

To date, twenty-eight genuine skulls have been found, and their guardians are people of conscience who understand the importance of this reunion. The Grandfathers chose to reveal the prophecy of the crystal skulls and the reunion because they need to find the remaining twenty-four. Unfortunately, however, this quest has been plagued by fortune hunters, forgers, and false messiahs who claim they possess the skulls and are able to activate them. Still, our Grandfathers are certain that enough of the true skulls will be retrieved in time. It will be catastrophic if they fail to complete this mission.

22

JOB AJAW AND THE
PROPHECY OF 2012

In the infinite immensity of *najt*, in that which we call eternity, destiny can be changed. It is not inexorable! We are not condemned! We just lost our way, but we can fix it. We can begin again!

—RAMÓN CARBALA,
Mayan Mam traditionalist and thinker

The most widely circulated Mayan prophecy is that of *Job Ajaw Nimahaab*. This particular prediction is of great importance. During this "prophetic time," as our Grandfathers call it, various prophecies converge.

As I've mentioned, our predictions for the *Tiku'* cycles have been very accurate. The start of the transition period, from 1987 to 1992, was an extremely intense time. On a broader scale, attention was drawn to the environmental damage wrought by humans. The Western world became more interested in the Maya when Rigoberta Menchú won the Nobel Peace Prize in 1992 for her efforts to bring attention to the plight of Guatemala's indigenous people during the civil war. Mayan traditions and spirituality gained a wider audience, and their knowledge—including the sacred calendar, the prophecies, and a harmonious awareness of Mother Earth—spread.

As the *Tiku'* cycle continued during what is known as the gestation period from 1992 to 2001, more political and socioeconomic transitions occurred. The truth about corporate greed was exposed: large companies declared hidden billion-dollar deficits, banks operated in the red, the New York Stock Exchange suffered a crash nearly as bad as the one in the 1930s, and the price of oil began to rise. Ethnic and racial divides grew worse, with fundamentalist extremists and racist groups speaking out openly. Other man-made catastrophes included the attack on the Twin Towers, the war in Afghanistan, the war in Iraq, the conflict between India and Pakistan, and the U.S. government's woefully inept response to Hurricane Katrina. There were also natural catastrophes, such as floods, extreme droughts, plagues, earthquakes, deglaciation, and volcanic eruptions.

The prophecy of Kaokan sets out the transfer of energy from Asia to America, its movement from India and Tibet to the Sierra Madre and Andes mountain ranges, to awaken energy centers that will act as spiritual hubs for Mother Earth and humanity. We've seen what a profound effect this energy has had on the countries it passed through. Having reached the jungle and been blocked at the Panama Canal, it returned to the Four Corners in the United States, with obvious disastrous consequences. This *k'atun* will end on December 20, 2012, and a new cycle of four hundred years, or twenty *k'atunes*, will begin.

Finally, the famous date of December 21, 2012, is the start of a new cycle called *Job Ajaw*, or the Fifth Sun. This new era will be ushered in by the solar meridian crossing the galactic equator and the earth aligning with the center of the galaxy. At sunrise on December 21, 2012, for the first time in 26,000 years, the sun will rise to intersect with the Milky Way and the plane of the ecliptic. This cosmic cross, traced in the sky, is considered to embody the sacred tree, the Tree of Life, known to all of the world's spiritual traditions.

Job Ajaw is one cycle in the *Nimahaab*, or Long Count, a period of 26,000 years divided into five periods of 5,200 years, each relating to the movement of the sun with respect to the Milky Way. The Grandfathers call this "a return to the beginning."

The *Nimahaab* macro cycle is divided into the following five cycles known as the *Ajaw*.

JUN AJAW—*The First Sun*   The first cycle of 5,200 years was governed by feminine energy, or matriarchy, and the element Fire. Jun Ajaw was a formation period. Fire played an important role, in both the survival and the development of human beings, as did Mother Earth, provider of nourishment and fertilization during the hunting, gathering, and agricultural stages. This led to a worship of feminine deities as procreators of the human race as well as conservers and preservers of food and the knowledge needed for survival: weaving, animal husbandry, social organization, worship, and rituals of a magic-spiritual nature.

CAB AJAW—*The Second Sun*   The second cycle of 5,200 years was governed by masculine energy, or patriarchy, and the element Earth. *Cab Ajaw* was a period of both economic and intellectual development. Agricultural techniques and architecture were perfected, ceremonial buildings and temples were constructed, and urban centers began to develop. Masculine deities were worshiped: the gods of knowledge (sacred architecture, astronomy, and mathematics), wisdom (astrology and adjustments to the sacred *Cholq'ij* calendar), creation (creators, makers, the Sun, Moon, Venus, and Pleiades), and war and hunting. There was also territorial expansion, which led to relationships with other civilizations in the world and a reshaping of the spiritual order (syncretic with respect to the previous cycle).

OXIB AJAW—*The Third Sun*   The third cycle of 5,200 years was governed by feminine energy (manifestation of women) and the element Air. Higher feminine deities were worshiped; the cosmic-telluric deity as manifest in feminine wisdom, the gods of love, the god of death, and cosmic-anthropomorphic gods. *Oxib Ajaw* was a period of development of the mind and spirit. During this cycle, great advances were made in the sciences of the psyche, art, and astronomy. This led to readjustment of the cosmic order, more precise determination of planetary orbits, Venusian, solar, galactic, and *Ab'* calendars, and community implementation of the sacred *Cholq'ij* calendar. Mathematics developed further with the implementation of the number zero and greater precision in measuring time. This ultimately led to the consolidation of the cosmo-vision.

KAJIB AJAW—*The Fourth Sun*   The fourth cycle of 5,200 years has been governed by masculine energy and the element Water. *Kajib Ajaw* has been a period of unification and interrelationship between city-states and a time when theocracy has reigned. Masculine energy and Water have influenced the civilizations of this world and the diffusion of a culture that is highly developed technologically and spiritually. This period has been complicated, because material energy brings the power to dominate matter. In spite of incredible scientific and technological development, we have become victims of our own unconsciousness. Rather than reflecting on ourselves and the world around us to attain wisdom, we are destroying our environment. We believe we are all-powerful, we worship reason and materialism, and we have become slaves of our own marvelous innovations. We must stop and remember what is truly valuable or we are heading toward the destruction of Mother Earth and all of humanity.

Events will occur toward the end of the *Kajib Ajaw* cycle marked by what we call "the purification." A period of warnings or awareness began in August 2001, and unless we take action, the destructive power of these events will only increase. We are living during a time when we will see major earthquakes, large volcanic eruptions (many from inactive volcanoes), floods, hurricanes, tsunamis, radical climate change, and other natural disasters. These will be accompanied by plagues and epidemics such as AIDS, diabetes, and drug-resistant infections. There will be wars and many other man-made disasters as we continue to participate in our own demise. The purification will end in September 2010 and will be followed by a period called "the definition," from September 23, 2010, to December 20, 2012.

Contrary to what many people believe, the definition will not mean the end of the world. It will be a time of cleansing, when all of the garbage in our minds, all of our consumerism, will be cleared away and replaced with a resurgence of true spirituality and a renewed respect for ourselves and everyone else on this planet. We will learn to take advantage of our technology without allowing it to consume us.

The reigning sign of this cycle is Water, which governs knowledge. Mass media and globalization have enabled different cultures to learn more about each other, and that has made the world more interconnected. However, racism and bigotry still exist. Every society thinks it has the best way of life and wants to impose its vision and religion on others and blames others for environmental chaos. Overpopulation and competing economic interests have made us distrustful. We have an abundance of information but no meaning or purpose.

Mankind is confused and has no idea what's going to happen next! This fear of the end of the world is making us feel helpless in the face of inevitability. Many prefer to escape through drugs, alcohol, sex, and a perennially libertine existence. Still others cling to quasi-religions that put a dollar value on salvation.

As we witness economic, social, and spiritual erosion, face intolerance, and listen to the drums of war beating in the four corners of the Earth, there is no light to guide us. Many cultures have used the great traditions' cosmo-vision as a basis for their belief systems, but rather than providing guidance for a harmonious life today and for future generations, these traditions simply assure believers that they will find happiness after death.

It is the responsibility of all humankind to leave behind a better world, to create awareness and unity, to stop the destruction. For those who haven't noticed, we outnumber our leaders. In a democratic society, those who govern work for those who elected them, but the system has become so distorted that we're lost, forgetting that ultimately we, as a unified group, hold the power. The leaders decide there will be wars. We have allowed them to decide when and who they will fight. They make deals and pass laws that benefit only a few. If ordinary office workers don't do their job well, they're given an opportunity to change. What happens if they don't? They're fired! We can't fall prey to inertia—we must take responsibility for our future! Don't let others decide for us!

JOB AJAW—*The Fifth Sun*   The fifth cycle of 5,200 years will be governed by both masculine and feminine energy (balance) and the element Ether. December 21, 2012, is the pivotal date that everyone has heard of. According to our tradition, this is when the period of Job Ajaw, or the Fifth Sun, is expected to begin. This period is of great importance because it will be a time when humans ascend to a harmonious, spiritual level.

This 5,200-year cycle begins in the year 2012. It is important to note that neither the feminine nor the masculine will be supreme, but that the two energies will be equally balanced. The two will support one another, and the qualities in one will elevate qualities in the other.

The element will be Ether, which combines with the other four elements on a higher level. Fire, Earth, Air, and Water will act together in a subtle manifestation, activating full consciousness in Mother Earth and humanity. The hope is that it will be a cycle of mental and spiritual growth, of true realization.

It's important to know that things will not change automatically on this date. It all depends on what happens to us in the meantime, at the end of the Fourth Sun. Much of humanity could disappear if we fail to become aware and take action during this preamble period of disasters.

As we have said and will continue to say, December 21, 2012, does not mark the end of the world, as some would have us believe owing to their own ignorance, fatalist tendencies, or failure to study the messages and prophecies in depth. Still others have taken advantage of this knowledge and misrepresented what our Grandfathers have said in order to manipulate people. This has caused a great deal of confusion.

The writer José Arguelles has combined Chinese and Mayan astrology to create his own version of the sacred calendar. We disavow this version because it is unfounded and contains errors. For example, the names of some of the *nawales* are incorrect. We emphatically reject his way of determining each person's sign, any *nawales* that do not exist in the sacred *Cholq'ij* calendar, and his interpretation of these signs.

Arguelles obtained his information from works written by the Franciscan priest Diego de Landa, who came to Yucatán, Mexico, shortly after the conquest in 1549 and became the bishop of that state. Known as the greatest destroyer of Mayan knowledge, one of his greatest "achievements" was to burn more than ten thousand Mayan codices in a single day, an act he boasted of. In the name of God, de Landa also tortured and burned our wise men and scientists because, in his eyes, the marvels they were capable of could only have been the work of the devil. Such was his insanity that his own companions reported him to the king of Spain, who ordered that they gather information about everything he had destroyed. De Landa wrote a book that recounts the stories told to him by his informants. Unable to differentiate between the agricultural and sacred calendars, he created confusion by reporting that they were the same. This is the book Arguelles used as the basis for his calendar, which he then combined with the Chinese calendar. While we have the utmost respect for Chinese astrology, what Arguelles presents is not part of the Mayan tradition.

When Arguelles came to Guatemala for the first time to visit ceremonial centers such as Tikal, the Council of Elders asked to meet with him and expressly forbade him to use the Mayan name, much less speak on their behalf in his writings and presentations. He was asked to explain to others that his teachings were the result of his personal combination of Chinese, Mayan, and Pleiadian astrology in addition to his own inventions.

Unsurprisingly, he never made any such clarification. He did stop using the Mayan name in his writings for a while and instead used the term "Pleiadian," but he took up the Mayan name again when interest began to wane. The *Job Ajaw* prophecy became his personal mission. He claims to be the reincarnation of Pakal Botan, a king of Palenque, and says he will enable Mother Earth to transition to the fifth element by mobilizing a photon belt from the Pleiades to our planet.

Arguelles is profiting from the general public's interest in the Maya. People believe his story out of ignorance. The Grandfathers don't want to waste their energy on such individuals, but they do ask people to be informed because Arguelles is not the only avatar out there passing on misinformation.

The Fifth Sun is a time of harmony, peace, tolerance, and balance. It ushers in a new framework that will modify the current socioeconomic system. Humanity's destiny depends on our reaction to the events we are experiencing now, our growing awareness, our seriousness, our ability to learn, and the action we take. It is important that we foster a positive outlook toward the Fifth Sun and avoid creating a mass hysteria.

It would be counterproductive to waste our energy fearing the worst. We cannot rely on government to lead this change, nor can we operate as individuals. We must find a way to work together. It is a joint problem given the way society and the economic order are formed. There may not seem to be any way out right now; the complicated, complex structures don't seem to want to give way, and instant gratification seems more important than humanity's well-being. But the prophecies are clear: all of the cycles come to an end with the arrival of *Job Ajaw*, and a time of peace, understanding, and harmony will come. It is up to all of us to ensure that the majority of humanity will be here when this happens.

We are in desperate need of this change. This is our opportunity—it is our responsibility—to elevate Mother Earth to a higher plane within the cosmic order!

Humanity will have access to a subtle dimensional form, and cosmic law will prevail. As we have already said, it is predicted that the *B'alameb'* will return for this period. These mythical beings, these Men-Gods, taught this humanity and are the cosmic guardians of the four corners of the universe. It is the descendants of the fourth *B'alam, Ik'i' B'alam*—the father of the energy in Water, the fourth element—who will reign during this new period.

This is just one of humanity's cycles of evolution. Four previous humanities have reached this very point but failed, and everything had to begin again when man was destroyed. Those who survived mutated and began to rebuild humanity. Each of these previous humanities went through a similar process, and it has taken thousands and thousands of years to reach this point again.

The Maya sage Don Ramón Carbala had the following to say in this regard:

"This is the fourth time that cycle convergence has come. This is the story of Mother Earth and us as her children. In reality, this is the planet's purpose."

We are now faced with a real opportunity to reach the next level, which is not Fire, Earth, Air, or Water, nor a time of polar opposites (hot/cold, light/dark, feminine/masculine, day/night), but a time when things will work together in harmony. Once this cycle is established, there will be unity between men and women, and between human beings and Mother Earth.

Ether will be added to the four original elements. Ether activates and synchronizes the essence of the other four elements so they can bear fruit, enabling us to once again become like the first humans: with our sight encompassing the whole of the earth, we will travel the universe in our thoughts and have the power to present ourselves to the Great Father, Heart of Sky.

We can indeed achieve this balance and bring humanity to a spiritual level, a new order of understanding, and transcend from this space-time to other dimensions, other levels we can't even begin to imagine; we can start down a new path within existence, structuring and creating the universe. On three previous occasions, negative polarity has been the one factor capable of preventing access to the next level and thus destroying previous humanities. Our Mayan Grandfathers called these humanities "those on the other side."

The other side is clear about what it wants. It would rather destroy so that it can continue to rule without sharing or ceding power. It is defined by this role and works on the side of negativity. It doesn't discuss, argue, or fight over positions—it knows who is boss.

It is interesting to note that other humanities that reached this point had developed such advanced technology that it was the greatest cause of their destruction. Present-day humanity has not come close to reaching that degree of scientific and technological development. We inherited the remnants of such innovations, and if we use them properly, we will be able to understand and utilize Mother Earth's inner energy and reconnect with the cosmic. Such technology includes the pyramids, more than 52,000 of which were built so that at least 5,200 would survive until the fifth cycle in order to bring about the convergence of cosmic and telluric energies. The crystal skulls, which contain all of the previous humanity's information, will be of invaluable help if we are able to activate them.

On the side of light, those who are competing to show who is best and who is the most illuminated have not realized that they are doing the other side a favor and losing ground that rightfully belongs to them. Our Grandfathers are calling out to all of humanity and to spiritual guides in particular. Enough fighting to be the best! Put your pride aside, stop looking for material gain, and assume your role once and for all. We need to humble ourselves to work together. Otherwise, we will have to begin again . . . and how many times can we do that? According to tradition, we have just one more opportunity, that's all.

23

HUMANKIND'S DESTINY

I was on my way to Don Isidro's and couldn't stop thinking about events that were happening around the world and the time of the prophecies. As soon as I saw him, I burst out with the question, "Don Isidro, *what is the Maya's destiny?*"

As usual, he furrowed his brow, remained silent for a few moments, and then replied. "The question you should be asking," he said, "is what is humanity's destiny? The destinies of the Maya and of all other inhabitants of this Earth are connected. It's not a question of races or nations, much less of sectors, and even less so of sects."

The planet is a living entity, and its fate affects all of us who inhabit it. We can see by current events and the state of the environment how serious things are. A great imbalance has been caused by humanity's unconsciousness, the obvious result of breaking with the Natural Order.

People speak of "freedom" and "democracy," but I wonder whose freedom they're talking about. We're silenced as soon as we contradict those who have assumed the right to shape the world's future. This happens not just here in Guatemala but in more developed countries as well. The freedom they espouse exists within the confines of their rules, which in the end benefit only those who made them. This is possible only through a sophisticated conspiracy: agreements are reached between the major players without taking anyone else's needs into consideration.

We are mired in a state of lethargy. This becomes clear when we look at the values that govern us. I'm not talking about false morality here, but about something far more serious: true freedom of consciousness. Now, that doesn't mean doing whatever we feel like. Instead, freedom of consciousness is a matter of being free in one's mind, inside oneself. Freedom is living in harmony, where every human being respects himself or herself, others, and Mother Nature.

With true freedom, we are honestly concerned about ourselves as a real premise of existence, about being healthy because we have no worries, about being wealthy because our most treasured possessions are truth and simplicity. Truth is an awareness of self, of one's virtues and flaws. We accept ourselves as we are without internal conflict. Some people may be born with certain abilities we wish we had, but we have abilities that others want. It's not a competition. The reality is that we all need each other. Our differences create balance.

The higher one's position in life, the more responsible and humble one should be. All of the world's ills can be attributed to the fact that we don't live this way. Rulers in my Grandfathers' time were loved and respected for their wisdom and ability to serve others. They earned their higher position by demonstrating lifelong service: the best political campaign was to work for the community. Being a leader was an honor, not something to brag about or take advantage of. They didn't believe they were all-powerful. The purpose was to maintain equilibrium and uphold our Grandfathers' vision. Democracy isn't about choosing the person we think will serve our individual purposes. Wouldn't it be better to elect someone who will work for the good of all?

These days, people with power travel with bodyguards in bulletproof vehicles. They're separated from real life, convinced that they are the be-all and end-all because someone's whispering sweet nothings to them, constantly reassuring them that they are wonderful, manipulating them all the while. I wonder what these people have to fear if they're truly serving the people and watching out for everyone's well-being.

The superpowers are not the only ones divvying up the world; small groups in power also start wars, turning countries upside down at the drop of a hat. Globalization has created little financial cliques that vie for the world's resources, goods, and services. We have no idea that we're being manipulated.

We constantly compete to accumulate material wealth to fill our houses with as many symbols of our riches as we can, but the struggle leaves us empty inside. Alienation takes over, and we remain directionless. We'd rather have the latest gadget than sit and watch the sun set. We'd rather have full pockets and empty hearts.

By imposing borders and creating divisions between nations, we have come to hate our neighbors. We arm ourselves to the teeth, ready for combat at the slightest provocation. Our children leave and never come back. They are willing to kill or die for our country. Vengeance is a never-ending cycle.

We live in police states where obedience and the law are based on fear and repression, not conviction or conscience. And now we have a world police that thinks it has the right to impose order according to its view of human rights and assumes the obligation to invade other countries, start wars, and discredit anyone who stands in the way of its designs.

Freedom is more serious but ultimately simpler. Freedom is peace. It's being comfortable with our actions. It isn't conformism or waiting for a better life in the hereafter. It's a better life now. This can be achieved by slowing down and spending more time playing with our children instead of rushing headlong to nowhere. Isn't it better to reflect on our lives than to sit in front of a television, numb to the lack of real purpose in our lives?

None of this can be solved by just one or two people. It's a communal problem.

Humanity's destiny will depend on how prepared it is for this change. It's up to us to take action and have a more positive outlook, to avoid a sense of impending doom. Everyone's obsessed with the "end of the world" when what they should be thinking about is the "ends for which they were born."

Remember, this life is not eternal. There will be an end sooner or later because every one of us dies. We will be the ones to judge ourselves. This is the final judgment we hear so much about, the moment of death, and we will not be able to avoid, lie to, or fool ourselves then. At that moment we will answer for what we have done with this marvelous opportunity called life. Our own existence is transitory and shouldn't be wasted by spending our time avoiding ourselves in the day-to-day madness.

Our destiny as a culture during these times is to be a light and a guide. Together with other native peoples, we are calling out to our younger brothers, asking them to stop playing the illusory game they're caught up in and return to a harmonious life. Whoever hears this call to reestablish our value as human beings, whoever understands that we cannot continue to destroy nature and live unaware, will survive to build a new world. The major crisis is one of values—each person's value as a human being. If we choose incorrectly, humanity could spin out of control like never before. We must become one people, one nation where respect for the individual reigns, no one is excluded, and nothing is imposed. It will be a utopia in which harmony and respect rule, where there will be no more falsehoods, only true freedom. The oppressive, punishing forms of spirituality will disappear because the truth will be in each of us. This is our destiny, humanity's destiny, the coming of the Fifth Sun, the year zero, the return of the *B'alameb'*, the return of the wise men.

24

A RETURN TO THE
NATURAL ORDER

Reality is the vision we have of what surrounds us, but there are other, much more subtle realities that are more important. As humans evolved, they lost this ability to perceive and are thus disconnected from the cosmos, in a state of neglect that they seek to fill with material goods. This only condemns them to self-destruction and is the reason a return to the Natural Order is imperative.

—RAMÓN CARBALA,
Mayan Mam traditionalist and thinker

The Mayan world follows an organic path based on the Natural Order, respect for Mother Nature, and both cosmic and earthly influences. After living with the Elders for long periods of time, I always felt uneasy back in urban centers, where I was unable to comprehend all the drama surrounding me. The Western approach to life is one of generalized disorder where anarchy reigns. Westerners' materialistic worldview is completely skewed: in their eyes, everything revolves around the principle that whoever has more possessions is valued more and people are willing to endure the stress of going into debt in order to keep up. In today's world, a car is coveted more than a relationship, frivolity abounds, and we are constantly bombarded with advertisements that make us feel inadequate unless we buy products that provide only momentary pleasure. The trend is to go into debt, live under pressure, remain unaware, and accept that everything is for show. Life is an endless list of wishes.

Technological advances haven't improved our quality of life either—they have just increased the quantity of things we can accumulate. Innovations occur so quickly that whatever we have today is obsolete in just a few months. I'm not saying that we should thwart technological advances; cell phones, for instance, have revolutionized communication, but at the same time they have become a status symbol. Today our lives seem to be not our own existence but more like a movie we're watching.

If beings outside the human race were to come and observe us, what would they say? They would most certainly call us crazy and self-destructive. Thousands of acres of forest all over the world are destroyed every day primarily to satisfy inexplicable corporate interests. We use far more wood than we actually need. We are obliterating the natural environment with endless pollution. We wage senseless wars, we're intolerant and heartless, and we live in a perpetual state of anxiety. If we don't respect ourselves, how can the other inhabitants of this planet expect us to respect them? Our brothers the animals live symbiotically with nature and we don't value them, reducing their habitat day after day. Plants and trees can expect even less of us.

This attitude of ownership toward the Earth has created enormous territorial problems. Human existence is negligible when compared to the age of the Earth, so why do we try to possess it? We behave as if we're entitled to destroy everything around us.

We ignore all of the signs of our excess. Climate change, el Niño, la Niña, the hole in the ozone layer, our increasingly contaminated oceans, disappearing plant and animal species—none of it matters to us. We would rather remain inert and unaware. It's easier to live with our heads in the sand than to recognize, and work to correct, our destructive nature. Global warming doesn't worry us; we'll simply install air conditioning! Floods, hurricanes, droughts—none of these calamities matter for more than a day or two unless we're directly affected by them. This is our reality as human beings, the pinnacle of creation, made in His likeness and image. . .

It sounds cruel, but any judgment rendered by another species would definitely not be favorable, to say nothing of the sentence we would receive.

We often talk about conserving nature, but can we truly live in harmony with nature? We manufacture and consume products that harm the environment every day. What about paper towels, soap, and disposable diapers? Isn't the food we consume fertilized? Doesn't it contain hormones and pesticides? What about the abuse of animals raised for food or lab testing? The list is endless, and we cannot deny responsibility for our part in polluting and destroying this planet. Whether we like it or not, humanity is heading toward a point of no return. At the risk of sounding apocalyptic, I must say that, unless we take drastic measures, the outcome is clear.

Life has become so hard to bear and so alienating that we've become a world of addicts. Drugs are the most dangerous form of self-destruction. We don't have to face ourselves if we are high. We need constant noise around us: the radio and television fill the emptiness inside and ensure that we never have too much time to think. We avoid self-reflection. Modern life has very little to do with appreciating the world around us; it is about rushing here and there, filled with an urgency that doesn't allow for personal growth. As each day passes, we become increasingly insensitive to others' pain, to the drama and misery we cause. We derive more satisfaction from wearing designer clothing than we do from feeding the hungry. When people travel, their greatest pleasure derives from going shopping and coming back with a series of purchases that proves how wonderful their trip was. Travel no longer has anything to do with the desire to see natural wonders and learn about other cultures.

At this stage, science will not be able to save us unless we reach a comprehensive awareness. We must return to the Natural Order. We must strive to live a simple, harmonious life that is ecologically conscientious. The time for speeches has passed— we must practice what we preach. We are now in a phase where immediate action is required. It is up to us to band together. Our children's future depends on it. The world we leave to them can still be wonderful if we make the required changes. It is up to us to demand that the big industries responsible for pollution stop immediately. Our consumption is their profit. If we cut back on what we buy and search for alternatives that are more respectful of nature, they will have to change their policies.

The solution lies within us. We all know this. What's left if we take away a person's car, credit cards, cell phone, and designer clothing? Nothing but a poor, depressed, lost individual who thinks he or she is a failure and has no reason to go on living because having things is the value on which we base success. Hundreds committed suicide during the Great Depression in the United States because they couldn't bear to exist without things. Their entire self-worth was based on material possessions.

We need to redefine our values and abandon this false, hypocritical morality. We need to respect ourselves and appreciate others simply because we are all human. Everyone is a master at his or her own craft. The wonder of creation is found in the little things. We need to live in harmony and expand our sensibilities. It's very simple: life is about finding the answers inside, awakening the knowledge and powers that lie dormant, controlling our desires, using the strength of our minds for spiritual growth, and projecting ourselves onto the supreme. The day we start believing this will be the day life smiles upon us.

25

THE AGE OF THE MAYA

Contrary to our assertions that the Maya date back at least twelve thousand years, many people still believe the theories proposed by the first serious researchers of the Mayan people. According to investigators such as Silvanus G. Morley, J. Erick S. Thompson, Richard E. W. Adams, and others, Mayan civilization arose only 3,300 years ago and was divided into the following periods:

> *Pre-Classic* – 1300 BCE TO AD 300
> *Classic* – AD 300 TO 900
> *Post-Classic* – AD 900 TO 1300
>   (*some say 900 to 1529, the time of the conquest*)

The majority of subsequent scholars have tended to agree with such thinking, based primarily on Stela C at Quiriguá. The date carved in Mayan glyphs on this monolithic stone indicates the start of *Kajib Ajaw* (the Fourth Sun), the period of 5,200 years that ends on December 20, 2012, and also refers to *Job Ajaw* (the Fifth Sun), which begins on December 21, 2012.

The Maya erected stelae in order to record important events that occurred within the twenty-year cycle called a *k'atun*, such as when a new king came to power after a ruler's death. Some stelae have been discovered on which dates from ten thousand, fifteen thousand, even hundreds of thousands of years ago are recorded.

Proof that the Maya have a history dating back thousands of years is also recorded in the texts that survived the conquest. The *Popol Vuh*, the sacred book of the Maya K'iche, recounts events that occurred hundreds, thousands, even millions of years ago, and the oral traditions have similarly been passed down by our Grandfathers for thousands of years.

Don Isidro once spoke to me about our origins: "Our world was created when the Creator and Maker, B'itol and Tz'aqol, created, made, and gave life to our first fathers. We don't know exactly when this happened, but we do know there was a great cataclysm: the world turned cold, the earth was covered in mud, the sun grew weak, and there was fog everywhere. This is how man before us was punished when he forgot the Great Father, Heart of Sky, the unnameable one, the great Jun Ab Ku. The Mam tribe existed before this cataclysm. They are the source of our tradition, the bearers of our wisdom, and that is where the plan to found the four Tulas plus the Tula in the center began, thus composing the five Classic ceremonial centers where my Grandfathers' tradition began."

The *Popol Vuh* has the following to say about this cataclysm:

...And then a great downpour began. He was lighting a fire for the tribes when hail began to fall on everyone and they no longer had fire. They said to B'alam K'itze', B'alam Aq'ab', Majukutaj, and I'ki' B'alam: We cannot bear the cold and ice. They were shivering, their teeth chattering. It was as if they were dead, hunched over, their hands and feet crippled, unable to grasp anything when they came. Oh, idol Tojil, we are dying of cold!

...And before the Sun rose, the Earth was wet and boggy. Then, as if it were a man, the Sun rose, but it did not have much strength; it simply showed itself when it dawned. Only its reflection remains, for it is certainly not this Sun that shines now, the traditions say.

...And when the Sun came out, B'alam K'itze', B'alam Aq'ab', Majukutaj, and I'ki' B'alam were overjoyed. They rejoiced when it dawned, when the fog dispersed and the Earth dried out. Men were not big but small there on the mountains of Hacavitz when it dawned. There they burned the incense copal and danced, looking east where they came from, where their homeland lies. ...

Based on this text, our Elders' oral tradition, and the information contained on the stelae, we can safely say that the Mayan world is older than we think. According to geologists, the last Ice Age, which this story seems to refer to, ended ten to twelve thousand years ago (at least seven thousand years prior to officially accepted dates for the Maya), while the peak glacial period dates back more than twenty thousand years.

What caused the Ice Age is unknown. Various theories range from giant meteors to a great cataclysm that caused the destruction and sinking of large tracts of land (Atlantis), to the approach of a moon, to the Austrian Hanns Hörbiger's theory that there were once four moons, three of which fell when attracted to Earth.

As further evidence of how far back in time the Maya reach, the remains of a pyramidal temple built after the dawn of the Sun, some ten thousand years ago, can be found on Hacavitz Mountain in the department of El Quiché in Guatemala. If we take into account the Mam's mandate to build the four other Tulas—the ceremonial centers spread across at least four hundred hectares, built equidistant, and together forming the shape of a large cross—these constructions predate the dawn of the Sun at the end of the last Ice Age. This culture, heir to another that possessed all knowledge, preserved its power, magic, and wisdom in Tula of the North in Hidalgo, Mexico, and their tradition spread out from there to the Teotihuacáns and Toltecs, then to the Mexicas or Aztecs and Tlaxcaltecs.

Charting time was almost an obsession for the Maya; they created twenty different calendars. One of them, called the Long Count, is still used today. Each cycle lasts for 5,200 years of 360 days each. According to this living calendar, we are about to enter the fifth cycle on December 21, 2012. From this we calculate that the Long Count calendar has been in use for more than twenty thousand years.

Discoveries approximately twenty years ago in the Mayan city of Cuello in Belize also yielded proof that the Classic Period spanned 5,000 to 7,000 years rather than the 2,600 to 2,800 years previously thought. These results came from the analysis of pieces of Mayan pottery and other items in various laboratories in Europe, Asia, and the United States. Unsurprisingly, however, the archaeologists who made this announcement were discredited. There were also astonishing discoveries in Palenque, Mexico, in early 1999, when three new tombs were found with dates that place the Classic period much further back.

Copan, Honduras, is believed to have contained an astronomical observatory where the greatest Mayan scientists lived. It houses a stone engraved with a mammoth surrounded by glyphs. Scientists say that mammoths disappeared from the American continent ten to twelve thousand years ago. In Cerro el Hacha, Costa Rica, approximately thirty-five miles from the Nicaraguan border, there is another mural portraying a mammoth surrounded by Mayan glyphs. Because experts say the Mayan civilization never extended that far, reaching only to northern Honduras, orthodox Mayanists still owe us an explanation for these.

Western archaeologists, researchers, and historians find it hard to acknowledge that such a highly developed civilization existed over 3,500 years ago, while Europeans were still living in caves. The mysteries noted here have yet to be fully investigated to establish the age and origin of the Maya, possibly because of manipulation by these scholars.

We accept our Grandfathers' tradition. The Maya are related to a culture that predates the Ice Age, the mother of ancient cultures such as the Egyptians, the Vedantics in ancient India, the Tibetans, the Greeks, the legendary Chinese, and the little studied but no less important Druids. Despite the distances that separate these cultures, all of them share characteristics and knowledge that do not show up in much of the history we have been taught.

The step pyramids in Indonesia, Cambodia, and Sri Lanka are reminiscent of the Mayan pyramids. Those scattered throughout Europe, specifically in France and Spain, are similar to the platformed structures of the Early Classic Mayan Period, while the pyramids in China are identical to those in Teotihuacán, Mexico. The base and architecture of the Babylonic ziggurats scattered throughout Africa are very much like the pyramids found in Cuicuilco, Mexico.

Moreover, apart from ritualistic differences, there are great similarities in the religious traditions of the Hindus, Mayas, Egyptians, Assyro-Babylonians, Taoists, and Druids. They all have a similar pantheon of gods, the supreme one being the essence. All of these cultures are based on the Sun, it being one of the higher deities, and on the power manifested by another of the most worshiped gods in the form of a thunderbolt: the Vikings had Thor, the Maya have Kaqulja' (the three manifestations of lightning), and the Greeks had Zeus. Finally, we must remember that both Hindus and Mayas worked with immeasurable periods of time.

26

THE MAYA IN
OTHER TRADITIONS

Our Mayan Grandfathers asked me to reveal a part of our tradition, a story that is real and gives meaning to our community. They say that our ancestors' influence spread to other civilizations, to the Egyptians, Hindus, and Greeks, and is reflected in a saga in the Mediterranean that culminates in Ireland.

The *Popol Vuh*, the *Annals of the Kaqchikeles*, and the *Title of the Lords of Totonicapán* all speak of events that occurred thousands, even millions of years ago. These sacred works tell of other humanities that preceded our own. The extraordinary thing is that on the other side of the ocean there is also a record of this relationship and the notion of a common origin in a mother civilization.

Mayan sages say in the old stories that four great masters were appointed at the start of this humanity to educate those who survived the great cataclysm that destroyed the continent of Atlantis. The first master, known as Naga Maya, went to India; the second, Maya Chez, went to Egypt; the third, Kara Maya, went to Greece; and the fourth, called Kukulkan, Quetzalcóatl, or the Plumed Serpent, went to the Americas.

EGYPT

Maya Chez arrived among the precursors of the Egyptian civilization. He and his children or companions mixed with the inhabitants now known as Nubians, a dark-skinned people with Caucasian features. Maya Chez taught the astronomy, pyramidal architecture, and science and technology that would later give rise to the Egyptian civilization. The first pyramid built in Egypt is a step pyramid known as Maya, and there are Mayan glyphs in one of its chambers. Just like the mother civilization, these people worshiped Osiris and Ra, the Sun god.

INDIA

Naga Maya went to India. ("Naga" in Sanskrit means "snake," an important symbol in Indian culture.) A chapter in the ancient Vedic chants known as Viveparitah Karani says: "When we were nomads and wandered through the Indo Valley, the Naga Mayas came from across the sea in their celestial cars of fire called *vimana* that flew through the air. They taught us agriculture, social organization, and construction [architecture], as well as mathematics and the mysteries of the heavens [astronomy]. They built their houses with nine platforms [step pyramids] in order to worship the Sun and left us the measurement of time. When their work was done, they left in their *vimanas*."

GREECE

Kara Maya crossed the ocean, bringing the ancient Maya's knowledge with him, and founded the mythical city of Helios, where the wisest people lived. Kara Maya civilized the Greeks. As guardian of the north, his strength was knowledge, the power of thought, and this is where the schools of Greek philosophy originated.

It is said that the Greek alphabet is an epic poem composed of words from an ancient poem by Kara Maya that remembers his ancestors who lost their lives when Atlantis was destroyed.

THE MEDITERRANEAN AND IRELAND

An old legend in Ireland is duplicated in a Greek myth and in another from ancient Egypt. The legend tells of two races, the Fir Bolg and the Tuatha de Dannan, who fought to the death. The first practiced black magic and the second white magic. The Tuatha de Dannan were defeated in the first battle at Magh Tuiredh and broke up into smaller groups. These groups took refuge with their Phoenician brothers, the Reds, who were a mystery to all of the tribes in the Mediterranean because no one knew where they came from. Of Mayan or Atlantan origin, the Reds settled particularly in what are now Lebanon and Jordan. Once the Tuatha de Dannan smaller groups reunited, they and the Phoenicians traveled around the Mediterranean teaching their magic. They founded the cities in Europe called Falias, Gorias, Munias, and Finias. In time, they moved north, seeking refuge in Ireland. A century later, those from the most northerly part of Ireland had grown strong and went to confront the Fir Bolg or black magicians. They carried four magic objects with them: the stone of destiny, the enchanted lightning bolt, the cauldron of the future, and the magic spear of Naga. After defeating the Fir Bolg, who took refuge in caves, the Tuatha de Dannan kings went to found their kingdom in northern Ireland and sent their sages down every river to civilize every other nation.

Vestiges of this culture show that their deities were very similar to the Maya's. The Tuatha de Dannan worshiped the god of thunder and lightning, one of whose names was Lugh—a great master builder who was wise to all of nature's secrets. Beings such as elves and gnomes exist in both cultures; the Maya call gnomes *tzitzimite*, and elves are called *chajal'eb*. The fire ceremonies of both cultures are also basically identical.

27

THE MAYAN CALENDARS

They were endowed with intelligence. They saw, and their sight was such that they were able to see, able to understand every-thing that exists in the world. When they looked, they immedi-ately saw all around them and contemplated the vault of sky and the round face of Earth.

—THE POPOL VUH

The counting of time is extremely important to the Maya, and they built astronomical observatories for exactly that purpose, such as those found in Uaxactun, Chichén Itzá, and countless other ceremonial centers throughout the Mayan world. Even after the Spanish conquest, the Maya continued to count time according to their tradition, only they did so in hiding. The priests thought that Mayan timekeeping was the devil's work and would have killed them for the practice.

As already indicated, one of the great Mayan cycles of time indicated that the Spanish would come to the Americas and that a disastrous period would follow. We are now in a different cycle, one of positive energy. In accordance with this new cycle, the Elders, wise men, and *Ajq'ijab'*, or day keepers, are now bringing their calendars to light. Much interest in these calendars is being generated among Maya and non-Maya alike.

Research done with our Elders, day keepers, and Mayan chroniclers shows that the Maya use twenty calendars. These can be divided into four types:

> Calendars that cover cycles of days
> Calendars that cover great cycles of years
> Calendars based on other celestial bodies
> Other calendars

CALENDARS FOR CYCLES OF DAYS

B'olom Ajaw: This calendar is based on the pulsation of the sun. It was used by archaeologists and is known in the West as the Nine Lords of the Night.

Ixim Tun: This is an agricultural calendar for the cycle of *ixim*, or corn. The Swiss anthropologist Rafael Girard calls this calendar the "Fixed *Q'ij*."

Cholq'ij, or Tzolkin: This is the sacred calendar, a human cycle consisting of 260 days, divided into 13 months of 20 days each. This calendar has been passed down from generation to generation since the date of creation—the year zero is depicted on Stela C at Quiriguá—through the last 500 years without any modifications whatsoever.

The *Cholq'ij* governs human aspects: it consists of 260 days or

Piedra del Sol
Tenochtitlan

Cuatro Soles
Tenochtitlan

Tizoc
Tenochtitlan

Tenochtitlan

Coatlán

Chichen-Itzá

Chalco

Humboldt

Cofre de Piedra

Xochimilco

Tzolkin y Haab

Malinolco

nine months of the Gregorian calendar, the time it takes for human gestation as well as the biorhythmic period after birth.

The following are the names of the twenty days:

1	B'atz'	2	E	3	Aj	4	I'x
5	Tz'ikin	6	Ajmaq	7	No'j	8	Tijax
9	Kawoq	10	Ajpu	11	Imox	12	Iq'
13	Aq'ab'al	14	K'at	15	Kan	16	Kame
17	Kej	18	Q'anil	19	Toj	20	Tz'i'

The *Cholq'ij* has been compared with the Aztec or Mexica *Tonalamatl* calendar. Both were found to have a similar structure and the same meanings for the twenty days. The twenty days were also compared between all of the Mayan groups in Guatemala—the Mam, Q'anjob'al, Popti', Ixil, Chuj, K'iche, and Kaqchikel tribes—and once again, all of the meanings were found to be the same.

Hab' Tun: This is a 360-day calendar in the cycle of a cosmic constant and can be considered an astronomical calendar. It is very well known.

Ikix: This is a lunar calendar that the Maya use to manage the tides and women's menstrual cycles. It is found in the Dresden Codex, and Rafael Girard refers to it as the "*Wo Ix*."

Hab' (*Jun Ab'* means "one year"): This is a 400-day year, and the cycle consists of 5,200 days. The Kaqchikel refer to this calendar as *Jun A*. It is narrated in the *Annals of the Xahil*, and the following dates are set out in the Spanish translation, where the day *Kej* is used as the regent:

Gregorian Date	Hab Date	Gregorian Date	Hab Date	Gregorian Date	Hab Date
Sept. 22, 1962	4 Kej	Oct. 27, 1963	1 Kej	Jan. 4, 1966	11 Kej
Feb. 8, 1967	8 Kej	March 14, 1968	5 Kej	April 18, 1969	2 Kej
May 23, 1970	9 Kej, 6 Kej	Sept. 4, 1973	3 Kej	Oct. 9, 1974	13 Kej
Nov. 13, 1975	10 Kej	Dec. 17, 1976	7 Kej		

Matuytun: This 52-year calendar is the cycle of the Pleiades when they are at their zenith in Mesoamerica. Archaeologists are familiar with this calendar.

CALENDARS FOR CYCLES OF YEARS

Ajaw K'atun Choltun: This is a cycle of 260 *tun* years. Since a *tun* is 360 days, this cycle lasts for 93,600 days. The energy of the Earth moves every 260 years. Therefore, during this cycle the Elders would evaluate whether the cosmic and telluric energies continued to be in harmony with and possessed the required power with respect to the element that governed every Mayan town (such as *itza*, or the energy of Water). If the energies were in conflict, the town would migrate to another location where this harmony existed. If the energies were favorable, however, the town would expand and construct other buildings over already existing structures.

This prophetic calendar is based on the numbers for the spiral of *najt* and uses the sign *Ajpu* (*Ajaw*) in 20-year cycles, equal to 7,200 days. The numbering for the date 4 Ajpu is counted in cycles of 20, and the resulting order is 8, 6, 4, 2, 13, 11, 9, 7, 5, 3, 1, 12, and 10.

Although there is no documentation, we are now in the process of understanding how our Grandfathers used this calendar in ancient times. Known in the West as the Short Count, this is the first time we are bringing its use to light.

Gregorian Date	Date Name	Numerical Date
	(baktun-k'atun-tun-winal-kin)	
May 13, 1914	1 Ajpu	12.15.0.0.0
February 14, 1934	12 Ajpu	12.16.0.0.0
November 1, 1953	10 Ajpu	12.17.0.0.0
July 19, 1973	8 Ajpu	12.18.0.0.0
April 6, 1993	6 Ajpu	12.19.0.0.0

Oxlajuj Majq'ij: This is a cycle of 13 *baktuns* (a 400-year period) and therefore a period of 5,200 years.

Waqxaqib' Mayaq'ij: This is a cycle of 8 *baktuns* and therefore a period of 3,200 years.

Juwinaq Mayaq'ij: This is a cycle of 20 *baktuns*, or 8,000 years, also known as a *piktun*.

CALENDARS BASED ON OTHER PLANETS

Maeqoq'ij: The cycle of Venus

Maymuluk: The cycle of Mars

Mayik kox: The cycle of Sirius, the brightest star in the sky

OTHER CALENDARS

Tiku': This is the prophetic cycle based on 52 years. It is divided into *B'olom Tiku'* and *Oxlajuj Tiku'*. The first is a period of 9

cycles of 52 years, for a total of 468 years. It is also known as the Nine Hells and is a period of darkness for humanity. The second is a period of 13 cycles of 52 years, for a total of 676 years. It is also known as the Thirteen Heavens and is a period of light for humanity.

Najxit Tun: This is a sacred calendar whose function we have not yet been authorized to reveal.

Eqomal May: This is a prophetic calendar, the cycle of what are known as the year bearers, or reigning energies.

Ninamay Q'ij: This is the great cycle of *Ajaw*. We are not allowed to speak of this calendar at this time, nor do we know exactly what it is.

13 Winal	20	280
14 Tun	360	4,680
13 K'atun	7,200	93,600
13 Baktun	144,000	1,872,000
13 Piktun	2,880,000	37,440,000
13 Kalab'tun	57,600,000	748,800,000
13 Kinchiltun	1,152,000,000	14,976,000,000
13 Alautun	23,040,000,000	299,520,000,000
19 Ab'	Fixed	
20 Ab'	Kaj (Sky)	

Fixed Ab': This calendar consists of 360 days plus another 5 known as the *Wayeb*, a time for introspection, meditation, and resolutions. After the sacred *Cholq'ij*, this is the most used calendar and the basis for counting time in the Long Count, a period of 5,200 years. Eighteen months of 20 days plus one month of 5 days make up this calendar, and each month has a particular meaning:

PO'OP: This means a weaving, a grass mat made from the tule reed that grows in lakes or marshes. The deeper meaning of the word is "space," "time," "period," "era," "cycle," "harvest," "events," "occurrences," and "stories." The Maya were very attentive to the passing of time, and all of the events they observed were used to count their days. They noted what the new year brought, what resulted from these phenomena, how often these events happened, and what memories they left with the Mayan people, whether they wrote of joy or pain.

WO: These are frogs that sing a very sad song. The Maya engraved this animal on their *tetunes*, or stelae, after observing that the frog's song was a plea for rain during times of drought. The year keepers, or *chaques*, as they are known in Yucatecan Mayan, believe these frogs are actually huge and that the little frogs, called *Wo*, whose songs announce the rain, are their assistants and musicians.

SIP: This is a tick, four to six millimeters long, that sucks the blood of certain mammals.

SOOTS': This is an insectivorous bat that hangs upside down from its feet during the day. Mayan "metaphorgram" glyphs were characteristic of their writing system. The vampire bat, common throughout the Mayan lowlands, gave rise to a glyph that the scribes combined with the glyph for sacrifice. To indicate ritual killing, which implies the concept of blood, it seems that the natural metaphor came from the story that vampires suck blood. The bat here is resting with its head hanging down. Only rare glyphs represent the bat with its head at the top, such as the glyph for the *k'atun* and its number to indicate that this *k'atun* in particular had come to rest, its interminable journey through time finally ended. What a surprising, logical metaphorgram for the abstract idea of rest!

TSEEK': This refers to punishment or correction, penitence or the justice one metes out to another. The Mayan phrase is *Utz'eqil ajsipil*, or "the punishment the delinquent receives."

XUUL: This means whistle, a voice that imitates, a small flute, or a sharp sound. *Xuul* is also a very common variety of tick in South America. In times past, the main agricultural tools were the pointed planting stick that was hardened in the fire (*xuul*), the stone ax (*b'wat*), and the fiber bag for carrying the corn seeds (*chim*). The most important tools added in modern times are the steel machete (a heavy knife with an iron blade, approximately two feet long), the steel ax, and the iron tip that was used to modify the planting stick. Modern agricultural tools are useless in the Mayan region, particularly in northern Yucatán, where the ground is rocky and the soil is very shallow.

YA'AXK'IIM: This means autumn, one of four seasons in the year, or temperate. In the Northern Hemisphere, autumn begins with the autumnal equinox on September 23 and ends with the winter solstice on December 21. In the Southern Hemisphere, autumn is the period between the spring equinox on March 21 and the summer solstice on June 21. *Ya'axk'iim* also refers to the second crop of grass or hay that grows in the fields during the fall, as well as the period between one's prime of life and old age.

MO'OL: This is the collection of fruit that is picked up off the ground once it ripens; the wine obtained from such fruit; the season when fruit is collected; the applause a person earns as a result of his or her actions; the thing that is harvested; the harvest itself, particularly the sacred red, black, white, and yellow corn; and the fruit of the community's labor.

CH'EN (YUCATECAN MAYAN) or AB'AJ (K'ICHE MAYAN): This is a mineral substance, relatively hard and compact, that is neither earthlike nor metallic in appearance, as well as a stone engraved with an inscription or figure, the finding of writings or other traces that prove this truth. Naturally, this was the material the Grandfathers used to record the most important concepts, stories, and cosmo-vision.

YA'AX: This word means green, but it is also used in Yucatecan Mayan in the sense of "new," "fresh," "first," "first-time," "recently," or "newborn." Given such connotations, *ya'ax* takes on a meaning similar to *sujuy*. For example, *sujuy aq'ab'* is late afternoon, when evening begins, with *aq'ab'* meaning night. *Yaxokinal*, meaning "the sun going down again" or a recent sunset, is essentially a synonym.

SAK: This means locust, a name that, like grasshopper, is given to various genera and species of Othoptera insects, of different sizes and colors, in the locust family. Some are migratory and move in great clouds, devouring all of the vegetation in their path. Others are sedentary and multiply in enormous quantities. The most important migratory species are the Moroccan locust (*dociostaurus maroccanus*) and the desert locust (*schistocera gregaria*). It is "that which destroys or consumes." *Sak* can also be a lobster, a fuchsia-colored marine decapod crustacean (*palinurus vulgaris*) that lives in deep water and whose meat is highly prized. Another variety, a dirty white color that turns pinkish when cooked, may be up to ten inches long.

SEJ or *KEJ:* This means deer. The Mayan metaphor for drought was *Cim Sehil*, or "the deer die." In one scene a figure of a deer in agony is accompanied by the glyph for drought in the text. "The deer die" is a metaphor for a very severe drought.

MA'AK: This means to eat soft fruit, honey, and eggs. It can also signify earth, the lid of a box, the covering on a container, or a lock, as well as a door that opens and closes.

K'ANK'IIN: This word comprises the words *k'an* or *q'an* (in K'iche) and *Kin*. The former means ripe fruit such as avocado, guava, or jocote. *Q'an* also means a person who can perform every kind of trick. *K'ank'iin* signifies the time to plant crops in the fields, take honey from the hives, and let the bees swarm. It is also the day of the dead. Kin is the name for Father Sun. It is the time when offerings are prepared and taken to the grave, the celebration of candles takes place, and the indigenous authorities, appointed to rule alongside the elected authorities, are confirmed or changed once a year.

MUAN: This is the owl, representing wisdom. It is the messenger from Xib'alb'ay (the underworld)—he who brings knowledge of the earth's inner fire. Its head turns 360 degrees, and when the *Kablikot*, or two-headed owl, appears, the lords of the underworld announce changes that usually bring destruction. The *Kablikot* appeared once in 1998 and twice in 2001. It reminds us that we must act with great thought and care during this cycle of changes.

PAAX, PAX ATAB'AL: This is a drum, tabor, tambourine, clavichord, monochord, harp, or organ, as well as the act of strumming stringed instruments.

K'AYAB: The root of this word is *kay*, which means "to sing." *K'ayab* means the singing of men, birds, nightingales, cicadas, and so on. It is the song of nature.

KUMK'U': This is the dance; it is also harmony and rhythm. *Kumk'u'* is a time to find unity and recognize one's place on the ritual dance where cosmic and telluric deities are represented. These are times to rediscover congruity and go deeper into the dance that opens the dimensional gates.

Wayeb: Unlike the eighteen months that consist of twenty

days each, this is a special five days that weren't considered part of the year. This short period was extremely dangerous because it could be expected to bring all sorts of ills. During these five days, people only did work that was absolutely necessary, fasted, and practiced self-restraint.

Ab' Kaj: Our Mayan Grandfathers created this numerical system in order to control and manage time based on distance, velocity, and movement. Despite its infinity, they never became lost in space because of their skill as great visionaries, physicists, and mathematicians.

Static Ab': The *Ab'* calendar consists of 365 days, divided into 18 months of 20 days each, plus an additional 5 called the *wayeb*. The year begins with the month zero, *Po'op*. The *wayeb* is a period in which to make offerings to Ajaw, the Great Father, for having allowed us to work for 360 days. This is why it is not counted in the *baktuns* or 400-year periods.

Correlative Ab': This counting of time was not used to determine agricultural and livestock activities because it does not deal with solar cycles. It loses one day each astronomical year, and as a result the date shown on the calendar does not coincide with the climate changes of the seasons.

Winaq May Kih, or *Oxlujuj Baktun*: This is a cycle of 5,200 years. Called the Long Count, it is a system for recording time in a linear manner. The formula for the Long Count consists of the following five units of time:

Q'ij or *kin*—1 day
Winal—20 days
Tun—360 days
K'atun—7,200 days, or 20 years

Po'op	Wo	Sip	Soots'	Tseek'
Xuul	Ya'axk'iim	Mo'ol	Ch'en	Ya'ax
Sak	Ke'ej	Ma'ak	K'ank'iin	Muan
Paax	K'ayab	Kumk'u'	Wayeb	

Baktun—144,000 days, or 400 years

Based on Stela C at Quiriguá, this system was first used as of the day 4 *Ajpu* of the 8th month *Kumku*, which fell on 13 *baktun*, 0 *k'atun*, 0 *tun*, 0 *winal*, 0 *kin* (13.0.0.0.0), which corresponds to approximately August 12, 3113 BCE on the Gregorian calendar.

Although we know the era of El Mayab (Mesoamerica) began at 13 *baktun*, there is a problem correlating the Long Count and Gregorian calendar systems to determine a precise date in the latter, owing to the inaccuracies in the Gregorian calendar, which has undergone several adjustments over time. It was replaced by the Julian calendar, which has even more imperfections.

THE CALENDAR WHEEL

The juxtaposition of the 260-day *Cholq'ij* calendar with the 365-day *Ab'* calendar causes the calendars to coincide on the same day and number every 52 years. This is what is called the calendar wheel.

Fifty-two years can be divided into 4 periods of 13 years each, for a total of 18,980 days—a number equally divisible by both 260 and 365. The period of 52 years was the result of constant, methodic observation of the Pleiades, which pass through their zenith precisely every 52 years.

To understand how these two calendars are juxtaposed, picture two gears with the day name and number written on each cog. The small wheel represents the 260-day *Cholq'ij* calendar, and the large one represents the 365-day *Ab'* calendar. If we start the small wheel at 8 *Kaan* and the large wheel at 0 *Po'op*, then begin to crank both, the small one will turn 73 times and the large one 52 times until they come back to 8 *Kaan* and 0 *Po'op*, respectively.

28

THE SACRED *CHOLQ'IJ* CALENDAR

The *Cholq'ij* is mathematically perfect; changes never have been and never will be made to it. Its precision is the result of centuries of observation and study by great Mayan astronomers, astrologers, mathematicians, and wise men. It is the perfect instrument for understanding our purpose in the marvel that is life. It is the best gift our Grandfathers could have left us.

—DON PASCUAL,
Mayan Mam sage

Picture thick fog, pure air, and children peeking out at a caravan of students walking behind their beloved master through an incredible primary forest in an unbelievable energy center deep in the heart of the Cuchumatanes Mountains. It was the late 1960s, and the movement toward change was reflected in our odd attire, long hair, and beards, which were quite out of place in a conservative country like Guatemala, let alone there in that forgotten paradise at the ends of the Earth, where innocence and nature still reigned supreme. We must have been quite a strange sight heading back to Don Pascual's house.

Don Pascual inherited the purest Mayan tradition, preserved for centuries orally as well as in documents, altars, and sacred books. Generation after generation, priests and wise men have taught their disciples the traditions particular to the various lineages—organizations of a magical, religious, and scientific nature. The honor of initiation is based on the sign under which a person within the family clan was born and can also be a result of special signs the *H-Men* sees in a particular person. Currently, more than one person from outside the family clan has been awarded such a distinction.

After a sacred fire ceremony at which we would perform some community work or a simple walk through those majestic forests in order to harmonize our spirits, we would make ourselves comfortable on Don Pascual's patio. This temple of knowledge came to feel like my true home. There in that humble place, my fellow students and I would learn about history, the calendars and their marvelous measurements of time and space, how to manipulate energies, how to use the Mayan signs, and high theurgy, and Don Pascual would also share his personal maxims.

One night he explained the transcendence of *najt*. For the Maya, space-time is the synthesis of reality, the place where we exist. *Najt*, where space-time converges as one unit, is this dimension. This unit is never separated, and when velocity is added, the result is the dimensional image of the form, or what we call reality.

It is difficult for someone born in the world of *kaxlanes*, or white men, to understand this concept because in the West space, time, and velocity are distinctly separate. This limits the true perception of the many dimensions that the Maya know. We inhabit this reality, shaped and modeled after the cosmos, and vibrate with respect to the cosmic dance. We react to both cosmic and earthly currents of energy.

To travel along this infinite road of *najt* is to evolve. The ability to stop moving and enter a state of stasis is the key to gaining access to a perfect dimension, the world of Paxil or Kayala, something akin to a lost paradise. "Understanding this mystery and living it," Don Pascual told us, "changes your priorities and values. It breaks down barriers and expands your perception as well as your approach to your own personal reality and allows you to see the energies."

At this point, our venerable sage fell silent, then spoke the following words with special emphasis:

"Our Grandfathers left an extraordinary legacy to humanity, one that synthesizes all of the wisdom of the ancient world. It is the most useful and transcendent instrument for both individuals and nations because it gives us the information we need for full, harmonious self-realization. I am speaking of none other than the sacred *Cholq'ij* or *Tzolkin* calendar, the count of days."

This instrument allows each of us to find our place in the world, understand our propensities, strengths, and weaknesses, and lead an existence that is in harmony with our individual life purpose and thus reach our full potential.

The *Cholq'ij* is a calendar with 260 days or energies: the 20 days in the Mayan month, or *winal*, multiplied by the 13 days of

the week (20 × 13 = 260). The *winal* arises from the convergence
of the 10 cosmic energy currents and the 10 telluric energy currents. It is also related to the 10 fingers on our hands, which are
connected to the cosmos, together with our 10 toes, which are
connected to Mother Earth. The 13 days of the week arise from
the 13 main joints in the human body: two at the ankles, two at
the knees, two at the hips, two at the shoulders, two at the el-
bows, two at the wrist, and one
at the neck.

Each of the 20 *nawales*, or
days, in the *Cholq'ij* is preceded
by a number between 1 and 13,
creating a calendar of 260 days.
Once the calendar cycle ends, it
repeats again without interrup-
tion. This system of measuring
time does not consider the positions of the sun, moon, or stars
because it is a dimensional-en-
ergy calendar, not an astronomical calendar.

"As guardians of the tradition, we *H-Menob'* have a special
commitment," Don Pascual said. "Our primary mission is to
keep a record of time and count the cycles because they contain
the history of the world. Every cycle or fold in the infinite spiral of
the great *Kan* [macrospiral] is an eternal return that results in
similar events in the following cycle. This is what makes it possible for us to know our destiny: just as we know the path that the
Sun and Grandmother Moon trace as they come and go day after

day, so do we as humans come and go. This is the way in which we know how to cast a fortune and predict events."

The *k'atunic* wheel (20-year cycle) of 360 days each has its own year bearers (or *nawal* energies, the reigning energies and signs), with their own positive or negative power. What happened once will happen again. Knowing this, living this, is what made our Grandfathers so great and wise.

The *nawal* energies symbolized in the signs of the *Cholq'ij* are related to the cosmic-telluric. From the moment we exist in their presence their strength and power govern us. Our way of life, both social and spiritual, is influenced or ordained by this energy form in this manifestation of what we call reality.

 Our Grandfathers' vision of this interconnection between *najt* and the *nawal* energies has been used forever in the ancient territory of El Mayab (Mesoamerica).

While the Mayan signs are based on cosmic influences, they are quite different from Assyro-Babylonian astrology. The latter is based on the day, time, and place of a person's birth. The appearances of various planets and the correlations between them are determined according to how they are distributed in zodiac constellations and houses. In other words, in that system it is as if a photo of the sky were taken at the moment of birth from the geocentric basis of our planet in a quadrant of the universe.

The Mayan signs are based instead on the cosmic-earthly rhythm. There is a direct projection of cosmic currents—the confluence of energies from the four corners of the universe. These are what underpin the Mayan Cross in each sign as the four main

elements (Fire, Earth, Air, and Water) and thereby provide us with information on aspects that govern both our conception and the moment of our birth. Both of these moments are particularly transcendent for human beings. Further, we are influenced by hemispheric energies, terrestrial currents, our birthplace, and the traditions of our people or ethnicity.

Every year is regulated by a reigning *nawal*, known as the year bearer. This energy protects us and is the catalyst for our power.

We need this knowledge so that we can harmonize ourselves with Mother Nature and therefore with the cosmos, find our path, and unify our purpose. Our Grandfathers warn that this ancient tradition is not to be treated as a curiosity, not to be indulged in as a form of entertainment, and not to be used selfishly. Instead, it should guide our growth on all levels—physical, intellectual, emotional, and spiritual.

29

THE *CH'UMILAL WUJ:*
THE *BOOK OF DESTINY*

The *Ch'umilal Wuj*, the *Book of Destiny*, is one of the most important Mayan books. It is preserved in absolute secrecy by the guardians of the tradition and used as the basis for the social and spiritual organization of the ancient Classic Mayan world as well as the traditional Mayan world of today. For many centuries, it was reserved solely for use by *Ajq'ijab'*, since it is the responsibility of the Mayan spiritual guides to direct human beings and astrologers who specialized in the Mayan sign.

This *Book of Destiny*, or *Book of Fate*, as it is called, is based on the sacred *Cholq'ij* calendar. It is the ancestral technique of using the information in the *Cholq'ij* calendar regarding the different meanings of the twenty *nawales* (days), the year bearer (reigning energy), and the Mayan

Cross. This advanced system provides the key to handling energies and predicting the future, especially for personal use. It is used to awaken our inner knowledge.

The energy and information in each day's *nawal*, both positive and negative according to the different stages of life, is used to guide people, help them find their purpose, indicate aspects that will allow them to achieve this goal, and thus shape their destiny. The relationship of the fixed or mobile cycles of change that govern people must also be kept in mind. Through a person's sign, we can establish the abilities, gifts, spiritual qualities, or paranormal properties that person possesses and outline the places or energy centers that will help him or her develop.

Every energy center, or altar, manifests a different strength based on the convergence of cosmic and telluric energies. Some are more powerful than others, and there are certain days when such places are particularly strong. A diagram that outlines potentially beneficial dates makes it much easier for a person to follow the correct path.

To activate these energies at the different altars we must perform a traditional ceremony according to the corresponding element on the appropriate day and time. When we are in tune and in harmony with the altar, the information we require can be transmitted to us so that we can activate or decode it. Activation occurs in our DNA by unblocking the knowledge and preparing our body to awaken our internal

powers. The altars possess information that various *H-Menob'* (Mayan priests) have kept there for thousands of years.

There are more than 5,000 natural altars in Mesoamerica, and at least 2,000 have remained active for centuries. Our Grandfathers also built more than 260,000 ceremonial centers, including the pyramids and temples that were created for energy purposes as narrated in the *Books of Chilam Balam*.

The practice of following Mayan signs enabled the traditional Classic Mayan world to be a harmonious civilization. No one lived in opposition to their own energies and destiny. Everyone respected each other because they knew they were all part of an evolutionary whole in the cosmic plan.

The mandate that each person was born with was honored. Thus, if a boy was born into a family of farmers on the day *Oxlajuj Tz'i'*, his mandate was to be a just man and a great judge; throughout his childhood, he would be taught everything to prepare for his future position. His higher status would be respected and accepted from the moment he was born. Everyone had a role. No one labored at anything other than what they were born to do as indicated in their sign. Everyone therefore grew in a unified and enriching manner, completely in tune with their own makeup and with Mother Nature.

This extraordinarily harmonious view of coexistence may seem idealistic, but according to our Grandfathers' prophecies, this is how humankind will return and reign when the changes in the new cycle have fully taken hold.

"We are living in prophetic times," Don Pascual told us. "The era our Grandfathers prepared us for has arrived, this time of 12 *baktun* 6 *Ajaw*, the Return of the Wise Men, after *B'olom Tiku'*, or the Great Night, a period that lasted almost five hundred years, from the time of the conquest until August 1987. Next came a period of five years, the transition, when the gates of knowledge were opened to all people, all nations. As of that date, according to orders from the Elders, anyone who came to the Great Tradition with a genuine desire to find their destiny would be given that opportunity. Many great sages have been reincarnated in different parts of the world, and they will be the ones to bring comprehension and harmony.

"The times we are living in require great clarity. It is a transcendent time. As a result, word will spread to the world's native traditions, including our own, all of which are extremely valuable. It's important to follow an active spiritual path without fundamentalism or dogmatism. These times require a tradition that is pragmatic, clear, and congruent with Mother Nature.

"We have reached the pinnacle of materialism, frivolity, and all that is transient. Everything has been dulled—our minds and our senses. Led by technology, we have lost our way. We are all responsible for this. Everyone lives for the minute and cares more about what's on the outside than the inside. Sadly, there's nothing but a great void, an enormous fear inside most of us. It's easier to dull our senses with vain delusions than to really look at ourselves. People are so afraid to be alone that they need distractions like the television and radio. Worse still, they avoid facing the true meaning of their existence by using drugs. Mayan drugs are made from the sacred plants we inherited and are only taken to help us reach our full potential through strict ceremonial usage, supervised by masters who are fully aware of their effects and how to control them. The chemical alterations these plants have undergone and the negativity surrounding them has overshadowed any benefits.

"Now many are coming back to the ancestral wisdom and the Natural Order. This is when the right guide and individual orientation are important. Great changes begin with just one person, oneself. Here I must highlight the significance of bringing the initial use of the *Ch'umilal Wuj* to light, in the hope that it will motivate people to move deeper into realizing their value and destiny.

"Remember, Carlos, that in both the ancient Classic Mayan world and today's traditional Mayan world a newborn is immediately taken before the wise day keeper—the *Ajq'ij* or *Chi-Mam* who knows the signs. A person should never go through life without being conscious of his or her life purpose, abilities, propensities, and different cycles, both positive and negative."

Based on this vision from my beloved masters and our desire that the use of this sacred tradition be transcendent in each person, we present the twenty *nawales*, or sacred days.

30

THE MAYAN SIGNS

Mayan life and spirituality are built on understanding and using the following signs, which governed the Classic Mayan world and have been preserved by our traditional Elders.

On August 17, 1992, the planet entered a new cycle, one of comprehension, wisdom, and harmony. This new cycle is a time of great change in the world's social and economic structure. For this reason, the doors of Mayan wisdom are being opened to humankind. Now that the period of darkness has ended, the Elders have resolved to publish the Mayan signs as an instrumental way of understanding our true purpose. The hope is that everyone will orient their life based on their sign and follow *Saq B'e* (the White Road).

Respect for historical accuracy is one of the strictest and most important rules: not a single word is ever added to or removed from our texts or oral tradition. This book is a commitment to reality—that is, to our Grandfathers' vision. Although as human beings we all have many limitations, we can find a way to overcome them in the depth and transcendence to be found in these signs. The task of using the signs in one's personal life, however, requires a real desire to conform to a new way of life that balances technology and harmony with nature.

Other works have already been published; those by José Arguelles are the best known and have aroused expectations of a Mayan resurgence. However, although Arguelles uses some Mayan concepts, he employs his own methodology and, like many others, confuses the agricultural and sacred calendars. Although the agricultural calendar uses the same signs and is 260 days long, it is designed to guide planting and harvesting. It is a fixed calendar that follows a different order, beginning on *Imox*, with its symbol *ixim* (sacred corn), the basis of the Mayan diet and economy. The *Cholq'ij*, on the other hand, is based on the *Ch'umilal Wuj* and is a mobile calendar that begins again every 260 days. It starts on 8 *B'atz'*, a date celebrated by millions of people in Guatemala and southern Mexico as the Mayan New Year. This calendar coincides with the *Ab'* and Long Count calendars, but not with the agricultural calendar.

B'atz'

ENGLISH	*Thread of Destiny*
KAQCHIKEL	*B'atz'*
YUCATEC	*Chwen*
NAHUATL	*Ozomatli*
DIRECTION	*East*
ELEMENT	*Fire*
KEY	*Look for answers in time and space*
GROWTH	*Creativity and community service*

SIGNIFICANCE OF THE KAB'AWIL   The top part of this glyph is a cone that has time rolled up in it. The cone descends to a triangle, which represents our dimension, and then to the sphere of the Earth, passing through the angles, which are the two polarities, masculine and feminine.

MEANING   *B'atz'* is the start of life, infinite time, and unity. Spiritual connections are history interwoven with time. This sign symbolizes cosmic phenomena and original wisdom. *B'atz'* is the deity that created Earth and Sky, the Creator of life and wisdom. *B'atz'* signifies the time it takes for a child to develop in the womb. The *tz'ite* that represents *Ajq'ijab'* (Mayan priests) contains 260 seeds, representing the nine moons or nine months of pregnancy. *B'atz'* presides over the future.

This sign symbolizes time unraveled, evolution, and human life. The Maya depict time as a thread wound around a giant reed underneath the Earth. This thread is unraveled as time goes by. History is woven from time, just as clothing is made from woven threads.

Before the Maya used thread, they wove with *pop*, or palm, and thus the *Popol Vuh* was originally called the *Pop Vuh*. This

sign indicates that time has unraveled, giving us life and existence. This is why we are happy and dance around the fire from right to left during a sacred ceremony, until we have circled it thirteen times. When the ceremony is about to end, we dance around the fire another thirteen times, from left to right, winding up the spool of time again. This symbolizes our

love and desire for more life. Ajaw, the Great Father, is movement, and dance is movement. The Creators and Makers tossed a thread to the end of the universe, then folded it and threw it back.

Climbing plants represent vegetation and signify unity and infinite time. *B'atz'* unites men and women and governs marriage.

It also symbolizes the umbilical cord. It is the start of life, infinite time, intelligence, and wisdom.

CHARACTERISTICS   People born on this day have the conception sign *Aq'ab'al*, and their destiny sign is *Kawoq*.

B'atz' is the sign of great planners—people with a comprehensive, futuristic outlook. They make excellent doctors who tend to combine natural or ancestral medicine with new technology. This ability to combine the old with the new influences all aspects of their life, although deep down they are conservative.

Great seekers of harmony, they tend toward any of the arts. They are planters of corn, orators, musicians, weavers, painters, sculptors, singers, poets, and writers. They are also great lovers of nature. People born under *B'atz'* may become *Ajq'ijab'* (Mayan priests), *K'exelon* (midwives), or spiritual guides. They are tenacious and achieve their goals with hard work. They are creative, superstitious, amusing, sensitive, and passionate.

They are demanding in love, seeking the perfect partner, and therefore tend to become quickly disenchanted. Once they find their mate, however, they try to protect that union at all costs.

As adults, they achieve success and prestige. They normally have a splendid future, attaining a level of comfort and material wealth through hard work.

POSITIVE ASPECTS   *B'atz'* are calm and frequently solve their problems easily. Ajaw listens to these people. Their judgments are accurate. They are generous, active, dynamic, and good defenders of the people. They are organized, they possess spiritual strength, and their ideas flow. They have a strong personality, and their actions are well defined. They have a deep love of family.

The Mayan New Year is celebrated on *Waqxaqi' B'atz'*, or 8 *B'atz'*, the day of masculine energy, while *B'eleje' B'atz'*, or 9 *B'atz'*, is the day of Mayan women and nature as a whole.

NEGATIVE ASPECTS   *B'atz'* have a strong, difficult personality. They are proud, arrogant, and insecure and may ridicule others in order to make themselves feel superior. They are ruthless, ignorant, and overbearing.

God of Medicine, Copán

ENERGY   This sign is the best day for marriage. It is also a good day to put things in order or to start planning a project. It is the day that protects artists and an auspicious day to ask for good crops. It is a good day to solve family problems.

PROFESSIONS   Artist, dancer, Mayan priest, midwife, physical therapist, chiropractor, matchmaker, obstetrician/gynecologist, ecologist

GOVERNING BODY PART   Blood vessels

NAWAL   Monkey

ENERGY PLACES   Forests, lakes, the clear night sky

COLORS   Red, orange

COMPLEMENTARY SIGNS   *B'atz'*, *Ajmaq*, *Imox*, and *Kame* are truly complementary signs. They make the best relationships in terms of love and business. They become lifelong friends.

HARMONIOUS SIGNS   *B'atz'*, *Tz'ikin*, *Kawoq*, *Aq'ab'al*, and *Kej* are harmonious signs. They combine good energy, and there is rarely any conflict between them. They sometimes make good friendships or lasting love relationships.

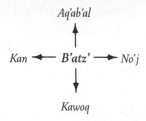

$$Aq'ab'al$$

$$Kan \longleftarrow B'atz' \longrightarrow No'j$$

$$Kawoq$$

B'atz' are community-oriented later in life, in both service and scope. Family is very important to them, although they and their relatives don't always understand one another. The greatest obstacles to their personal growth are ego and avarice. At times they are detached from the material and financial and therefore need to learn balance. Their *nawal* is the monkey, which signifies wisdom in many cultures. It is said that being near a person with this sign brings great fortune. In Mayan mythology, the first divine twins were Jun B'atz' and Jun Chowen, whose names translate as One Monkey and One Artisan, respectively. Both were great sages and the fathers of fine art, but they succumbed to their egomania. Duality marks this sign. *B'atz'* are children of the night. This is when they are energized and feel a sense of freedom. They have a great deal of sexual energy and can be tempted to act on strong passions or violent sexual impulses. Writing is their most natural form of expression. Great strategists with strong mental acuity have been born under this sign.

Having *Aq'ab'al* as their conception sign means that they will grow spiritually. This life is a product of their past. Now they have a new opportunity and must take advantage of it. Life will bring many changes. The energy of *Aq'ab'al* has one foothold in the past and another in the future. The greatest problem for *B'atz'* will be to find themselves in the present. They will always appear young and ready for adventure.

Kan in the right hemisphere brings additional strength and energy. The inner fire it brings to *B'atz'* can be their greatest virtue or their greatest vice. Their right hand will work incredible healing miracles. They tend to lose a lot of sexual energy, magnetism, and power over material things.

No'j in the left hemisphere brings nobility and a spiritual nature. The knowledge that *B'atz'* acquire throughout life will become wisdom.

FAMOUS PEOPLE BORN UNDER *B'ATZ'*　　Dustin Hoffman, Jacques Cousteau, Sean Connery, Stanley Kubrick, Neil Armstrong, Robert De Niro, Harrison Ford, Serena Williams, Joan Miró

ENGLISH	*Path*
KAQCHIKEL	*E*
YUCATEC	*Eb'*
NAHUATL	*Malinalli*
DIRECTION	*West*
ELEMENT	*Earth*
KEY	*The sacred way*
GROWTH	*Experience acquired through travel and from wise Elders*

E

SIGNIFICANCE OF THE KAB'AWIL   The upper right-hand side of this glyph signifies the ear, the path. The dots are stones placed alongside the path.

MEANING   *E* symbolizes the path of destiny, travel, the road of life, the guide, and the means. The how and what of the journey called life is the energy of action; that which moves us toward a precise objective, it is the part of life that searches for realization in every situation and aspect of life. *E* represents the stairs between the world, the overworld, and the underworld. It indicates where to walk. It also symbolizes the staircase and individual steps on the spiritual path, represented by teeth. *E* lays out the vertical and horizontal lines we need to follow as individuals and as members of society.

E is the strength, power, and energy a person possesses for undertaking journeys, jobs, commissions—anything having to do with human realization. It is the sacred way, *Saq B'e* (the White Road), purity, and the second level. The White Road leads from one temple to another, from one city or ceremonial center to another.

E is the unfolding of history, which begins with *B'atz'* and ends with *Tz'i'*. *E* provides action. It is intermediation, it is the search for what is new and yet similar between different visions, and it brings an innate, innovative strength.

E guides and protects merchants. After diplomats and wise men, merchants were next to walk along the roads. This energy satisfies their needs once they have gone the distance.

CHARACTERISTICS   People born on this day have the conception sign *K'at*, and their destiny sign is *Ajpu*.

E are *Ajq'ijab'* (Mayan priests), leaders, diplomats, and political experts. They are travelers and make good guides and successful merchants. They are natural leaders and great storytellers and orators. Very sensitive, they like to surround themselves with works of art; with focus and hard work, they can become great artists.

They are skilled at the art of conversation. They know something about everything, like history, and are always respected.

They are obedient, resolute, and brave and share their wealth with the community. They are highly creative and self-motivated. They have an adventurous, restless spirit, needing to move and travel frequently and take risks. They are speculators, constantly changing their opinions. They are very noble, particularly with children and the younger generations, and they share their experience and wisdom. They are deeply understanding, tolerant, and kindhearted, and they genuinely care for their fellow man.

This sign is one of the luckiest in love. Those born under it need several relationships throughout life and aren't exactly the most faithful people. When they are comfortable and free of pressure, however, they feel no need for extramarital affairs, and home is where they are happiest. They generally make good parents. Despite being very communicative, they are actually quite vulnerable and distrustful beneath their outer shell.

POSITIVE ASPECTS   *E* are generous, kindhearted, resolute, understanding, cheerful, and affectionate. They readily and immediately help others and are happy to show them the proper path. They ask Ajaw for whatever other people need and are sincere. They make good *Ajq'ijab'* and may become *K'amol B'ey* (community guides).

NEGATIVE ASPECTS   *E* can argue ideology with their enemies. They have a tendency to see the negative side of actions and events. They are prone to serious illnesses. They may envy those who are wealthy. They are manipulative and not very trustworthy, using negative strategies to get what they want. They are liars and tend toward infidelity.

ENERGY   This is the best day to begin any type of business or negotiation or to sign a contract. It is an auspicious day to

Teotihuacán messenger in Tikal

begin a trip, whether long or short. It is a very good day for communication, especially from abroad, and for receiving news about loved ones who live elsewhere.

PROFESSIONS   Merchant, administrator, mathematician, broker, salesperson, real estate agent, art or antique dealer, philosopher, psychologist, chef

GOVERNING BODY PART   Sole of the foot

NAWAL   Wildcat

ENERGY PLACES   Mountains, highland forests, rivers

COLORS   White, light blue

COMPLEMENTARY SIGNS   *E, No'j, Iq',* and *Kej*

HARMONIOUS SIGNS   *E, Ajmaq, Ajpu, K'at,* and *Q'anil*

THE MAYAN CROSS

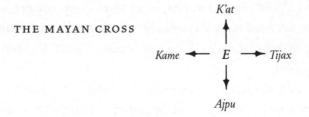

E make excellent merchants and brokers. Their people skills and attention to detail inspire confidence, as does their positive attitude. In Mayan mythology, *E* is the second step in creation. It is creative action, where the infinite path of time finds a space in which to manifest. The image is one of naturally achieving balance and harmony. It gives those born under this sign a deep sense of spirituality. It is destiny, the path of life, and *E* are great travelers on the sacred path. They are facilitators and bringers of news.

E provides a special gift for understanding all of the arts relating to divination. Males should surround themselves with feminine energy that extols their virtues, while women should surround themselves with masculine energy, where they will find true friendship. *E* are often very well informed about other cultures. They are not usually prophets in their own land. Life for them is better lived outside their place of birth.

K'at as the conception sign speaks of a life governed by previous lives and is the reason for the entanglements and obstacles *E* face throughout life. This same energy, however, also helps them crystallize their purpose.

Kame in the right hemisphere denotes an old soul inclined toward the past and all things ancestral. It opens good communication with other dimensions. *E* will be respected later in life. They are protected from accidents or illnesses and feel confident about taking risks. They are surrounded by a halo of mystery and have great magnetism.

Tijax in the left hemisphere indicates that *E* may be able to pull aside the veil of secret knowledge. *Tijax*'s energy protects them from those who seek to deceive, telling them when to withdraw from a bad situation. It also makes them categorical when making decisions, which may be impulsive. The *nawal* energy is the double-edged knife—half-positive, half-negative. *E* have to find balance in order to make use of this strength.

Ajpu as the destiny sign means that *E* will find certainty and rest later in life, after a great deal of agitation, emotion, and travel in their younger years. This energy provides them with security and stability. They will manage to overcome the obstacles and tests that life places in their path.

FAMOUS PEOPLE BORN UNDER E   Stevie Wonder, Yitzhak Rabin, Anne Frank, David Beckham, Earvin "Magic" Johnson Jr.

ENGLISH	Authority, Sacred Altar
KAQCHIKEL	Aj
YUCATEC	B'en
NAHUATL	Acatl
DIRECTION	North
ELEMENT	Air
KEY	Abundance and rebirth
GROWTH	Return to the origin, social influence

SIGNIFICANCE OF THE KAB'AWIL   The vertical lines or stalks at the top of this glyph that come only partway down signify spiritual growth. The horizontal line, symbolizing multiplication and the horizon, is an altar table, and the sacred trees, such as the ceiba and coral tree, with their roots, trunk, and canopy, also represent a table or altar.

MEANING   *Aj*, represented by sugarcane and cornstalks, symbolizes the strength of power. It means abundance and the renewal of nature in order to be in harmony with others. It is a pillar that connects cosmic and telluric energies. It is unity, power, and the seven virtues of the divine power: Fire, Earth, Air, Water, Heart of Sky, Heart of Earth, and the Center. *Aj* is also clairvoyance, sacred words, love of humanity, telepathy, body signs, unexpected dreams, and sacred knowledge of sex.

Aj symbolizes Grandmother Ixmukane's first rite before the cornstalks, when she cried for some sign of life from her grandsons Jun Ajpu and Ixb'alamke, who were alive in the underworld, Xib'alb'ay. It is triumph over all evil and bad spirits. It is the triumph of life over death.

Aj is the sacred staff that symbolizes both earthly and divine authority, providing leadership and autocracy, and the posts that hold up a house, the pillars of strength. It is male strength and conviction combined with poise and communication *par excellence* during difficult times.

The sugarcane crop is the community that provides abundance, the sweetness of knowing how to grow by sharing. It is the return home, the place of origin, the *tab'al*, or sacred Mayan altar, the place where higher energies converge and manifest. *Aj* also represents the spinal column, developing the internal serpent of fire that moves and awakens secret strength. It activates the powers that result in heroic acts.

Aj cultivates the knowledge of human nature gained through joint, community work. It personifies integrity, honesty, and rectitude. It is the mother of confidentiality and purity and has characteristics of cosmic expansion.

This sign deals with ethics, prudence, and morality. *Aj* invokes simplicity and justice as the path to life harmony. It is a sign of prestige and status, bringing the energy needed to attain the sublime.

CHARACTERISTICS People born on this day have the conception sign *Kan*, and their destiny sign is *Imox*.

Aj are masters of knowledge, *Ajq'ijab'* (Mayan priests), and *K'exelon* (midwives). They understand the physical. With hard work, they can develop the ability to receive spiritual messages.

They are readers, researchers, and scholars. They seek refinement and education, becoming great academics. They are intelligent, strong, and persevering. Their search for perfection is a great asset but could also be their greatest obstacle. They suffer but succeed in the end, achieving the goals they set for themselves. Those born under this sign attain prestige and renown. Great politicians, statesmen, and psychologists born under this sign have gone down in history as a result of their honesty and good work. They are deep thinkers by nature.

POSITIVE ASPECTS *Aj* possess sacred knowledge and strong spiritual power. They are cheerful and decisive and able to take secrets to the grave. With their respect for plants and other species, they make good farmers. They are trustworthy at home with their family and love their children. They are great moralists, always thinking about rules. They need to be constantly stimulated and easily lose interest if they are not. They may hold public office or attain senior positions within their profession and will be known as authorities.

NEGATIVE ASPECTS Some *Aj* may live in poverty. Their lives are changeable, and their powerful emotions can result in great sadness and pain. They are often ill during childhood, but not as adults. They like to test their fellow men. They are obsessive and angry, not very sensible, insensitive in some situations, proud, and gluttonous.

 ENERGY This day protects the home, plants, and animals. It brings good weather and good harvests, and it bears fruit. It is the energy that brings rebirth, a return home, a sign of life. *Aj* facilitates the renewal of nature in order to be in harmony with others.

PROFESSIONS Artist, counselor, educator, poet

GOVERNING BODY PART Spinal column

NAWAL Armadillo

ENERGY PLACES Beaches, lowland forests

COLORS Brown, white

COMPLEMENTARY SIGNS *Tijax, Aq'ab'al*, and *Q'anil*

HARMONIOUS SIGNS *No'j, Imox, Kan*, and *Toj*

THE MAYAN CROSS

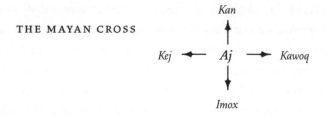

Aj represents authority. Those born under this sign are often known throughout life as experts in their field. However, they are usually the power behind the throne, preferring to avoid the spotlight. Theirs is a minor power. These people will always have a special connection to their place of birth. They love the Earth and nature. Their lives are almost always successful, though not without obstacles. The combination of these energies results in a certain seriousness, although deep down they are somewhat eccentric. Others often find them strange. This perception does not distract them from earnestly pursuing their work, which can lead them to be obsessive. The mind plays a big role in *Aj*. Their brains are always working, and they like to delve into the mysteries of psychology.

Kan as the conception sign will bring additional, boundless energy. This sign is associated with the eternal search for knowledge. The greatest weakness of *Aj* is their sexual energy—their sensuality in particular. They must keep their spinal column flexible, for their energy seeks to be channeled. They will develop paranormal powers if they are able to use their internal energy. Self-discipline is their closest ally. *Kan* in this position indicates a spirit that is far along the path and needs to live intensely in order to grow. This intensity makes *Aj* either very desired or very disliked.

Kej in the right hemisphere provides exceptional imagination and inspiration. It tempers *Aj*'s usual pragmatism. *Kej* makes those born under *Aj* sensitive to art, particularly music and painting. They have an equal understanding of the feminine and masculine visions.

Kawoq in the left hemisphere influences the tendency to make big plans as well as to seek social justice and work for the wellbeing of all. *Aj* are emotionally dependent on their partner and maintain strong ties with their family. Family comes first, and despite their sexual appetite, they seek fidelity. Family and close friends respect them.

Imox as the destiny sign creates conflict for *Aj* with their inner personality, manifesting as nonconformity. This sign brings unrestrained impulsiveness, and this enriches *Aj*'s lives with unusual experiences and makes them particularly intrigued with mysticism, though they do not make this the focus of their life given their affinity for pragmatism and provable facts. *Aj* are passionate about the countryside, and this is where they will become highly spiritually refined.

FAMOUS PEOPLE BORN UNDER *AJ*   Barack Obama, Larry King, Quentin Tarantino, Maria Callas, Sigmund Freud, Carl Jung

ENGLISH	*Jaguar, Magic*
KAQCHIKEL	*I'x*
YUCATEC	*Ix*
NAHUATL	*Ocelotl*
DIRECTION	*South*
ELEMENT	*Water*
KEY	*Patience, astuteness, and action*
GROWTH	*Inner learning and high magic*

SIGNIFICANCE OF THE KAB'AWIL   This glyph signifies the heart of the planet, the feminine reproductive organs, the face of a jaguar, and points on the map of Mother Earth.

MEANING   *I'x* is the jaguar or tiger, signifying feminine and feline energy. It represents the four *B'alameb'* (Men-Gods), intelligence, the strength of Mother Earth, the power of the jungle, and the protective spirit of hills, plains, and mountains.

Signifying the creative forces in the universe, *I'x* is the day of high magic. This energy develops higher powers. Great magicians and prophets are born under its auspices. It provides innate intuition and curiosity. Those born under this sign could practice magic-scientific techniques. It is particularly favorable for divination. The power of this sign mediates between the real and the unreal, the positive and the negative, the possible and the impossible. It is therefore referred to as the Day of Magicians. Psychic powers and abilities are favored on this day.

Of all the signs, *I'x* expands the mind the most, providing the strength to reach the highest level of consciousness. This strength, combined with mental acuity, benefits the highest levels of mysticism.

I'x is represented by the jaguar, an *Ajpop* (higher deity) of the American jungle. It is related to strength, power, astuteness, and firmness. The mythical Men-Gods who led this humanity were the four *B'alameb'*, or jaguars, regents of this sign, who saved and guided the Mayan world twelve thousand years ago.

It is a special day for spiritual and community guides to ask for strength and positive energy and for a good life for all animals. It is a day on which to ask Ajaw, the Great Father, for good crops. The day's energy is related to sensitivity; it is therefore auspicious to establish good relationships based on clarity.

CHARACTERISTICS   People born on this day have the conception sign *Kan*, and their destiny sign is *Iq'*.

I'x are strong, brave, energetic, and passionate. They rule in love and can always find someone to fulfill their desires. Feminine energy favors the development of magic powers. They have a knack for raising animals and farming. They are warriors and dreamers. They have an excellent imagination. They are changeable, easily distracted, and quick to make decisions. They are brave risk-takers, and their destiny is unpredictable. They possess a physical strength and power that makes them especially resilient.

Their energy is totally feline, and this makes women born under this sign especially feminine. They are natural hunters, both loved and feared. They make protective fathers and love the security that family provides.

If there is one word that describes them well it is "astute." Although they are somewhat daring and never show their anxiety, they are always realistic and prudent. They have a strong personality. They keep their problems to themselves and have difficulty sharing them.

POSITIVE ASPECTS *I'x* are able and agile in their actions. They possess the strength and energy to meditate. They love being popular. Highland traditions can be good for them. They are interested in success, possess good health, and have the courage to confront any of life's difficulties. They can be *Ajq'ijab'* (Mayan priests).

NEGATIVE ASPECTS *I'x* are presumptuous, vain, quick-tempered, and proud. They like to be the center of attention, seeking fame and success. They love power and are willing to do anything to attain it, which can unbalance their energy and quickly derail them on the path of life. They can hurt others if they aren't careful. They can be arrogant, resentful, foolish, and fickle.

They are influenced by the *nawal* of the Seven Sins, or *Wuqub' Qak'ix*: pride, ambition, envy, lies, crime, ingratitude, and ignorance.

ENERGY This day has a special power to change negative aspects. It is a day on which to withdraw, meditate, and reconsider life, to formulate a new strategy, and to solve problems. It is also a good day for inner strength and for magic and handling occult forces.

PROFESSIONS Warrior, philosopher, mathematician, doctor

GOVERNING BODY PARTS Muscles, nerves

NAWAL Jaguar

ENERGY PLACES Jungles, ceremonial centers, step pyramids

COLORS Yellow, brown

COMPLEMENTARY SIGNS *I'x, Kawoq, K'at*, and *Toj*

HARMONIOUS SIGNS *I'x, Tijax, Iq', Kame*, and *Tz'i'*

THE MAYAN CROSS

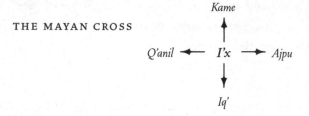

I'x is the sign of great mystics and powerful magicians. The first Fathers of humanity govern this sign. The virtues and sense of magic of those born under this sign are therefore demonstrated throughout their lives, even if they try to reject or deny this talent. As pragmatists, they hesitate to disrupt the status quo.

Kame as the conception sign indicates continuity from a previous life connected to their ancestors. This sign is drawn to what is old and allows *I'x* to successfully look inside themselves. It also provides extraordinary intuition: they must follow their instincts in order for their undertakings to turn out well. Protected by higher, interdimensional beings, great knowledge is revealed to them in dreams. They are an object of envy and betrayal among their own sex. They will have to find alliances with the opposite sex, which understands them better.

Q'anil in the right hemisphere directs their energy toward agriculture. Everything *I'x* plant bears fruit, even if it's not immediately apparent. Those born under this sign who want to start their own business would do best to partner with someone who has a complementary sign. *I'x* are able to embark on new ventures very successfully, but others need to see them through. They will have problems with young people throughout their lives; they are likely to have few children, and only later in life, although this could change if their partner is very fertile.

Ajpu in the left hemisphere is an energy that passes tests, particularly ones of a spiritual nature. In Mayan mythology, the twins Jun Ajpu and Ixb'alamke, the beginning of masculine and feminine, went down to the underworld and passed the tests set for them by the Lords of Xib'alb'ay. This day brings certainty, security, and the achievement of goals, provided the mind doesn't play tricks and engender doubt. People involved with *I'x*, particularly in love relationships, must be very patient because they can become highly suspicious and demanding, even obsessive. They will always find someone willing to serve them and satisfy their pleasures. They need their achievements to be recognized and complimented.

Iq' as the destiny sign feeds their mind and imagination, making them particularly intelligent. That intelligence will grow if they let their imagination run free, although they have a tendency to overthink or fabricate.

FAMOUS PEOPLE BORN UNDER *I'X*   Richard Nixon, Arnold Schwarzenegger, Tiger Woods, Paul Newman, David Blaine, Viggo Mortensen, Ernest Hemingway, Julie Andrews

Tz'ikin

ENGLISH	*Intermediary between Earth and Sky, Bird of Power*
KAQCHIKEL	*Tz'ikin*
YUCATEC	*Men*
NAHUATL	*Cuauhtli*
DIRECTION	*East*
ELEMENT	*Fire*
KEY	*Intermediation between earth and sky*
GROWTH	*Intuition, dreams, and divination*

SIGNIFICANCE OF THE KAB'AWIL   This glyph symbolizes an eagle's head. The top part is bald, and the vertical lines are the feathers on the back of the head.

MEANING   *Tz'ikin* is the intermediary between God and man. It is the intermediary between Mother Tz'aqol, Father B'itol, and human beings. It is intermediation between Ajaw, the Great Father, and human beings, represented by everything that exists in space: air, clouds, cold, and heat—powers that Heart of Sky created to help us. It represents the sacred vision.

Tz'ikin means bird, the guardian of all Mayan lands. It is the *maq'uq'*, or quetzal, the first bird to sing when the Sun and all the

animals appeared. It is liberty, the messenger, treasure, luck, and money. It also
means fortune. It is a special day on
which to dedicate the *Xukulem Chuwach
Ri Qajaw*—the Mayan ceremony to ask
for good luck.

This sign brings good relationships. *Tz'ikin* provides magnetism and is the perfect day to negotiate, particularly in love and
business. It is a special day for increasing intuition and vision.

The energy of this sign is accompanied by global awareness. It
instills idealism and focus in the community. It is an indepen-
dent, mutable energy.

It represents abundant harvests, good business, love, and art.
It is a sign of liberty and the search for experience, the sign of
love. The energy of this sign breaks with the status quo and can
find a solution to anything. *Tz'ikin* brings broad vision, unlimited
by time or space. It is the panoramic, acute vision of an eagle.

The name of the sign derives from *Tz'i'*, the Authority, and
Q'in, Father Sun. In other words, *Tz'ikin* is the Sun's authority,
the representation of the Father on Earth. The image is of an
eagle, whether in majestic flight or as a god on its rocky outcrop,
representing social life and the status quo. On the ground, it represents the mundane.

CHARACTERISTICS   People born on this day have the conception sign *Kej*, and their destiny sign is *Aq'ab'al*.

Tz'ikin are merchants and artists. They are cheerful, kind,
generous, friendly, and intuitive. They are lucky with money. Because they are very socially adept, they are popular and have good
friendships. They are sophisticated but eccentric. *Tz'ikin* are the

power behind the throne, and they make very good strategists. They give the impression that they can solve any problem. As the most erratic sign, however, they easily grow bored and can abandon everything in a flash. The same thing happens with their friendships, though they may later come back to a friend they had forsaken.

Tz'ikin are very lucky in love; they were born to be loved. They are susceptible to becoming involved in base passions and like to live intensely. Flattery is their greatest weakness.

They were born to be their own boss, and they need space and freedom. Generally, their energies are most alive when the sun is setting and at night. They are therefore the perfect bohemians. Life to them is a party.

They possess extraordinary mental acuity. They are *Ajq'ijab'* (Mayan priests), and they develop far-reaching vision, receiving revelations through dreams.

POSITIVE ASPECTS *Tz'ikin* are kind, cheerful, and communicative. They manipulate invisible powers and are visionaries. Their predictions are accurate. Some possess great spiritual strength. They have a good vocabulary and express themselves easily and are thus great communicators. They are ingenious, mystical, and generous. They transmit the sacred word and are protected by Ajaw.

NEGATIVE ASPECTS *Tz'ikin* are very temperamental, insatiable, and forgetful. They are stubborn, licentious, ambitious, envious, opportunistic, arrogant, lazy, extravagant, frail, proud, verbose, prone to exaggeration, irresponsible, and vindictive. They can be spendthrifts, liars, and cheats.

ENERGY This is the best day for love and to ask for personal or community abundance. It is also a good day to ask for protection for businesses. It is an auspicious day to ask for a partner or friend. Intuition, vision, precognition, and revelations through dreams prevail in spiritual matters.

PROFESSIONS   Poet, sculptor, painter, clairvoyant, scientist, merchant, diplomat, psychologist, adviser, broker

GOVERNING BODY PART   Eyes

NAWAL   Eagle, condor, quetzal, butterfly

ENERGY PLACES   Mountains, lakes, highland forests

COLORS   Dark blue, light blue, white

COMPLEMENTARY SIGNS   *Tz'ikin, Ajpu, Kan,* and *Tz'i'*

HARMONIOUS SIGNS   *Tz'ikin, B'atz', Kawoq, Aq'ab'al,* and *Kej*

THE MAYAN CROSS

$$Kej$$
$$\uparrow$$
$$Toj \leftarrow Tz'ikin \rightarrow Imox$$
$$\downarrow$$
$$Aq'ab'al$$

Tz'ikin is Father Sun's representative on Earth, the Sun's Authority, and this is what makes it such a fortunate and charismatic sign. The extraordinary intuition of those born under this sign will save them from countless problems. Rules, schedules, and commitments were not made for *Tz'ikin*. They are free-spirited children of the night. Life is a party they never want to end. They are quickly excited and then bored by things that attract their attention, and they are well aware of the damage they can inflict as a result of their fickle nature. *Tz'ikin* are lucky in love and oblivious to the broken hearts they leave in their wake. They are always looking out for their own well-being.

Tz'ikin make great confidants throughout their lives and are sought after as advisers and psychologists. They are capable of performing heroic acts. Although fascinated by fame and power, they seek to remain anonymous. The word "gadabout" fits them like a glove and they will only begin to settle down later in life. They weren't made to be faithful, even though they love home life and are very responsible there.

Kej as the conception sign gives *Tz'ikin* a need for and love of nature. They adapt well to every situation and place they live in. They will have excellent friends and admirers of the opposite sex. Men need feminine energy and protection in order to survive, and women need male energy and protection.

Toj in the right hemisphere provides human warmth. The law of action and reaction in this and previous lives will follow *Tz'ikin*: those born under this energy are not exempt from paying the price for former lives. This is their misfortune, but they will always come out ahead. They resolve everything at the last minute, as if always testing their good fortune and ability to live on the edge. They need contact with fire for personal harmony and balance. Fire speaks to them and is critical to their ability to decipher knowledge. This does not mean, however, that heat or warm places are always beneficial to them.

Imox in the left hemisphere is the sign of all that is unexpected, eccentric, and unconventional. It orients *Tz'ikin* toward mysticism, giving them strength and developing their internal powers and senses.

Aq'ab'al as a destiny sign and catalyst leads *Tz'ikin* to search for answers in the past. They are intrigued and affected by where their family came from, as well as by periods of change in humanity such as in ancient Greece and Egypt, classical Rome, the Renaissance, and the Belle Époque. Their counterpart will have an affinity with and projection toward the future, to the new technology they admire but fear. They are youthful, and their vocation will tend toward innovation.

FAMOUS PEOPLE BORN UNDER *TZ'IKIN* Woody Allen, John F. Kennedy, Diego A. Maradona, Rigoberta Menchú, Michael Jordan, Adam Sandler, Sean Penn, Winston Churchill

ENGLISH	*Curiosity, Sin, and Pardon*
KAQCHIKEL	*Ajmaq*
YUCATEC	*Kib'*
NAHUATL	*Cozcacuauhtli*
DIRECTION	*West*
ELEMENT	*Earth*
KEY	*Search for expression and transmission*
GROWTH	*Forgiveness and personal service*

Ajmaq

SIGNIFICANCE OF THE KAB'AWIL   This glyph signifies the mind in a state of forgiveness and illumination. It is a brain with rays, lines of expansion, reaching out in all directions.

MEANING   *Ajmaq* is a favorable day to ask for and receive forgiveness, to manage harmony and discord, and to focus on the word, the message, ancestral lines, and the energy that emanates from living bodies, called an aura.

This day brings an energy that is the mother of all mistakes, offenses, and lack of responsibility before Ajaw, the Great Father, and all manifestations of life and creation. Our Grandfathers said that sin is a direct offense against Ajaw.

Ajmaq is forgiveness and a day of introspection. In antiquity it

was a day to stay home and reflect on one's acts and their consequences, whether intentional or unintentional. On that day, one would go out only to make an offering, to ask forgiveness from those who had been wronged, or to go to the ceremonies and listen to the traditions. The summing up of their lives in general and the last *winal* (twenty days) in particular was a way for Classic Mayans to maintain balance. They asked Mother Earth to forgive their abuses and gave thanks for the benefits they had received. This was the day when the great sages would share their teachings with the whole community and the community could speak with the Elders.

Ajmaq is earth, the spirit of our Grandfathers. *Maq* is like a curtain of smoke that hides us from the presence of Ajaw. It is planetary awareness and outer space. It represents our Grandfathers and ancestral wisdom. In the eyes of the Grandfathers, the greatest error and irresponsibility—*maq*—is not believing in Ajaw and not serving or remembering Heart of Sky and Heart of Earth. It is a day that reminds us of and connects us to a universal vision as well as to our own reality. On this day, we can delve deeper into the purpose and direction of our lives. It is a day when questions arise and we explore the wonder and mystery of our expression as individuals. It is a day to remember our Grandfathers, our ancestors, and Mother Earth in her manifestation as the protector and procuress of humanity, she who always forgives. It is sweet honey.

The energy of *Aj* is the experience and virtue of a long walk through life. It is represented by old age, which does not have the same meaning as it does in the West. To become an Elder in the Mayan world one must have completed 4 cycles of 13 years and thus be 52 years old.

CHARACTERISTICS People born on this day have the conception sign *Q'anil*, and their destiny sign is *K'at*.

Ajmaq may be Mayan doctors. They are likely to have a long, healthy life. They are analytical, shrewd, quiet, and able to keep secrets. They have the virtue of taking life slowly and reaching their goals. They have a special talent for getting along well with everyone. They are very sweet and have many long relationships. In the Yucatecan tradition, the energy of *Kib'*, which means candle, was created on this day and means inner light, the divine spark in the infinite interior of our body.

Ajmaq have a strong personality and quick temper. Although they embody the duality of curiosity and prudence, it is not unusual for them to have vices. Their essence is impenetrable, though they appear to be open and direct. They aspire to be sincere but often shift blame onto others. Deep down, they are insecure.

Given the importance of this energy, those born under this sign are sentient, sensitive, and potentially prone to depression. Their greatest challenge is to accept other people's faults. Luckily, they often live a long life, and this allows them to gradually accept other ways of being. They can be extreme and get caught up in religious fundamentalism.

Maq is *Wuqub' Qak'ix* (the Seven Sins): pride, ambition, envy, lies, crime, ingratitude, and ignorance.

POSITIVE ASPECTS *Ajmaq* have the courage to solve problems. They have a talent for mixing with all types of people and acting as their defenders. They dominate the cosmic force. They are analytical and accountable for their actions. They ask the Grandmothers and Grandfathers who have already come back to truth to grant them intelligence and show them the proper path to follow. They are strong in both the material and spiritual sense.

NEGATIVE ASPECTS *Ajmaq* blame others for their bad behavior. They are frail, undisciplined, jealous, and irresponsible. They are liars and have a strong personality. They are likely to have vices and to cause problems in the home, and they tend to be unfaithful to their partner.

ENERGY *Ajmaq* is the most auspicious day to ask for and offer forgiveness, atone for our sins, and avoid confrontation. It is also a good day to cure all types of illnesses, defend the dispossessed, seek justice, and achieve harmony with Mother Earth.

PROFESSIONS Strategist, politician, mathematician, orator, doctor, public relations, accountant, lawyer, international jurists

GOVERNING BODY PARTS Genitalia, aura

NAWAL Owl, bee, insects

ENERGY PLACES Caves, caverns, streams, oceans

COLORS Gray, black, white

COMPLEMENTARY SIGNS *Ajmaq*, *B'atz'*, *Imox*, and *Kame*

HARMONIOUS SIGNS *Ajmaq*, *E*, *Ajpu*, *K'at*, and *Q'anil*

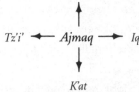

Ajmaq influences those born under this sign to be quite curious. This life is a direct consequence of their previous lives, and this is a new opportunity to discover the path to comprehensive evolution. Their challenge is to not get lost in the illusion of the material world and instead to expose their inner light. Few signs have the opportunity that *Ajmaq* have to let their inner light shine and the power to understand themselves. It is also the sign most likely to bring many changes and provide many wake-up calls. Deep down they are aware of their life purpose, but this doesn't mean it is easy for them to find their way. Their power comes from inner strength and the ability to take control of any situation. This only makes them seem more mysterious to others. If they awaken their conscience, they will be high-ranking public servants with a strong social conscience and spiritual balance. They will become defenders of the people. Their life, which is generally long, is about finding balance and making use of their intense experiences.

Q'anil as the conception sign provides the seed that will grow slowly but steadily, and this is reflected in all aspects of life for *Ajmaq*. They have a special duty to children and plants; working with either of these is the most beneficial for balancing cause and effect. They get along and communicate much better with other people's children than their own. They are well suited to planning projects and being able to carry them out.

Tz'i' in the right hemisphere indicates a tendency toward material law, which benefits *Ajmaq* in financial terms. They do very well in banking and finance. They can also be distinguished litigators. Their right hand has the power and authority to cure many illnesses, and they may specialize in alternative medicine.

Iq' in the left hemisphere catalyzes the depths of the mind, resulting in a very profound and focused intelligence. It also manifests in *Ajmaq* as a tendency toward exploring the mysteries of spirituality, which leads to an expansive mind and universal awareness.

K'at as the destiny sign provides challenges and entanglements. This energy always influences the future with uncertainty. The task for *Ajmaq* in their later years is to have learned from all of the entanglements and intense experiences they have faced in life. Their curiosity and *K'at*'s influence combine to create an alliance that is hard to control. It is difficult to keep them from becoming involved in other people's problems.

FAMOUS PEOPLE BORN UNDER *AJMAQ*   Arthur C. Clarke, Bob Dylan, Anthony Hopkins, Valentino, Truman Capote, Marlon Brando, Reggie Jackson, Pablo Picasso

ENGLISH	*Knowledge, Thought*
KAQCHIKEL	*No'j*
YUCATEC	*Kab'an*
NAHUATL	*Ollin*
DIRECTION	*North*
ELEMENT	*Air*
KEY	*Knowledge and wisdom*
GROWTH	*Mental transmission and clarity*

SIGNIFICANCE OF THE KAB'AWIL   This glyph symbolizes learning. The drawing in the middle represents the brain, and the circles are degrees of increasing human spiritual betterment.

MEANING   *No'j* turns knowledge and experience into wisdom. It is the connection between the Universal Cosmic Mind and the human mind—intellect, knowledge, wisdom, and spiritual learning. It is the energy that governs the mind, knowledge, and memory. It also governs education, the humanities, and psychology. It is the interaction between expansion and the infinite, on the one hand, and on the other, the rigid concept of reality, the limitations imposed on humans. It symbolizes the movement of earth and sky. It is the power of thoughts and ideas, the brain, development, and earthquakes.

Nobility is the greatest virtue of *No'j*. This day champions all virtues, particularly patience, prudence, and sublime love. Renunciation brings clarity. Nobility leads to power; this is the sign's greatest challenge.

No'j is the guide to life as long as all experience and knowledge are imparted in wisdom. Wisdom belongs to Ajaw, the Great Father. According to the Maya, no single person is wise. Humans must therefore consult Ajaw by means of the Mayan ceremony and the *tz'ite* divinatory technique using the seeds from the coral tree. People have good ideas but aren't wise and therefore need to meet as a council in order to share them, develop theories, and ask Ajaw for wisdom. The Elders meet as a council under the protection of *No'j*.

No'j brings the power of communication in both day-to-day matters and the sublime as manifested through art. This communication is intergalactic and interdimensional. *No'j* involves the mystery of *najt*. We can journey in space and time through the subtle instrument of the mind, thus providing advanced spirits with a plenitude of action and awareness.

Great sages and practitioners of white magic have been born under this sign, most notably the heirs to the great lineage of Kukulkan, one of the greatest spiritual guides in the ancestral world. This sign activates the positive side of the spirit of this dimension. It is the reality of the transparency of contents in invisible space. It contains synchronicity, the great vibration, and collective memory.

CHARACTERISTICS   People born on this day have the conception sign *Toj*, and their destiny sign is *Kan*.

No'j possess the qualities of wisdom and intelligence. They are *Aq'omanela'* (Mayan healers), *Ajq'ijab'* (Mayan priests), and diviners. They are brave and prudent and have good body signs. They are extremely trusting and don't realize when others want to hurt them. They convey a sense of security.

No'j is one of the most noble and persevering signs in terms of love. They are good-natured and understanding in marriage. They are faithful by nature, enjoy calm relationships, and give their partner room to develop.

They make good students and fight for justice. Although conservative, they break from tradition by fighting for their forward-thinking ideas. They are idealists and dreamers. Their greatest challenge is to come down to reality. *No'j* were born to initiate change. They are visionaries and prophets of the new way of life, and so deep down they aren't happy with the status quo. Their existence is marked by clarity of being and the search for the profound. If one word could describe them, it would be "knowledge."

Great seekers of their own truth, they are tireless investigators and avid readers. Eventually, they use art to communicate and express things that can't be put into words. They need to transform and allow for self-reflection and growth. They are less thought, more action. They will grow by taking knowledge and making it wisdom.

POSITIVE ASPECTS   *No'j* are merchants and *Aq'omanela'* (healers). Those born on 12 *No'j* are great defenders of justice. They are prudent and studious. Good artists, their spirits are lifted by music and the visual arts. Noble, idealistic, and romantic, their most notable characteristic is service to others and a deep concern for children and the elderly.

NEGATIVE ASPECTS   *No'j* may hurt others with their extreme honesty. They lack the self-awareness to achieve their goals. They are very conceited and proud, slow to act, frail, angry, imposing, arrogant, individualistic, verbose, and inflexible.

ENERGY   This is a very good day for nourishing the mind, improving the memory, and asking questions of the sacred ceremonial fire. It is also a good day to ask for body signs, to harmonize relationships, to request clarity, and especially to turn knowledge and experience into wisdom.

PROFESSIONS   Artist, doctor, spiritual guide, mathematician

GOVERNING BODY PARTS   Brain, pineal gland

NAWAL   Coyote, woodpecker

ENERGY PLACES   Tropical forests, woodlands, lakes, mountains, clouds

COLORS   Dark blue, light blue

COMPLEMENTARY SIGNS   *No'j, E, Iq',* and *Kej*

HARMONIOUS SIGNS   *No'j, Aj, Imox, Kan,* and *Toj*

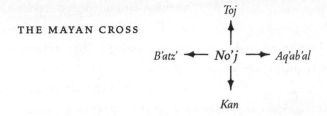

No'j have a special virtue: this is the sign of learning that leads to wisdom. The lives of those born under this sign are graced with nobility and extreme trust. Life will generally be easy in a material sense; No'j attain financial well-being without much effort. Study and reading are the main tools they use to achieve their purpose in life. They have a strong tendency toward simplicity; too much excess can complicate their lives. Their view of the world is idealistic. They seek community, peace, and balance. This sign blazes trails; the adjacent energies provide courage and power.

Toj as the conception sign indicates an emotional suffering, mainly during childhood. It is difficult for No'j to find their place. They wish that the illusion and protection afforded by their early years had never been shattered. Encounters with strangers may have been frightening during this period. This life is a direct result of their previous life, where all of their suffering or atonement began, even if they are honorable and upstanding now.

B'atz' in the right hemisphere endows No'j with special growth in the arts and great manual dexterity. They tend toward writing, music, and painting. They make very good doctors, surgeons, and psychiatrists and are successful with ancestral or alternative forms of medicine. The interaction between B'atz' and No'j results in a strong, analytical mind. The thirst for knowledge stays with them throughout life. They are particularly interested in philosophy and anything to do with new technology. Their artistic expression requires nurturing to evolve.

Aq'ab'al in the left hemisphere brings many changes, especially on a spiritual level. *No'j* need to focus their attention on one discipline in order not to waste their energy. *Aq'ab'al* is the sign of changing opportunities. The greatest experiences in life for *No'j* come through travel and, above all, contact with nature. *No'j* is a rejuvenating, changeable sign that needs to make an effort to settle down and have a base.

Kan as the destiny sign provides a great deal of energy for *No'j*. The power of their inner fire is manifested in their sexuality, alternating between times of extreme action and others of great calm. Ruled by *No'j*, they tend toward romanticism and have many platonic loves. They will always find a partner who is more realistic, someone who is their compass in life.

FAMOUS PEOPLE BORN UNDER *NO'J*   Ronaldinho, Richard Gere, Alfred Hitchcock, Antoine de Saint Exupéry, Jay Leno, Barbara Walters, Joseph Barbera

ENGLISH	*Double-edged Knife, Obsidian*
KAQCHIKEL	*Tijax*
YUCATEC	*Etz'nab'*
NAHUATL	*Técpatl*
DIRECTION	*South*
ELEMENT	*Water*
KEY	*Double-edged knife*
GROWTH	*Warrior, cutting negative energy*

Tijax

SIGNIFICANCE OF THE KAB'AWIL   This glyph symbolizes the tip of a flint knife, seen from the front, and the pyramid as seen by the *nawal* energies from the sky.

MEANING   *Tijax* means separation, the cut, the knife, the pyramid, the healing and harmonizing of any of the four bodies (physical, mental, emotional, and spiritual), and spiritual liberation in the physical body. It represents the genitalia and miracles. *Tijax* is the *nawal* of doctors' intelligence. It is the energy of synchronicity, orientation, and navigation. It is a rational, liberal strength that causes controversy. *Tijax* must overcome extremism, intolerance, pride, and egoism. Revelations come in the form of fleeting images. This is the best day for purifying the balance of our actions, whether

positive or negative, making us atone and showing us a physical, mental, and/or spiritual map. On *Tijax*, one should ask Ajaw, the Great Father, for wisdom regarding minerals and crystals.

Tijax is the power of thunder and lightning. Its *nawal* is lightning, and this is what gives the stone named *chay*, or obsidian, its strength and form. Black and transparent, it is sharp but fragile, hard to polish, and difficult to manipulate. Once finished, however, it is highly prized for its integrity. Great diviners can see inside quartz and *chay*. It is the fundamental stone for diviners and warriors.

Tijax represents the cave or house where Chay, the sacrificial knife, lives in Xib'alb'ay, the underworld, and the place of punishment or flint stones. It means the obsidian knife, the double-edged knife, the strength and power of the warrior.

Symbolized by the double-edged knife, it is the image of both sides of a coin that converge at the tip where it is no longer clear where one ends and the other begins. In other words, there is positive in the negative and negative in the positive. However, the image itself is clear in telling us that *Tijax* is good when positive and extreme when negative. It has the power to cut through mysteries. It opens the way to another dimension. It also means pain, hurt, and sadness. It is the arrow or lance and brings danger.

Tijax is the power of directed thought and the strength of intelligence, the inner force of the planet, magma, the power of the volcano, the touchstone of sacred fire. It represents telluric power and its expression, whether in the form of tremors or earthquakes, and the energy of change or collapse. In other words, it is a good shaking—the strength or action we need in life to understand our true path.

CHARACTERISTICS   People born on this day have the conception sign *Tz'i'*, and their destiny sign is *Kame*.

Tijax are guardians of justice and healers of incurable illnesses. It is *Tijax* who make offerings in serious health situations. They are frail. They suffer from illnesses, accidents, arguments, or gossip and have to atone or make an offering so as not to be penalized. They make very good *Aq'omanela'* (Mayan healers) and doctors, and they are extraordinary surgeons. They possess great power in their hands.

They are brave, tireless, intelligent, and very good with good people. They have excellent ideas and great talent. They are rational, on the one hand, and intuitive, on the other. They are imaginative dreamers and good students.

They can be extreme; they are easily offended and can end a long relationship in the blink of an eye, although for the most part they are sensible and just. They are categorical. It is hard for them to manage love relationships because they would rather not formalize them. When they do take this step, they generally look for someone submissive because their personality is so dominant.

They can attain power and fame and amass great wealth. They enjoy luxuries and the high life. They desire everything in the world but are happy to share. They are very kindhearted. Although traditionalists, they are open to new proposals, particularly in the area of mysticism. Their lives are filled with many enriching experiences.

Social humanists, they value the things of the mind. They take on responsibilities at a young age. They are leaders or intermediaries in any situation and good at public relations, although they can be vindictive if they feel wronged.

POSITIVE ASPECTS   *Tijax* are optimistic when faced with life's difficulties, and they are excellent collaborators. They understand love and make great friends. They may be *Ajq'ijab'* (Mayan priests), spiritual guides, and *K'exelon* (midwives). They possess good body signs and interpret signs in sacred ceremonies and dreams. They are clairvoyant, intuitive, honest, spiritual, and regimented. They take on other people's problems as their own. They don't like to be violent and don't get carried away by passion.

NEGATIVE ASPECTS   *Tijax* can be angry and irascible. They sometimes choose the wrong friends and have trouble controlling their temper and vindictive tendencies. They are prone to being slandered, losing good jobs, and taking lovers. They steal or are stolen from. They don't have much family. They are proud, sensitive, and frail.

ENERGY   This is the day to ask for health, to cure difficult illnesses, and to eliminate grudges and the negative energy that surrounds us. It is a good day to end negative relationships or partnerships. It is also the day to ask for intelligence and a good memory.

PROFESSIONS   Mayan doctor, gynecologist, analyst, politician, judge

GOVERNING BODY PARTS   Teeth, nails, tongue

NAWAL   Swordfish, owl, toucan

ENERGY PLACES   Cliffs, waterfalls, caves, caverns, lightning storms

COLORS   White, red, black

COMPLEMENTARY SIGNS   *Tijax, Aj, Aq'ab'al,* and *Q'anil*

HARMONIOUS SIGNS   *Tijax, I'x, Iq', Kame,* and *Tz'i'*

THE MAYAN CROSS

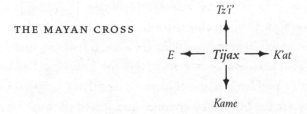

Tz'i'

E ← *Tijax* → *K'at*

Kame

Tijax has extraordinary power and strength. Because those born under its auspices have these elements in their personality, they bring unusual dedication and energy to their work. Their lives are marked by drastic changes, usually without warning, and they can be impulsive. They are destined to become warriors. It is their duty to help others with their problems, especially to cure illnesses. They are great doctors and possess a special power in their hands. It is also their duty to eliminate envy, hatred, and other negativity. The combination of these energies ensures that those born under this sign will have extraordinary spiritual experiences such as paranormal phenomena.

Tz'i' as the conception sign connects *Tijax* to justice and brings them recognition as an authority. They ascend rapidly in judicial professions. They make good lawyers or intermediaries, and they are also good judges whose decisions may be extreme but just. They have a propensity for politics and medicine and make great advisers and psychologists.

E in the right hemisphere provides fortune and wealth when *Tijax* are young. It also brings sudden trips or changes in residence, away from their place of origin. They will have relationships with foreigners throughout their lives, and many *Tijax* will marry someone from another country or culture. They bring luck to businesses, particularly those in which they act as a broker.

K'at in the left hemisphere indicates a life full of experiences and changes. This energy is responsible for involving *Tijax* in other people's problems. *K'at*—the net—traps them in situations where they are confronted by enemies and forced to think carefully before they act. This energy is auspicious for spiritual development and artistic expression. *Tijax* will have to seek a balance between their fertile imagination and reality. This is a sign that makes leaders and provides many followers.

Kame is the destiny sign and the indicator that the future protects them. *Kame* is death, the sign of security and ancestors. *Tijax*'s knife in the middle gives those born under this sign the power to cut through the curtain that shields our vision from other dimensions or realities. The knife also protects them from accidents and death. *Tijax* usually complete their life cycle and fulfill the purpose for which they were born.

FAMOUS PEOPLE BORN UNDER *TIJAX* Fidel Castro, Kiefer Sutherland, Keanu Reeves, Laurence Fishburne, Sophia Loren, Louis Armstrong, Martin Scorsese, Francis Ford Coppola, Benito Mussolini, Jules Verne

ENGLISH:	*Abundance, Family*
KAQCHIKEL:	*Kawoq*
YUCATEC:	*Kawak*
NAHUATL:	*Quiauhuitl*
DIRECTION:	*East*
ELEMENT:	*Fire*
KEY:	*Abundance and community*
GROWTH:	*Community work and detachment*

Kawoq

SIGNIFICANCE OF THE KAB'AWIL The group of spheres represents the members of a family and a group of families that belong to a community. The crosshatching means assistance or collaboration.

MEANING *Kawoq* is family, meetings, groups, society, community, country, and continent—anything that can be grouped. It is a community day, generally beginning with the individual. It means group relationships and descent, the eternal return to life of future generations. It is society, the village, the town, the country, the continent, the planet, the planetary system, the galaxy, the universe, and expansion. It means the strength of unity, greater consciousness, the unfolding of the cosmic plan, growth, and fertility. It is the energy for abundance, in both the material and spiritual sense. It is the energy that brings the rains for good harvests.

It is a special day on which *Ajq'ijab'* (Mayan priests) and *K'exelon* (midwives) burn *pom* to the Sacred Pouch in their brazier. This is the copal incense that the four *B'alameb'* offered in the ceremony when they asked the Sun to come out for the well-being of the people. It is a special day to ask that one's people, house, family, and heart benefit. *Ajq'ijab'*, *K'exelon*, and spiritual guides burn copal to their Sacred Pouch to ask for the well-being of the people. It is an auspicious day to hold the sacred ceremony for cures. On *Kawoq*, one should ask for the knowledge to use medicinal plants because it is a day of energy, nature, and the elements.

It symbolizes the woman or the wife and the sacred spiritual staff. It is dignity, the Mayan priest, the representation of power and authority. It symbolizes total realization: rain, lightning, fire, wind, and water. It is group consciousness, individuals seen as a unit, and the assumption of an imaginary leadership role. Everything one does is for the benefit of the community, thus eliminating egoism and taking advantage of others.

The role of *Kawoq* is the passing of time, the accumulation of days, and the teaching each one brings. It is the cycles of time in each of the calendrical sets, and the changes these bring represent the various stages of life.

CHARACTERISTICS   People born on this day have the conception sign *B'atz'*, and their destiny sign is *Kej*.

Kawoq are brave, intelligent, noble, and imaginative. They are good-natured, kind, calm, generous, and caring. They are motivators and good communicators and presenters. They guide and defend the people. They are spiritual guides, diviners, and prognosticators. They are clairvoyant, receiving messages through dreams and body signs.

They attract abundance and will never go hungry. The arts, which are not foreign to them, are one means for them of attaining wealth. They are friendly and get along well with others. They have a great capacity for interaction and fit in anywhere, in any situation, although they always yearn for home. Not ambitious, they accept things as they come. They are somewhat conformist and obedient but have the gift of leadership when they are in power. They let themselves get carried along by gossip and what others say. Other people are very important to them. They like to put things in their place and will therefore not hesitate to make claims against anything they consider incorrect. They tend to get involved where they're not wanted. Their fulfillment comes through transformation and regeneration.

Kawoq live for their families and find it hard to break away. They are good children and concerned parents. They have to fight the inclination to live other people's lives for them. Although their intention is to prevent others' suffering, they are often manipulative and may impose their own vision. They are respected in love, although it is difficult for them to find a partner. They are quite conservative in this regard. They will have problems with their spouse unless they can become less dependent on their family, particularly their mother.

POSITIVE ASPECTS   *Kawoq* behave rationally and are sure of themselves. They are observant, noble, imaginative, and judicious. They tend to be generous community leaders and dedicated to their families. They never go hungry. They are responsible with family. They are diviners and receive good body signs and dream signs. They deepen their knowledge and refuse to tolerate injustices.

NEGATIVE ASPECTS   *Kawoq* sometimes get involved where they don't belong. They can also be blamed when something bad happens. They refuse to back down in arguments whether they are right or wrong. They are prone to illness unless they do their spiritual work. They can be combative and intrusive and are likely to experience divorce and infidelity.

ENERGY   This is the best day to ask for the common good and the well-being of the family, as well as to settle family disputes or problems of a financial nature. It is a good day to attract affluence and abundance in business. It is a day on which to ask for good weather for crops.

PROFESSIONS   Ecologist, neuropath, community leader, politician, mathematician, gynecologist, orator, writer, artist, forecaster

GOVERNING BODY PARTS   Heart, nerves

NAWAL   Turtle

ENERGY PLACES   Forests, especially pine or cypress

COLORS   Green, blue

COMPLEMENTARY SIGNS   *Kawoq, I'x, K'at,* and *Toj*

HARMONIOUS SIGNS   *Kawoq, B'atz', Tz'ikin, Aq'ab'al,* and *Kej*

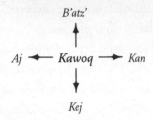

Kawoq in people's hearts attracts them to small groups and the local community. It makes them responsible and attentive to detail, which can verge on perfectionism. They will hold leadership positions and are very well prepared for anything to do with community service, politics, and government. *Kawoq* is a sign of abundance. The presence of those born under this sign draws others even if they don't realize it. They inspire confidence and maintain a strict sense of justice, although their idea of justice can be very rigid. Their greatest challenge in life is family. Their family ties are very strong and hard to break; *Kawoq* have trouble separating from their parents in order to start their own family. When they do break those family ties, however, they are exemplary spouses and parents.

B'atz' as the conception sign makes *Kawoq* good planners and doers. They attain a great deal of prestige and fame in the area of community service. This energy also enables them to be visionary planners. They are drawn to traditional medicine and can balance the use of plants and energies or currents with the physical and chemical.

Aj in the right hemisphere manifests in *Kawoq* as a strong, authoritarian personality, although deep down they are vulnerable and seek protection. This energy is responsible for their success and prestige, which are envied, particularly in the family circle. *Kawoq* are good conversationalists and make excellent friends. They are overprotective parents and need a great deal of attention as children.

Kan in the left hemisphere allows *Kawoq*'s mind and spirit to become one. The image is of a spiral, inner fire, the DNA that is projected onto the spiritual as a catalyst that awakens innate occult powers. *Kan* makes their love relationships sublime, and *Kawoq* generally fall in love with those who are unattainable or unavailable. However, they will always find someone with whom to create a home. The person born under this sign will be similar to one of his or her parents. As the sign of family, *Kawoq* ensures unity and protection, at times to excess. They can become obsessive in this regard, and that obsessiveness is their greatest obstacle to growth.

Kej as a destiny sign marks *Kawoq* as sensitive, agile, nervous, and somewhat impulsive. As walking trees, they find peace and harmony in woodlands. This is where their mind and spirit will be nourished. Although this sign ensures that they are firmly rooted in all four corners of the world, it also points to their need to take precautions because betrayal can occur where they least expect it. Those born under this sign need harmony, and it is therefore best to be surrounded by artistic expressions and to have their own space, their own refuge.

FAMOUS PEOPLE BORN UNDER *KAWOQ*   Isabella Rossellini, Nicolas Cage, Diana, Princess of Wales, Brad Pitt, Yves Saint Laurent, Kurt Cobain, Joe DiMaggio, Jerry Seinfeld, Al Gore, Nicole Kidman, Joseph Stalin

ENGLISH	*Blowgun Hunter, Sun*
KAQCHIKEL	*Ajpu*
YUCATEC	*Ajaw*
NAHUATL	*Xochitl*
DIRECTION	*West*
ELEMENT	*Earth*
KEY	*Hunter, certainty, and security*
GROWTH	*Passing spiritual tests*

Ajpu

SIGNIFICANCE OF THE KAB'AWIL   This glyph signifies the face of the hunter who uses a blowgun. He has a beard, and his mouth is rounded, about to shoot.

MEANING   *Ajpu* is overcoming negative energy. It is the victor, the male, the man, the boss, the spiritual warrior, the hunter, Jun Ajpu, and Ixb'alamke. It is the day of Ajaw, the Great Father, and his solar representation, a day of greatness and the strength of life.

It is the power of the great Jun Ajpu and Ixb'alamke, the twin Men-Gods, the mythical figures of creation, the grandsons of the first Grandparents, Ixpiyakok and Ixmukane. The twins went down to Xib'alb'ay, the dwelling place of the Lords of the Underworld (who, according to tradition, hid underground in order to

survive the great catastrophe twelve thousand years ago). There the twins passed all of the tests that were set for them, died, and were reborn—an allegory for spiritual awakening. They are the great hunters, accurate and sure, the possessors of great magic, the fathers of fine art, and the teachers of this civilization.

This is a special day for Mayan ceremonies that protect against *Wuqu' Qak'ix* (the Seven Sins): pride, ambition, envy, lies, crime, ingratitude, and ignorance.

It is the energy of *Wuqub'Ajpu*, also known as Ixb'alamke, the *nawal* of fertility and hunting. Jun Ajpu and Ixb'alamke planted stalks of corn in the patio of Grandmother Ixmukane's house. If the corn flourished, it meant the twins had survived; if it withered, they had died. Ixmukane performed a ceremony to revive the plants; this is the regenerative power, the cycle of life.

Ajpu governs lunar and solar eclipses and represents the ball game. It brings material and spiritual certainty. It is the realization of the solar body. It is transformation, mutation, and acuity. It is the warrior, the companion, the traveler, the dancer, and the artist, maker of wonders. It is the soothsayer—the diviner and vanquisher of spells—the lord of flowers, master and heir to the power of light.

CHARACTERISTICS People born on this day have the conception sign *E*, also known as *B'ey*, and their destiny sign is *Q'anil*.

Ajpu are orators, writers, carvers, silversmiths, wise men, sculptors, comedians, travelers, dancers, and thespians. They are good, kind, and generous with everything. Romantic dreamers, they are brave, mercurial, intelligent, and sure of themselves. They have a sunny vision of life and are well liked. They tend to dilute their energy by following several paths at once and acting impulsively. They have a futuristic outlook and could be *Ajq'ijab'* (Mayan priests).

They are very observant. They aren't always right even though they are certain, so life will teach them many lessons. They tend to be domineering and manipulative. They are natural warriors and always get their way. Their ego is their greatest obstacle along the spiritual path.

Ajpu came to shine, to shed light. Their mission is to guide humanity. Their task is to convey wisdom, not their idea of the truth but real spirituality. They are a light and a guide during times of human crisis.

They are good at creating and managing a social circle. They are very selective about who they choose as companions and will go to heroic lengths to defend or help a friend. They need their own space but rarely give space to others. They want to shine everywhere. They know how to take advantage of their personality, which is their true fortune.

Romantic yet practical, they will have many relationships before settling down. They often realize too late that the opportunity for true love passed them by. They are good lovers and have a taste for good food—to them these are true arts. As talented craftspeople themselves, they admire art and antiques and will become collectors if they have the means to do so.

POSITIVE ASPECTS *Ajpu* are spiritual defenders, great friends, and companions. They are astute, strategic, direct, and clear. They are facilitators and forerunners. They are the spirit of sunlight, illuminators, and the hub around which their family revolves.

NEGATIVE ASPECTS *Ajpu* could have a spouse who dies suddenly, and death may come to their children. To avoid such tragedies, they should make offerings to Ajaw every twenty days. They are hunters of wild animals and could commit murder. They are exceedingly distrustful and too selective with their friends. They can be cunning, angry, categorical, resentful, and sickly. They avoid responsibility, don't take well to being corrected, and feel overly self-confident.

ENERGY This is the day to obtain certainty and security, to plan and achieve goals. It is a day of renewal, a day to ask for female fertility, to feel emotionally secure, and to sharpen the intellect. It is a day that brings the strength, courage, and energy to overcome obstacles.

PROFESSIONS Writer, actor, economist, lawyer, farmer, scientist, hunter, fashion designer, photographer, filmmaker, marketing, communications

GOVERNING BODY PARTS Thorax, chest, eyes, lungs

NAWAL Human being

ENERGY PLACES   Beaches, jungles, sunlight, sunrise, sunset
COLORS   Red, yellow, terracotta
COMPLEMENTARY SIGNS   *Ajpu, Tz'ikin, Kan*, and *Tz'i'*
HARMONIOUS SIGNS   *Ajpu, E, Ajmaq, K'at*, and *Q'anil*

THE MAYAN CROSS

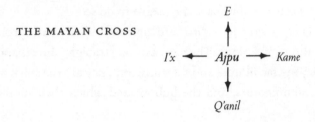

Ajpu have a clear, strong personality and strive to be just. As the sign of the hunter, they always have their blowgun ready. Their vision runs deep, beyond the superficial. They are called to do great things in life, no matter where they are born. It is the energy of the light that makes them shine. Their greatest challenge is not to be dazzled by their own brilliance. Their mission is to pass the tests they are given on the path to self-realization. These tests may come from past lives. They feel strongly compelled to search for the spiritual, which can manifest early or late in life, depending on when they are faced with such tests. Ancient cultures and ancestry influence them. They would like to go back to such times, undoubtedly because they lived through them with such intensity that the memories are still fresh. When they travel, which they tend to do, they often feel as if they already know the place. They can be lonely if they let their opportunity for love pass them by. At times they will miss the company of a loved one, but such loneliness does not cause them too much pain because they are quite self-sufficient.

E as the conception sign speaks to *Ajpu* of being a stranger in their own land. This doesn't mean, however, that they don't love their native land. They are destined to travel a great deal and will live abroad for periods of time. Further, this energy favors love with a foreigner. Their relationships will be intense and passionate. They need a very understanding, mature partner because they are highly demanding and seek people who are at their intellectual level.

I'x in the right hemisphere gives *Ajpu* men an understanding of women, whom they dominate. Feminine energy is vital for their survival. In *Ajpu* women it brings femininity. As well-rounded women, sensuality and astuteness are their best weapons. They prefer relationships in which they can dominate. *I'x* energy gives them the power to be good intermediaries as well as artistic talent.

Kame in the left hemisphere protects the life of those born under *Ajpu*. This is a rejuvenating alliance that brings constant change. It makes them very curious, courageous, and adventurous. They need to see with their own eyes and don't simply believe what others say.

Q'anil as the destiny sign means that *Ajpu* are planters. Their mission is to show the way and plant the seed but not necessarily stay to see their actions bear fruit. Given their imposing personality, relationships with their children are difficult unless the children are born under a complementary sign. If *Ajpu* don't have their own children, they will focus their parental instincts on other children who need help.

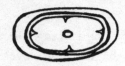

FAMOUS PEOPLE BORN UNDER
AJPU Pope John Paul II, Frida Kahlo,
Roman Polanski, Mikhail Gorbachev,
Helen Mirren, Richard Bach, Michelle
Pfeiffer, Shaquille O'Neal, Albert Einstein,
Rabindranath Tagore, Vincent van Gogh,
Benjamin Solari Parravicini

ENGLISH	*Energy of the Left Hemisphere*
KAQCHIKEL	*Imox*
YUCATEC	*Imix*
NAHUATL	*Cipactli*
DIRECTION	*North*
ELEMENT	*Air*
KEY	*The left side and the unusual*
GROWTH	*Increasing internal powers*

ꓘMOX

SIGNIFICANCE OF THE KAB'AWIL   This glyph signifies a glass of water. The top part is the mouth where it is filled up, and the vertical lines represent its roundness. *Imox* also represents the rain.

MEANING   *Imox* puts the mind in a receptive mode, increases spiritual strength, and manages the energies of change. It provides the power to understand nature's messages in order to plan the next steps in one's life.

Imox means the essence in every sense of the word. It is everything that corresponds to the left side, the subtle part of humans. It is the unusual and the eccentric. We need a positive equilibrium on this day because it could lead to lunacy. It is lizards or crocodiles, the energy that manifests the hidden or internal side

of humans, the powers that are dormant. It is the essence of our consciousness, our mind. It represents the inner space of the mind and the connection between concepts. It is the power that keeps ideas together, the strength of our mind.

This energy is favorable for performing ceremonies in which we invoke the element Water. It is the source of life in its simplest and purest form. It has an extraordinary power over humans, given that we are 80 percent water. This is an auspicious day to ask for rain, for the rivers to continue to flow, for wells and lakes to remain full. If these are not taken care of, if trees are cut down and no offerings are made, the rivers and wells and lakes will dry up.

Imox is the spirit of rain, represented by snakes in the sky that hurry through space, causing a downpour. This sign also governs coexistence with the beings that live in the water and favors communication with them, particularly dolphins, whales, and crocodiles.

The fixed agricultural calendar begins on the day *Imox*, and the appropriate ceremony for the advent of the corn harvest is also performed on *Imox*. Corn and beans (*ixim*) are the nutritional foundation of the Mayan world, and this day is used to prevent those crops from becoming diseased.

Imox represents the fertility of nature, humans, and other species. It is the source of life, both material and spiritual nourishment. It is linked to comets, which are the seeds that germinate in space. It also represents madness or the unusual, anything that breaks from the status quo. It is an energy that brings strange things.

CHARACTERISTICS   People born on this day have the conception sign *Aj*, and their destiny sign is *Toj*.

Imox are home-loving, the lords and guardians of houses. They are spiritual, sociable, and sensitive. Their ideas and actions are pure. They adapt to situations as they come and prefer pleasure and comfort to work and sacrifice. Those born under this sign are considered eccentric, reckless, daring, and unusual. They have a strong personality and are receptive to clairvoyant vibrations. It is easy for them to develop their intuitive gifts, particularly revelations through dreams. They can become hypnotists.

They are very proud of their strong, domineering personality. There is no middle ground as far as they are concerned, and there is no going back once they make a decision, however crazy it might seem. They can experience periods of extreme joy or depression. They feel that no one understands them and continually try to attract attention.

They are warm, caring, loving, and romantic. They become involved in stormy relationships, creating love stories that combine passion, dependence, and madness. They are shrouded in a halo of mystery, which makes them enigmatic and further enhances the magnetism of their charismatic personality. They become involved in countless love affairs. They are very lucky in love and always find a partner who fills their needs. *Imox* is not exactly the most faithful sign, but those born under its auspices are good

providers and love home life. Older people are attracted to *Imox* when they are young, as are younger people when they are older.

They usually do well in whatever they undertake. They are fortunate and protected, particularly by the opposite sex. Although they can be the quintessential freeloader, they also like to do things for themselves and often attain a good position in society. They rarely face difficulties and are lucky in their finances.

POSITIVE ASPECTS   *Imox* do not like to deceive. They are lively, productive, and creative and like to help their fellow dreamers. They receive cosmic messages. Those born on even-numbered days become *Ajq'ijab'* (Mayan priests). Clairvoyant, they feel other people's pain.

NEGATIVE ASPECTS   *Imox* are indecisive, violent, disorganized, distrustful, and dishonest. They could suffer from a temporary mental disorder. They are temperamental and prone to exaggeration. They tend to lie and like to argue. They are changeable, egotistical, and stubborn. Some are freeloaders. They quickly grow bored with their amorous relationships, becoming cruel and lustful. They leave children scattered all around the world.

ENERGY   This day brings good energy for increasing internal powers and strengthening the spirit. It is a day to ask for rain and the purification of rivers, lakes, and oceans.

PROFESSIONS   Teacher, psychologist, sociologist, doctor, artist, poet, orator, politician, writer, judge, spiritual healers

GOVERNING BODY PARTS   Blood, ganglia, genitalia

NAWAL   Lizard, crocodile, shark, turtle
ENERGY PLACES   Rivers, streams, oceans
COLORS   Yellow, green, light blue
COMPLEMENTARY SIGNS   *Imox, B'atz', Ajmaq,* and *Kame*
HARMONIOUS SIGNS   *Imox, Aj, No'j, Kan,* and *Toj*

THE MAYAN CROSS

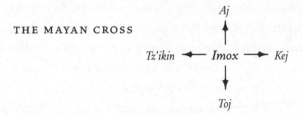

Imox's purpose in life is to follow an unusual path. Others will find them strange, and some may even think they are crazy. This sign has a strong connection to marine mammals, particularly whales and dolphins. They are joined with these animals in spiritual brotherhood and therefore are the ones best able to receive their messages and understand them. This sign is the quickest to develop paranormal powers. It is natural for *Imox* to be born with extraordinary intuition, which they must heed closely in order for things to turn out well. They also have many visions. These increase during storms because lightning unblocks their channels. They constantly have revelations in dreams. They need to create a personal code to understand the messages they are given.

Aj as the conception sign orients their life and provides *Imox* with a sense of order and seriousness; otherwise, their madness would have free reign. *Aj* allows for social coexistence. Love is what finally settles *Imox* down and could even take them to the other extreme and make them overly serious. This energy is quite lucky in itself, providing certainty and security in life and allowing others to recognize *Imox*'s merits. They must learn to rely on more than their seemingly endless good luck, however, because it could one day be reversed.

Tz'ikin in the right hemisphere brings luck and good fortune in work and business and allows *Imox* to live comfortably. The union between *Tz'ikin* and *Imox* makes those born under this sign romantic, affectionate, and warm, but they have flashes of insensitivity that can destroy their relationships.

Kej in the left hemisphere brings a closeness to nature and allows *Imox* to find their way anywhere, in any situation. This sign gives them the quick thinking they need throughout life to solve the entanglements they encounter. They have to be very careful with drugs and sex. Although they may seem to be in control, at any given moment these vices could take hold of them and prove difficult to escape.

Toj as the destiny sign will ensure that *Imox* pay for their mistakes. Although they always come out ahead because of the protection they are afforded, there will be an inner price to pay and setbacks that could delay the attainment of their goals. It is therefore best for them to atone by means of spiritual offerings or by providing direct, material help to those in need.

FAMOUS PEOPLE BORN UNDER *IMOX*   Claude Monet, Walt Disney, Federico Fellini, King Juan Carlos I, Frank Sinatra, Tom Hanks, Mark McGwire, Jennifer Aniston, Thomas Alva Edison

ENGLISH	*Wind*
KAQCHIKEL	*Iq'*
YUCATEC	*Ik'*
NAHUATL	*Ehecatl*
DIRECTION	*South*
ELEMENT	*Water*
KEY	*Wind and what is crystal-clear*
GROWTH	*Purity and clarity*

SIGNIFICANCE OF THE KAB'AWIL   This glyph signifies a window like the ones our Grandfathers used in the Classic Mayan era to let the air through.

MEANING   *Iq'* is the wind, the element that governs ideas and change. It is life and represents the renewal. It is a good day for performing ceremonies for the spirit of air and wind. The wind was born on this day, and so began life. It is Heart of Sky representing the acts of divine beings on the ritual stage, giving power to life, *Nim Kaqulja'*, or the power of nature. *Iq'* symbolizes the vital spirit, lightning, tempests, and air currents. This sign animates energy and represents the space inside our body.

It symbolizes the cleanliness and purity of glass. It is also the windows in Mayan temples. These served a dual purpose. The

first was to determine what type of wind was blowing based on sound. Giant, vibrating flutes were placed on top of the pyramids, and their music directly influenced those who heard it, altering their energy in a positive way. The second purpose of the windows, which were aimed toward the four cardinal points, was to observe and record equinoxes, solstices, and the transit of important stars such as Venus and the Pleiades.

Iq' is an element and one of the manifestations of Majukutaj, one of the four *B'alameb'* (Men-Gods) in Mayan mythology. It is the purifier of the body, mind, and spirit. The image is that of great nourishment for the mind. It is the divine breath that sustains existence, the energy of words and communication.

This sign animates energy and is represented by subtlety. It provides visions and brings beauty and harmony. It is the element that governs ideas. It is the space between the earth and sky, the invisible space between material things, the space inside of us.

CHARACTERISTICS   People born on this day have the conception sign *I'x*, also known as *B'alam*, and their destiny sign is *Tz'i'*.

Iq' are deeply devout people who possess cosmic energy and are spiritual healers. Impulsive, they immediately fall ill if they cease making offerings to Ajaw, the Great Father. Unless they follow the proper path, they are unable to develop their power as *Ajq'ijab'* (Mayan priests) and instead develop negative energy.

Iq', the Creator and Maker, endows those born under this sign with an impulsive, inopportune, and changeable nature as well as a strong personality. *Iq'* can be gentle one minute and angry the next for no apparent reason. They tend to be either capricious or obsessive about certain things. They have a good memory, and their nimble minds comprehend things easily. They make the best mathematicians. They can adapt to any situation and usually make good use of it. They are master manipulators and manage others both subtly and overtly. Although they are somewhat shy, they face up to any crisis. Their greatest obstacle is their imagination, which toys with them. They may confuse their premonitions with their fertile imagination because they come to believe that the conjurings of the latter are real. They can spin an entire story based on one event, and this gets them into difficult situations. They will not back down even when they are aware of their folly.

They may be incredibly successful, particularly as fiction writers. Their ability to communicate also makes them great orators. They are good with words and are extremely convincing if they are able to keep their active imagination under control.

They may suffer from mental illness, and the moon's energy has a strong effect on their moods, taking them from exaltation to excitement to periods of quiet withdrawal or depression.

POSITIVE ASPECTS   *Iq'* adapt well to any situation. Their actions are pure. They are dreamers, merchants, and innovators. They make excellent executives and are brave enough to confront any sort of crisis. They are physically strong. They may be *Ajq'ijab'*. They receive divine visions and have a futuristic outlook. They are extreme thinkers, and they are fond of traveling.

NEGATIVE ASPECTS   *Iq'* have a very strong personality.

They are fickle, impulsive, temperamental, and irascible. They tend to be very unfaithful to their partner. Impure, violent, and dishonest, they may suffer from social and financial problems. They are proud, vindictive, and unpredictable. They are erratic—calm at times and demanding at others.

ENERGY   This is the day to ask for renewal as well as beneficial winds to nourish our minds and purify us. It is also good for healing those who have psychological problems and for eliminating passions, hates, and depressions. It is a day that reinforces our prayers to the Great Father and a good day to develop the power of the mind.

PROFESSIONS   Philosopher, mathematician, singer, musician, doctor

GOVERNING BODY PARTS   Respiratory system, throat

NAWAL   Hawk, hummingbird

ENERGY PLACES   Snowy mountains, canyons

COLORS   White, dark blue, light blue

COMPLEMENTARY SIGNS   *Iq', E, No'j,* and *Kej*

HARMONIOUS SIGNS   *Iq', I'x, Tijax, Kame,* and *Tz'i'*

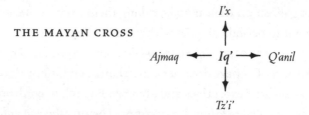

THE MAYAN CROSS

Iq' is the most sensitive sign. With the wind as their element, those born under this sign possess quick, nimble minds, and their lives are ruled by the brain. They are highly imaginative, but also the most analytical of all the signs. Their actions are based on impulses and the stimuli they receive. They will make inopportune decisions for no apparent reason. When they do reflect, however, they will take a long time to make a decision. Their vivid imagination can be a blessing or a curse, depending on how they use it. If any sign needs to learn to

God of Wisdom. Copán

control their personality, it is *Iq'*. They suffer when they don't, and some end up alienated and lonely. They have a very strong connection to the moon; no other sign is so affected by its influence. They should therefore verify which phases of the moon lift them up or sap their energy by monitoring how they feel over several weeks during the various phases of the moon. This is key because this influence will affect them their entire life.

I'x as the conception sign brings *Iq'* understanding and harmony with the opposite sex. They instinctively want to protect or attack, like felines, and should trust their instincts. *Iq'* women will have to be careful of those who claim to be their friends, and they can expect betrayal. This energy makes them warriors. They will have to accept other realities and realize that they aren't always right because they tend to go against the grain.

Ajmaq in the right hemisphere makes *Iq'* curious. When applied properly, this curiosity allows them to discover and invent things and engage in analytical thinking. Many scientists are born under this sign. *Iq'* have a tendency to experiment with the unusual, and that tendency, in matters of sensuality in particular, could get them branded as sinners. Their right hand possesses good energy. It transmits their power and can heal.

Q'anil in the left hemisphere is the seed. The image is one of harmony and inner beauty. Although they might not realize this, *Iq'* are interdependent with nature and are required to defend it in some way. Their spiritual growth depends on being in harmony with Mother Earth. *Q'anil* brings a special sensitivity, and art is *Iq'* best form of expression. When agitated, it is best if they go for a walk, especially in a park or anywhere there are trees.

Tz'i' as the destiny sign is the sign of law—tailor-made in this case because *Iq'* make their own laws. For those who didn't learn their lessons when they were younger, the suffering caused by their extremism and inflexibility will end in later years and their life will become calm. They make great advisers and will undoubtedly be very successful.

The combination of these signs results in highly intelligent and dynamic people. This energy, both physical and intellectual, needs to be channeled; the best options are art, music, dance, and writing, which awaken their sensitivity. It is very easy for *Iq'* to develop their gifts. When going into a spiritual discipline, they need to be careful not to become fanatical.

FAMOUS PEOPLE BORN UNDER *IQ'* Michael Jackson, Elizabeth Taylor, Hillary Clinton, Al Pacino, George Lucas, Maria Sharapova, Roger Federer, Will Smith, Denzel Washington, Bono

ENGLISH	*Dawn*
KAQCHIKEL	*Aq'ab'al*
YUCATEC	*Akb'al*
NAHUATL	*Calli*
DIRECTION	*East*
ELEMENT	*Fire*
KEY	*Dawn and duality*
GROWTH	*Opportunity through change*

Aq'ab'al

SIGNIFICANCE OF THE KAB'AWIL   This glyph signifies the owl and represents light and dark at the same time. The two circumferences at the top represent the energy of creation, and the dots below represent receptive energy.

MEANING   *Aq'ab'al* is polarity: dusk and dawn, cold and heat. It represents light and dark, two sides of the same coin, two opposing and harmonious energies. It is sunrise and sunset. When the mythical twins passed the tests of darkness and left this world, Jun Ajpu became the Sun and Ixb'alamke became the Moon. It means the darkest time of night and the first ray of sunlight. The duality of this sign is apparent but not extreme. Who can say exactly when night ends and day begins? There is always a little light at night and a little darkness during the day.

In the *Popol Vuh*, the Earth was blanketed in fog and mud after a great cataclysm twelve thousand years ago. The four *B'alameb'* performed various ceremonies to clear the air and get the sun to shine to provide all of its warmth. These ceremonies were held on Mount Waq'xaqi Aq'ab'al, also known as Hacavitz, and each Man-God brought his own incense as an offering. It was the first tribute to the Great Spirit, and they watched the Sun come out. *Maq'uq'*, the quetzal, was the first bird to sing. All of the people and animals bowed down to give thanks for this new dawn, this new chance at life, this regeneration of creation.

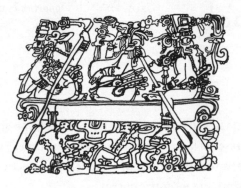

Aq'ab'al is the renewing force, a break from the routine, from monotony; it represents letting go of the reins and heading in a new direction. All of us undergo chronological, cyclical, and individual changes in our lives that alter or transform our destiny.

Aq'ab'al is a good, strong, sacred day for ceremonies to ask Ajaw, the Great Father, for humility, blessings, and pardon for our errors, whether conscious or unconscious.

CHARACTERISTICS   People born on this day have the conception sign *Tz'ikin*, and their destiny sign is *B'atz'*.

Aq'ab'al are cheerful. The word "gadabout" fits them like a glove. Strong, dynamic, creative, and astute, they can achieve all of their goals. They are highly intelligent, and if they study and are stimulated, they can achieve the impossible.

Aq'ab'al are realistic about the situations they're faced with in life. They are spiritual, devout, and charitable and are nice and well respected by family and friends.

With one foot in the past and another in the future, they are particularly interested in history and have a futuristic outlook. They appear young and hold on to their youth, only maturing late in life. They hold power over darkness and negative forces, although their duality could become trapped in such energy.

They are the light of hope. The first rays of sunshine, *Aq'ab'al* are genuine in their attempts to help. They make good confidants, though that doesn't prevent them from having a hidden side. Their secrets are rarely discovered. They value their privacy a great deal and need their own space and time to themselves. Many literary people, statesmen, and leaders are born under this sign. They are calm despite life's many inopportune changes. They become frustrated when they are unable to finish what they have started, but there is no going back once they decide to end something. They are very lucky, as if protected by an invisible power. *Aq'ab'al* seek the truth, and if they try, they will find an inner path that provides real answers to their purpose in life. They are not usually prophets in their own land. They will find fortune and success outside their place of birth.

They are passionate lovers and tend to go to extremes, being either very sweet or very radical. It is difficult for them to find their true partner, and they constantly move on in search of their soul mate.

POSITIVE ASPECTS   *Aq'ab'al* show courage in the presence of enemies and have the strength to solve problems. They are realistic and take responsibilities very seriously. They remain forever young.

NEGATIVE ASPECTS   *Aq'ab'al* can be plagued by failure and suffering. Their tendency to steal or hoard things may lead them to commit robbery and assault, and they may be unfaithful. They are prone to illness as a result of their own irresponsible actions. They tend to lie and may make enemies.

ENERGY   This is the day to ask for clarification regarding our path, to ask for fresh opportunities, to renew our life, to achieve clarity, to bring light into the darkness, and to reveal mysteries. It is a good day to ask for stability and to find a good job.

PROFESSIONS   Doctor, physiotherapist, writer, artist, mathematician

GOVERNING BODY PARTS   Lungs, kidneys, stomach, intestines

NAWAL   Bat

ENERGY PLACES   Caverns, valleys, dawn, dusk

COLORS   Red, navy blue, orange

COMPLEMENTARY SIGNS   *Aq'ab'al, Aj, Tijax,* and *Q'anil*

HARMONIOUS SIGNS   *Aq'ab'al, B'atz', Tz'ikin, Kawoq,* and *Kej*

THE MAYAN CROSS

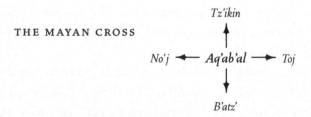

Tz'ikin

No'j ← *Aq'ab'al* → *Toj*

B'atz'

Aq'ab'al is a sign of constant renewal and hope during difficult times, but those born under it will also have to struggle with a dual nature. It will provide many opportunities, and the challenge is to choose the right one. A youthful, modern appearance is the most attractive quality of those born under this sign, and some are also drawn to their mystery. The constant changes they experience aren't always for the better, so they need to analyze each situation carefully and avoid impulsive decisions. Their inner strength will protect them from many dangers, but they tend toward self-deception and pride.

Tz'ikin as the conception sign brings *Aq'ab'al* the power of Father Sun, indicating that the previous life as a talented, well-known person with unlimited possibilities influences this life. That life wasn't fully appreciated, and much was left undone; this life is a new opportunity for evolution. *Tz'ikin* brings good luck, fortune, and protection.  Even those of humble origins will be afforded every advantage because of the positive balance from their previous life. *Tz'ikin* energy restores the gifts they developed previously (intuition, dreams, vision, and telepathy), so it is easy to find the path to spiritual fulfillment.

No'j in the right hemisphere indicates special nobility, determination and deep thoughtfulness. Life presents *Aq'ab'al* with important opportunities to ensure their financial well-being in middle age. They make good students and professionals. They are very influenced by and interested in their family and national history, both of which they love dearly. They need to discover the past in order to move forward. *No'j* provides control over material things.

Q'anil in the left hemisphere signifies the seed; waiting for a new form or vision of humanity to germinate—the being that will change the future. *Aq'ab'al* have many followers who seek advice regarding all aspects of life. *Q'anil* indicates a talent for sowing the seeds of innovation in the minds of individuals and the masses. *Aq'ab'al* may have conflict with their children because the children do not share the same vision. *Aq'ab'al* parents must make an effort to let everyone move at their own pace and pursue their own interests.

B'atz' as the destiny sign is the path to the future. It confirms for *Aq'ab'al* that their lives are the result of the past and a projection into the future. Although they can see their way forward, they must give thoughtful consideration to their day-to-day actions.

The composition of the Mayan Cross indicates that the whole world lies ahead; there are no negative signs to stop *Aq'ab'al*. They are their own architects, however, and their evolution could easily come to a halt. Love is their biggest potential stumbling block. If they do not pay careful attention to the search for a soul mate, they could fall for the wrong person.

FAMOUS PEOPLE BORN UNDER *AQ'AB'AL*   Pelé, Eva Perón, Jack Nicholson, Penelope Cruz, Donald Trump, Bruce Willis, Drew Barrymore, George Clooney, Morgan Freeman.

ENGLISH	*Net*
KAQCHIKEL	*K'at*
YUCATEC	*K'an*
NAHUATL	*Cuetzpallin*
DIRECTION	*West*
ELEMENT	*Earth*
KEY	*Nets and entanglements*
GROWTH	*Inner clarity without interference*

SIGNIFICANCE OF THE KAB'AWIL   This glyph signifies the energy of gravity. It is represented by the sphere, trapped in the groove at the bottom, which divides the base into the two magnetic poles.

MEANING   *K'at* is the net, the snare, the problems that entrap us. This sign is the power to unite the people and elements required to do what we need to do.

The net is used to store the things that will feed us in the future, not only the physical things, such as corn and panela, but also what is invisible: our memories, everything we learn, our experiences, and the transcendent moments in life. It also repre-

sents entanglement—the problems that are of our own making or those created by destiny in order to teach us.

A net can be thrown into the water to fish, or it can be used to set a trap. Similarly, it can hold things set aside for the future, symbolizing abundance. *K'at* means everyone shapes their own thoughts, either positively or negatively. This sign is corn silk, which can cure various ills. We are offered it as a sign of plenty if we know to make offerings to our Creator. The image is one of incense in its wrapper. When we open the offering with our own hands, we are clearing away the obstacles that prevent us from succeeding. This sign brings life's tricks and tests. It is the spider's web, rewarding patience.

The lizard that represents this sign, like the pregnant iguana, symbolizes fertility and longevity. Represented by a fish, it is another sign of abundance relating to the fishing net and symbolizes the rebirth of the mythical twins Jun Ajpu and Ixb'alamke as fish.

K'at is the essence of the fire that consumes. It is captivity or oppression, the absence of freedom in prisons that can be physical, mental, emotional, or spiritual. It symbolizes the god of dance. Rituals that use harmonious strength to awaken telluric energies benefit from this sign.

CHARACTERISTICS   People born on this day have the conception sign *Ajmaq*, and their destiny sign is *E*, also known as *B'ey*.

K'at are sincere, organized, and extremely energetic. They are leaders and spiritual guides. They possess a powerful energy that allows them to overcome obstacles. This sign brings a lucky star that will ensure they are comfortable and accumulate wealth with ease.

They are curious. Our Grandfathers say that *K'at* are sinners willing to investigate. Like test pilots, they offer to be guinea pigs, and this causes problems, although it also gives them the experience they need for self-realization. Their projects and plans are often cut short or abandoned midway as a result of this curiosity.

 They will be able to achieve whatever they want or need to once they learn to control their emotions. They have a great ability to feel. This is developed as they search to satisfy their emotions through their senses. They may be prone to nervous conditions, and it is therefore dangerous to place extreme pressure on them, because they feel lows as strongly as highs. It is important for them to constantly analyze their life and find a safe harbor, which usually happens when they find a partner. If unsure, they can easily be manipulated. They may be very absolute when making decisions and ending relationships. They were born to be loved and have a special physical or spiritual attraction that makes them desirable.

Their greatest challenge centers on material things, which they must learn to manage. Greed and avarice are the order of the day unless they balance their energy with community service or work in the arts. This sign denotes an organized, meticulous mind that can easily become obsessive.

POSITIVE ASPECTS   *K'at* are studious and strive to better themselves intellectually. They are organized and frank and can take on the responsibility of being a spiritual guide. It is a day that strengthens women.

NEGATIVE ASPECTS   *K'at* face problems and difficulties that could imprison them physically or spiritually. They may abuse the law or even commit murder. Poverty and illness could result unless they pray and perform ceremonies to Ajaw, the Great Father, and carry out the mission they were destined for. They are irascible, nervous, miserly, insecure, proud, and arrogant. They don't follow through with their plans and often don't consider other people's feelings.

ENERGY   This is the day to ask for abundance, female fertility, and protection against fanaticism. It is the best day to unravel problems. It is a day to eliminate bad energy and influences, to loosen the ties that bind us to vices, and to fix emotional or romantic problems.

PROFESSIONS   Doctor, farmer, gynecologist, manager

GOVERNING BODY PARTS   Ribs, nerves

NAWAL   Lizard, spider

ENERGY PLACES   Oceans, jungles

COLORS   Brown, yellow, beige

COMPLEMENTARY SIGNS   *K'at, I'x, Kawoq,* and *Toj*

HARMONIOUS SIGNS   *K'at, E, Ajmaq, Ajpu,* and *Q'anil*

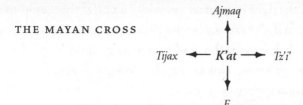

K'at means "net" and brings many challenges in life. Those born under this sign can easily become involved in other people's problems because they think they can fix anything. They offer without being asked. Eventually they learn to mind their own business. Their interference will always turn out poorly even if it is well intentioned. Just as they cast their net to find problems, they can learn to use it to bring success in whatever they undertake. They have a negative balance from past lives that needs to be cleared, so they must do a great deal of social work.

Ajmaq as the conception sign makes *K'at* very curious. *Ajmaq* and *K'at*, acting together, is the best combination for creating challenges of all kinds. Acting separately, these two forces place many obstacles in *K'at*'s way. These tests are placed in front of *K'at* to cleanse them, teach them, and help them find their destiny. They must simply accept these tests as their fate, rather than regard them as bad luck. On the bright side, this is the path of learning they've been given. One serious caution: they must keep in mind that the combination of *Ajmaq* and *K'at* can have a negative effect on people by promoting a tendency toward vices. This is particularly true of drugs and sex, which can become an obsession in the absence of self-discipline. *K'at*'s pride is their greatest challenge and will play tricks on them.

Tijax in the right hemisphere provides a power that could spin out of control if *K'at* are not careful. It is a categorical energy that leads them to behave rashly and to routinely make impulsive or precipitous decisions. This energy, however, will also free them from any trouble they get themselves into. Rather than untying the knots in the net, it simply cuts them away. If they learn to use this power, they will be greatly appreciated and sought out by many who need their help. They have curative powers in the right hand because the combination of *K'at* and *Tijax* is favorable for curing all ills and diseases. *K'at* can be extraordinary surgeons.

Tz'i' in the left hemisphere indicates the law, a person whose authority is recognized, although in roles of authority *K'at* tend to be dictatorial. They must be careful not to impose their will. No one can live for others, even with the best intentions. Everyone must learn for themselves. *K'at* can be great advisers in all fields, particularly in spiritual matters.

E as the destiny sign provides the best aspects. Rarely will *K'at* be prophets in their own land. Their best love relationships will be with those from elsewhere. They are likely to travel and may live outside their place of birth. Their life will be influenced by other countries or have something to do with them. *K'at* do better abroad. Since they are naturally good merchants and their network of contacts could reach as far as they choose, international trade suits them.

FAMOUS PEOPLE BORN UNDER *K'AT*   Martin Luther King Jr., Henry Kissinger, Pope Benedict XVI, Gérard Depardieu, Queen Isabella II, Osho, Christian Dior, John Galliano

Kan

ENGLISH	*Transmutational Energy, Snake*
KAQCHIKEL	*Kan*
YUCATEC	*Chikchan*
NAHUATL	*Co'atl*
DIRECTION	*North*
ELEMENT	*Air*
KEY	*Energy and inner fire*
GROWTH	*Revealing inside information and handling energy/power*

SIGNIFICANCE OF THE KAB'AWIL   This glyph signifies the serpent. The drawing in the upper left is the one who has snakes painted on his back, as are the dots. This is seen in every representation of Kukulkan, or Q'uq'umatz.

MEANING   *Kan* is serpentine fire, the energy of the inner fire that begins at the base of the spine, the coccyx. We all seek its ascension. This fire activates sexual energy as both a reflection of that energy and the force of life.

The telluric energy of Mother Earth means plumed serpent, Q'uq'umatz, or movement. Q'uq'umatz went down to the under-

world to demonstrate his greatness. After seven days, he became a snake; after seven more days, he became an eagle; after another seven days, he became a jaguar; finally, seven days later, he became a pool of blood that was poured on both the eagle and the snake.

Kan is the Creator and Maker of the universe. *Kan* is human evolution and spiritual development. It is every kind of growth. It is DNA in the shape of a double helix, which contains our genetic code and humanity's collective memory.

Kan is also truth, justice, intelligence, and peace. It is the orbit of the planets. It symbolizes the cycles of time and change. It is integration, autonomous functions, the ability to act, and the agility of action. It is the energy of knowledge, its transmutation into wisdom, serpentine strength and power, and sexual magic. It is also a very angry day when *Ajpop Katuja*, the great deity in Mayan mythology, went down to the underworld.

CHARACTERISTICS   People born on this day have the conception sign *No'j*, and their destiny sign is *Aj*.

Kan are strong when faced with a problem or difficult situation. The conception sign *No'j* makes them intelligent. Travelers and leaders, they prefer not to be out front because they themselves are slow to recognize their own worth. Although they are the brain, they need someone else to be the face. They don't like to look bad and tend to justify everything.

They are good athletes who are physically strong and have a great mental ability. Very active as children and young adults, they need to channel their energy more than any other sign. They are easily distracted and always plotting something, and therefore they don't do very well in school despite their intelligence.

They are avid readers and have a very good memory. Discoverers and scientists, they want to know about everything. They have the conscious, or unconscious, ability to retrieve information and memories stored in their DNA. It is therefore very easy for them to weave together all of the knowledge they possess to reveal both new and ancient wisdom. They are very good at cybernetics; it is as if they were born to work in this field. They are perfectionists, dedicated but capricious. Extremely just, loyal, and sincere, they have a giving spirit but need to be recognized for their deeds. Their greatest obstacles are ego and overthinking. They adhere to tradition and family and tend to depend on others. They would rather remain in the protection of the shadows. They are lucky in love and always find those who will pamper and support them— this is one of the most vital aspects of their lives. Although they aren't exactly the most expressive, they are very concerned about making a good impression and what others think about them.

They must learn to manage their strength and energy, particularly their sexual power. Many will be drawn to them because of this power, which can cause them to lose their way. Lovers of comfort and luxury, they undergo drastic changes in life.

POSITIVE ASPECTS   *Kan* may have many jobs or professions. They enjoy good health, are athletic, and have a great deal of strength and energy. They are knowledgeable and wise, have an excellent memory, and know many arts. They are always just and sincere and can be *Aq'omanela'* (Mayan healers) and spiritual advisers.

NEGATIVE ASPECTS   *Kan* can be irascible and envious. They may speak ill of others, and they can be proud, opportunistic, miserly, distrustful, and prone to exaggeration. They tend to rely on others both spiritually and materially and can be overly needy. They like to be spoiled. They are sometimes overly critical and controlling.

ENERGY   This is a special day for increasing physical strength, developing one's inner fire, and evolving spiritually. It is a good day for the return of what has been lost or forgotten, for a loved one to come back, and for reconciliation between couples. It is also a good day to ask for a partner and sexual balance.

PROFESSIONS   Astronomer, scientist, obstetrician

GOVERNING BODY PARTS   Nervous system, spine, genitalia

NAWAL   Snake

ENERGY PLACES   Beaches, mountains, starry nights

COLORS   Green, red

COMPLEMENTARY SIGNS   *Kan, Tz'ikin, Ajpu*, and *Tz'i*

HARMONIOUS SIGNS   *Kan, Aj, No'j, Imox*, and *Toj*

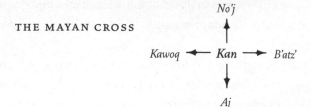

No'j

Kawoq ← *Kan* → *B'atz'*

Aj

Kan is one of the most respected signs. It means snake, and because in many other traditions snakes are stigmatized, it can be misconstrued. For the Maya, having a *Kan* nearby is a blessing, for they are wise, energetic people who are valued by the community. They are noble but do have to be careful of their pride, their greatest weakness. This sign brings a very intense life. Those born under it will be clouded by confusion during childhood; they need a great deal of attention and guidance to channel their internal energy and varied interests. In later years, their desire to teach and learn will grow. Middle age is usually the most difficult time for *Kan*. They are very analytical and easily distracted, but if they direct their energy toward sports, they may excel in this area. Their sexual energy is their greatest attraction, and their animal magnetism competes with their intellect. Quick to adapt, they are welcome everywhere, even though, deep down, they do not know their own true intentions. Because this sign is protected by energy, they possess incredible resilience. They will make good advisers because they inspire confidence while appearing kindhearted and noble.

No'j as the conception sign indicates that *Kan*'s intelligence and thirst for learning are results of their growth in previous lives. They possess an encyclopedic database of information.

Their greatest challenge is to put that knowledge into practice in order to attain the wisdom they seek. This sign brings nobility and idealism.

Kawoq in the right hemisphere provides *Kan* with a very enriching family life that can lead to codependence. This must be overcome in order for them to fly solo and let others learn for themselves. They will become overanxious if they're not careful. They generally rush into marriage, which will be fraught with problems if their partner is controlling. Their domineering personality can bring many ups and downs to their relationship with their family, resulting in the need for space. *Kawoq* makes them popular enough to attract followers. *Kan* are very skilled at cybernetics and at incorporating past knowledge into new forms of technology.

Tz'i' in the left hemisphere means that *Kan* are recognized as authorities, whether in intellectual or spiritual matters. They may be great professors or advisers. Many philosophers and psychologists are born under *Tz'i'*. This sign is also marked by law and justice, so it is important that they keep their affairs in order and enter into contracts cautiously.

Aj as the destiny sign brings *Kan* a very special relationship with Mother Earth. They are protected by the element Water. They should be prepared to travel in later life, as this is when they will attain their true power and knowledge. Life will become simpler then, and they will find their own destiny without needing to be protected or assisted. During this period, they will shine with a light that is very much their own.

FAMOUS PEOPLE BORN UNDER *KAN*   Jim Morrison, Marilyn Monroe, Sylvester Stallone, Alberto Fujimori, Angelina Jolie, Luciano Pavarotti, Yasser Arafat, Clint Eastwood, Venus Williams

ENGLISH	*Great Cycles, Death*
KAQCHIKEL	*Kame*
YUCATEC	*Kimi*
NAHUATL	*Miquiztli*
DIRECTION	*South*
ELEMENT	*Water*
KEY	*Clarity and rebirth*
GROWTH	*Resurgence of spirituality*

Kame

SIGNIFICANCE OF THE KAB'AWIL This glyph signifies death and is represented by closed eyes and a closed mouth, with the teeth sticking out. The circular line represents the cycles of reincarnation.

MEANING *Kame* is birth and death, the cycles that manifest during this period. It is reincarnation, the family and spiritual line, the invisible guardians. It symbolizes death, harmony, and rebirth. *Kame* is the only sure thing: we are all born, and one day we will all return to the origin.

Contrary to the way it is viewed in other cultures, death in the Mayan world is beneficial energy. That dimension is where our ancestors dwell, where we find true peace and harmony. Our needs are simpler there, and competition, ambition, and suffering are

completely absent. It is a place similar to Paxil and Kayala—the equivalent of the Western notion of paradise.

Kame is communication with entities from another dimension. It is the power or strength of our ancestors who advise and protect us throughout existence. Those who do not remember them, who do not safeguard their memory, will not have a proper guide for their destiny. It is the protective energy of those who die suddenly, those who are taken. It is the connection with the forces of the underworld.

Kame both debilitates and strengthens a person's powers. It predicts the good and the bad. It is prudence and protection in order to prevent accidents. It represents divine revelations, influenced by *Wuqu' Qak'ix* (the Seven Sins): pride, ambition, envy, lies, crime, ingratitude, and ignorance. It is the energy of fear, suffering, shame, shyness, and obscurantism.

CHARACTERISTICS   People born on this day have the conception sign *Tijax*, and their destiny sign is *I'x*.

Kame predict the future, both the good and the bad. They may be *Ajq'ijab'* (Mayan priests). They have revelations. Darkness, the manifestation of the unknown, gives them the power to solve mysteries. It offers clairvoyance and intuition that will make them famous. If they direct these talents to serving others, not for profit or to achieve personal glory, they will be great diviners and advisers whose fame will transcend borders.

They are astute, intelligent, wise, and frail. They are good with people, very pleasant, and endowed with a great deal of spiritual strength.

Those born under *Kame* are extremely magnetic. This trait can lead to power and fame with a strong inclination toward leadership. Their talent as leaders combined with their people skills makes them very popular.

People born under this sign are protected from death. The sign will save them from accidents, assault, violent acts, and illnesses as long as they believe in its protection. They should not fear death. They will witness many fatalities throughout their life.

Kame brings ups and downs, times of suffering and times of joy, and great changes even while those born under the sign remain deeply rooted in their convictions and traditions. They are destined to travel the world, to move from place to place, and to settle down only later in life.

Those born under this sign are marked by a suffering that they bring from previous lives; however, their magnetism will help them find good protectors. They will lead an intense life, full of honors that are at times undeserved. This sign is strongly influenced by the unknown, both internally and externally in other dimensions. This protects and helps them throughout life. They find that it is good to take up their ancestors' projects, for they are here to conclude what was left undone.

Kame is one of the luckiest signs in terms of love, although those born under this sign may not be aware of that. Often *Kame* seek only momentary pleasure, without stopping to realize the hurt they leave behind.

Kame are leaders who often don't understand the transcendence of their life purpose. They may fulfill this purpose without even realizing it. Their greatest virtue is giving to others and helping others understand their destiny.

POSITIVE ASPECTS   *Kame* are intelligent and strong in the face of adversity. They have a positive destiny and will be close to people of wealth and power. It is a sign of women and spiritual guides. They possess a great deal of magnetism, charisma, and leadership qualities, but they are always cautious. They are protected and will have a comfortable existence. Life has much travel in store for them.

NEGATIVE ASPECTS   *Kame* are at times extremely violent and vindictive. They could even commit murder. They suffer a great deal unless they atone for their debt to nature. Others look down on them for being stubborn and lazy. They have a tendency to lie and be unfaithful to their partner.

ENERGY   This is a special day to contact the ancestors, cure potentially fatal illnesses, prevent accidents, ask for protection during travel, and find access to spiritual knowledge. Communication with higher beings is possible on this day, as is access to dimensional gates.

PROFESSIONS   Philosopher, judge, spiritual healer, prognosticator

GOVERNING BODY PARTS   Cerebellum, heart, genitalia

NAWAL   Owl

ENERGY PLACES   Home, temples, ceremonial centers

COLORS   Yellow, orange, black

COMPLEMENTARY SIGNS   *Kame, B'atz', Ajmaq,* and *Imox*

HARMONIOUS SIGNS   *Kame, I'x, Tijax, Iq',* and *Tz'i'*

THE MAYAN CROSS

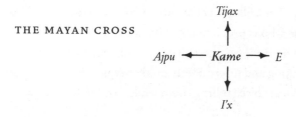

Kame provides those born under the sign with a never-ending source of protection and charisma. If they take advantage of this, they will have a leadership role that could result in a great deal of fame. The sign allows them to socialize in the upper echelons and gives them a particularly strong connection to their ancestors. It is said that those born under this sign have been reincarnated several times in the same family line. They always prepare the way for their future reincarnation, though they may not be aware of it. Being protected by *Kame* means being exempt from accidents, illnesses, and enemies, and this protection makes them very attractive to others. They will have to work hard not to leave a trail of devastation behind them, not to take things lightly, and not to abuse their good fortune. This comes with stability in later years. Life will take them in many directions, and they will change professions and residences several times. Their sign offers access to unusual situations. They will have many premonitions, and they can make great doctors if they work hard to develop their internal powers. It is easy to make deals with *Kame*. They will be loved and lucky in relationships but must learn to respect others. They run the risk of being alone and bitter in their old age if they do not attain this awareness.

Tijax as the conception sign protects *Kame*. This is the double-edged knife that will get them out of bad situations and away from anyone who is problematic. This knife will cut through the veil of mystery and, on the spiritual side, open doors to other ways of thinking and interdimensional energies. It is not unusual for *Kame* to hear voices telling them what to do or how to fix their problems.

Ajpu in the right hemisphere places many obstacles throughout their lives, but Kame will always surmount them. *Ajpu*, the hunter, is very astute and aware of others' tendencies and movements. It is an energy that provides certainty. It has a duality, however, that can lead to unbalance, and *Kame* will have to be careful that their friends and acquaintances don't get them into trouble. Just as *Ajpu* can lift *Kame* up, it can also cause a painful fall, particularly if they are proud and let their ego grow.

E in the left hemisphere is good for carrying out projects, particularly if these are of an intellectual or spiritual nature. It favors writing and other artistic pursuits.

I'x as the destiny sign will provide an intense life filled with ups and downs. *Kame* will often be recognized as authorities, especially in activities that have to do with nature, wealth, or fame in their own land. *I'x* is feline, feminine energy. It protects and supports *Kame* women in later life. In *Kame* men, it awakens sensitivity and the search for harmony through art.

FAMOUS PEOPLE BORN UNDER *KAME*   Bill Gates, Robin Williams, Freddie Mercury, Charlie Chaplin, Paul McCartney

ENGLISH	*Four Corners, Deer*
KAQCHIKEL	*Kej*
YUCATEC	*Manik'*
DIRECTION	*East*
ELEMENT	*Fire*
KEY	*Harmony and nature*
GROWTH	*Working with the four elements*

Kej

SIGNIFICANCE OF THE KAB'AWIL   This glyph represents a closed hand creating a circuit of energy that charges the four cardinal points, as represented by the four fingers, boosted by the thumb.

MEANING   *Kej* is the four elements: Fire, Earth, Air, and Water. It represents the four manifestations of humans: physical, mental, emotional, and spiritual. It is the four colors of humanity: red, black, white, and yellow. It means the four *B'alameb'* and their respective wives. It is the four cardinal points and the four paths. It is also solidity and stability.

In the ancient Mayan world, *kej*, or deer, were big and strong and used as a means of transportation, like horses. When the conquistadors arrived with horses, the indigenous people called that animal by the same name they used for deer. The deer signifies the four pillars that hold up the earth and sky and the knowledge of power through physical existence: *Releb'al Q'ij* (sunrise, the East); *Ruqajib'al Q'ij* (sunset, the West); *Rajtz'uk Ya'* (the path of Water, the South); and *Rajtz'uk Kaq'iq'* (the path of wind or Air, the North). These are the forces and powers that fuel human destiny.

Kej represents harmony. It has one foot in each of the four cardinal points and therefore the four basic elements. It is said that those born under this sign will be balanced. Their very nature is equilibrium. Harmony is the greatest power demonstrated by this sign.

Kej is the guardian of forests and nature and safeguards the balance between humans and Mother Earth. It is a good day to be thankful for life and the process by which an *Ajq'ij* (Mayan priest) acquires power. It is also a good day to give thanks for the elements that nourish life: Sun, Earth, Air, and Water. It is the sign *par excellence* of thorough investigation. Great advisers have been born under its auspices.

CHARACTERISTICS People born on this day have the conception sign *Kawoq*, and their destiny sign is *Tz'ikin*.

Astute and agile, *Kej* hold very important senior positions. They are sensitive leaders. They generally seek acceptance and are happy to climb the ladder in both work and social situations. They need to be very careful with business partnerships. Great advisers, they possess an analytical mind and extraordinary strength combined with a notable gentleness, both in expressing their ideas and in dealing with others. They make excellent diplomats. They have a strong inner personality that they're able to hide quite well. They appear submissive but are capable of doing anything to reach their goals. Unable to resist the depths of the mind, they make very good psychologists. *Kej* need to learn not to simply theorize but to temper their intellectualism with reality based on experience. They have the gift of divination and a highly developed intuition that should guide them in the face of problems. They make good *Ajq'ijab'*, appointed to give thanks and to ask for protection and spiritual strength.

The guardians of nature, *Kej* have the duty of preserving and renewing life. They are resilient and get right back up after a fall, as many times as necessary. They are reserved and prefer not to share their problems. They have a romantic soul; many bohemians are born under this sign. Art is one of their greatest virtues, particularly music and writing. They are seductive with words. The search for truth is their greatest purpose in life, and it will be very intense. They need to learn from experience so as not to suffer when they are old. They are fortunate and protected, always able to find a new opportunity and redeem themselves from prior problems.

They fall deeply in love and tend to hold on to their partner at all costs. Giving their word in matters of love may be the only oath they respect. They tend to be with the wrong people, and their relationships involve a good deal of obsession. Not all *Kej* can stand up to the challenge of being faithful. Betrayal is a word they know very well, either as victims or as perpetrators. They are masters at the art of deception and are rarely discovered because of the protection of those who believe them.

POSITIVE ASPECTS   *Kej* are defenders of the people. They possess wealth and enjoy good health. They make good spiritual guides. They have the courage to be activists. They are strong, intelligent, responsible, positive, and victorious. They are balanced in marriage.

NEGATIVE ASPECTS   *Kej* defend others but are unable to defend themselves. They have a strong personality, are very angry, and can do harm with their thoughts. They appear calm and affectionate on the outside but are quite obsessive/compulsive on the inside. They like fame and power. They are captivating, domineering, and manipulative. They are reserved, overly responsible, strong, demanding, foolish, depraved, selfish, and rash. They like to crush and destroy others. They are prone to illnesses of the hands and feet.

ENERGY   This is the best day for harmony with nature, finding balance with the elements, and avoiding betrayal.

PROFESSIONS   Social scientist, judge, psychologist, mathematician, merchant, writer, researcher

GOVERNING BODY PARTS   Arms, feet

NAWAL   Deer, coati

ENERGY PLACES   Forests, mountains

COLORS   Beige, yellow

COMPLEMENTARY SIGNS   *Kej, E, No'j,* and *Iq'*

HARMONIOUS SIGNS   *Kej, B'atz', Tz'ikin, Kawoq,* and *Aq'ab'al*

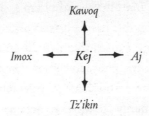

$$Kawoq$$

$$Imox \leftarrow Kej \rightarrow Aj$$

$$Tz'ikin$$

Kej are governed by beauty, art, and harmony. Those born under the auspices of this sign are unlikely to find happiness unless they pay attention to such things. As guardians in charge of preserving and regenerating life, *Kej* must have contact with nature for their own personal evolution. The four elements protect them. Fortune and success will smile on them if they balance their lives with moderation. This doesn't happen overnight and is usually achieved in middle age.

Kawoq as the conception sign represents a connection to family in this life and to one started in a previous life. One of *Kej's* parents usually possesses an energy that will be a negative influence. *Kej* will never leave either the family they were born into or the family they start. They will devote all of their attention to their family, and they cannot be happy if any one of their family members is doing poorly. They need the protection and security of home; however, this need generally results in codependence. *Kej* combined with *Kawoq* often brings many children, though not necessarily their own. Many people will depend on those born under this sign throughout their lives, adopting them as protectors. *Kawoq* brings opportunities and good times that can lead to abundance if they are prudent. They must learn to save for when the hard times come.

Although *Imox* in the right hemisphere enlivens *Kej* and makes them more flexible in life, it is a conflicting sign in terms of position. This sign causes them to do unusual things or gives them slightly eccentric characteristics. *Imox* fills their lives and gives them direction through art, the search for beauty, and harmony. This is the energy that makes *Kej* love and makes them lucky in love. It is a sign that provides grace, beauty, sensitivity, and good taste. It gives them the ability to develop their intuition. However, they could become fatalistic unless they are properly oriented. *Imox* also gives them the opportunity to be successful in the divinatory arts.

Aj in the left hemisphere is lucky. It brings *Kej* many opportunities and relationships abroad, even love that could lead to marriage to a foreigner. Even though they are closely tied to their original home, it must be remembered that *Kej* are not prophets in their own land and they will travel extensively. *Aj* favors spiritual development, and *Kej* will find it in a tradition other than their own. They can successfully make use of their natural diplomacy as long as they don't let opportunities pass them by.

Tz'ikin as the destiny sign is the force that brings *Kej* true fortune and luck. It provides last-minute solutions during the most difficult times. Their luck and protection seem endless. *Tz'ikin* is a great benefactor, but it does bring instability, owing to its changeable nature. This energy will provide *Kej* with good friendships and ensure that they will excel.

FAMOUS PEOPLE BORN UNDER *KEJ*   Mother Teresa, His Holiness the 14th Dalai Lama Tenzin Gyatso, Elton John, Giorgio Armani, Johnny Depp, Stephen King, John McCain

ENGLISH	Seed
KAQCHIKEL	Q'anil
YUCATEC	Lamat
NAHUATL	Tochtli
DIRECTION	West
ELEMENT	Earth
KEY	Seed, planting
GROWTH	Germination, realization

Q'anil

SIGNIFICANCE OF THE KAB'AWIL   This glyph represents the hole made in the ground with a *tixjob'*—the stick used to dig in the soil so the seed can be planted—as well as the four seeds that represent the four colors of corn: red, black, white, and yellow.

MEANING   *Q'anil* means germ, seed, life, and creation. It is a day of abundance, the symbol of sharing harmony, the fruit of love and understanding.

It is the Creation of the Universe, and humans are bearers of the spiritual seed. It is constant regeneration. It carries all of the codes for potential life. It is the divine semen, the cosmic seed that the creator planted on the day *Q'anil* when B'itol and Tz'aqol,

the Creator and Maker, sowed life in this part of the universe and placed man on this planet.

Q'anil is the creation of life, and Mother Nature in particular. It is the day to ask for the germination of sacred corn and everything else that Mother Nature produces. The four cardinal points are present in this sign. It is procreation and symbolizes the four colors of corn in Mesoamerica. It is the day of full realization and knowledge.

Eight *Q'anil* is a day of blessing, for giving thanks. It is the day of pregnant women and a day for reviving sterile ground. It is fertility in humans, plants, and animals. It is a day to ask for what you want, whether in business, crops, travel, or love.

Everything that begins on this day has a positive future. Growth is not to be expected immediately; it will happen slowly but surely. *Q'anil* is a day of good beginnings, a day to start things again or win back a lost love. It is a cyclical day, a day of comprehension.

CHARACTERISTICS People born on this day have the conception sign *Ajpu*, and their destiny sign is *Ajmaq*.

Q'anil are very intuitive. It is a creative sign. They possess love and knowledge and are easily influenced by either element. They are responsible and have an inner spiritual strength that makes them good advisers and administrators. They have many opportunities to travel. They are filled with a love and caring that they need to share.

As a cyclical sign, they live a life full of changes; they are extraordinarily adaptable, and their greatest virtue is that everything they begin is assured of success as long as they are patient and water the plant so that it can grow.

Q'anil is a sign that brings wisdom about life. The information possessed by those born under this sign is like a seed inside that just needs the space to grow. This knowledge is genetic experience and universal memory. The best way for *Q'anil* to find that knowledge is through reading and going anywhere that relaxes them, such as forests, lakes, or rivers. It is ancestral, intuitive knowledge that seeks roots, like a germinating plant, then rises to the surface and grows to great heights. All of this occurs step by step and in due time.

It is a sign that loves tranquillity and security. If either is absent, *Q'anil* feel incomplete and suffer a great deal. This sign brings protection but also requires protection. They need security and are usually willing to put up with anything to obtain it.

Q'anil normally either have children when they are young or not until later in life. However, just because *Q'anil* is the sign of the seed doesn't mean that those born under this sign will have many children. Further, any they do have will take a toll because of the sign's overprotective nature. They will have to learn to let others be.

Their challenge in life is to believe in themselves. They must have faith in their own abilities and dare to do things that could bring happiness, even when these things fall outside their usual norms. They must not take themselves too seriously.

They need to learn to be as patient with themselves as they are with others. They can be their own worst critic. Each stage of life is important for their self-esteem. They also need to remember that they are responsible for their own life and they shouldn't burden someone else with this responsibility, especially their partner.

POSITIVE ASPECTS   *Q'anil* make good *Ajq'ijab'* (Mayan priests) who ask for good germination and fertilization on earth. Very fertile, they are also responsible and harmonious. They are good defenders of the people, as well as intelligent, sensitive, and successful.

NEGATIVE ASPECTS   *Q'anil* may believe they are superior. They can be proud, neurotic, and weak. Egotistical, they work only for themselves and are prone to slander. They create discord and loathing between people. They have a tendency toward alcoholism and mental illness.

ENERGY   This is the day to begin any sort of love or business relationship and to win or take back something that was presumed to be lost.

PROFESSIONS   Farmer, philosopher, mathematician, doctor, artist

GOVERNING BODY PARTS   Genitalia, sperm, eggs

NAWAL   Rabbit, harvests, plants

ENERGY PLACES   Forests, rivers, lakes, highlands

COLORS   Gray, white, green

COMPLEMENTARY SIGNS   *Q'anil, Aj, Tijax,* and *Aq'ab'al*

HARMONIOUS SIGNS   *Q'anil, E, Ajmaq, Ajpu,* and *K'at*

THE MAYAN CROSS

$$Ajpu$$
$$\uparrow$$
$$Iq' \longleftarrow Q'anil \longrightarrow I'x$$
$$\downarrow$$
$$Ajmaq$$

Q'anil is a good omen for life, although it will bring many changes. Those born under it will always seek harmony and tranquillity, making them calm and peaceful. This does not make them conformist, however. This sign provides good opportunities, particularly in business, even though *Q'anil* often aren't the ones who see those opportunities through to fruition. Since they aren't always daring, it is best for them to associate with those who are. They make good but sometimes overly trusting administrators. This sign brings many opportunities in love. *Q'anil* need to remember that everything they sow will be successful.

Ajpu as the conception sign is one of great power, the one that overcomes challenges. In the Mayan tradition, it was *Ajpu* who passed the tests of the underworld. It is therefore expected that for *Q'anil* tests will arise throughout life. They will always come out ahead if they are tenacious and patient in the face of adversity. The payoff will be that they will grow stronger and slowly gain self-confidence. This sign brings certainty and develops intuition, which they must heed. It endows them with the desire to be of service and to help others. They will never lose faith in humanity.

Iq' in the right hemisphere makes *Q'anil* dreamers. It provides them with a sharp mind that grasps things easily. It is a sign that brings a great deal of sensitivity and arouses a vivid imagination. *Iq'* awakens a special appreciation for the arts, particularly literature. Many poets and musicians are born under *Iq'*. The moon will affect all of *Q'anil's* actions, and they should observe it carefully for several weeks in order to understand how it influences them.

I'x in the left hemisphere brings dignity and responsibility in everything *Q'anil* undertake. Sooner or later, superiors or employees will recognize their work. Great advisers in all disciplines have been born under *I'x*. Their vision is comprehensive, they have an aptitude for planning, and their predictions are often correct. Although *Q'anil* are calm and at times even submissive, *I'x* makes them strong enough to terminate anything that isn't in their best interest. It also brings the energy to make great sacrifices, but *Q'anil* shouldn't take on others' responsibilities. They must first satisfy their own needs and attain their own peace; only then can they help others.

Ajmaq as the destiny sign has the most influence on *Q'anil's* future. It brings slow change, which suits them best. They should avoid making impulsive decisions. *Ajmaq* is curiosity, all things novel, and the energy that takes one to new worlds. This influence is exactly what *Q'anil* need, because life shouldn't be taken so seriously. Those born under *Q'anil* are inclined toward spirituality and the search for inner powers, which brings equilibrium and a more balanced view of life. Their spiritual growth will be comprehensive. Seriously searching for and integrating such growth into their life will bring them closer to the truth.

FAMOUS PEOPLE BORN UNDER Q'ANIL   Carl Sagan, Jimi Hendrix, Elvis Presley, Paulo Coelho, Sidney Sheldon, Oscar de la Renta, Daniel Radcliffe, Babe Ruth.

Toj

ENGLISH	*Fire, Atonement*
KAQCHIKEL	*Toj*
YUCATEC	*Muluk*
NAHUATL	*Atl*
DIRECTION	*North*
ELEMENT	*Air*
KEY	*Fire and atonement*
GROWTH	*Liberation from the past*

SIGNIFICANCE OF THE KAB'AWIL   This glyph represents a wheel and its axis. It represents Grandfather Sun and his strength. It is a circle, symbolizing the law of cause and effect.

MEANING   *Toj* means Grandfather Sun and his representative on earth, *Tojil*, the sacred ceremonial fire. It represents the law of cause and effect and atonement to Mother Earth, all of the elements, and the Creator and Maker. It is the sign of payment, the energy that repays us for all the good or bad we have done in our lives. We must also repay this energy for the benefits and challenges it gives us. It is the result of the law of action and reaction, or what in the Hindu tradition is known as karma.

The sign means *Tojil*, the Sun God, atonement, offering, payment. It is the fire of the spirit of Ajaw, Heart of Sky and Heart of

Earth. It is the raindrop, the start of communication from higher life.

As *Tojil*, the sign also represents the power of B'alam K'itze', who at the dawn of this new humanity made an offering to Father Sun. That power is one that attracts the light. Ceremonial fire is believed to represent Father Sun, and it is this fire we ask to meet our needs. It is capable of curing all our illnesses and freeing us from any negative energy.

It is a day on which to make offerings to *Tojil*. This day lifts us up to the same level as the supreme deity so that we can be judged benevolently. It reconciles us with life and brings hope. It is a day on which to perform *Xukulem*, the Mayan ceremony to be at peace with Ajaw, the Creator and Maker, nature, and the cosmos.

CHARACTERISTICS   People born on this day have the conception sign *Imox*, and their destiny sign is *No'j*.

Toj is a very auspicious sign because it brings a series of gifts. It provides a special strength that places those born under it ahead. It is their job to pay the Father on behalf of others. Because the Father listens to them, they make good intermediaries. Many Mayan priests are born under this sign. They are great guides and natural leaders.

As good spiritual guides, *Toj* possess a light and strength in homes, families, and communities. They are strong and respectful, and they like to atone in order to attain justice. It is *Toj*'s destiny to atone for themselves and others; this sign brings protection as well as an intense life filled with emotion.

This sign is warm and therefore magnetic, sensitive, and very energetic. *Toj* must learn to channel that energy or it will be wasted. Great athletes are born under this sign.

Toj possess wealth, fertile energy, and a malleable personality. They are emotional, hardworking, and responsible. Home-loving and very fertile, they need company for all of their undertakings. They are concise and make decisions quickly, even impulsively. With their strong personality, they engage in passionate love affairs and can become extremely jealous or proud. *Toj* need to temper their impulsiveness and their emotions. In particular, they need to avoid imposing their will on others, a tendency that will cause them many problems.

Things may not turn out well for *Toj* because they will suffer in this life for events from past lives. There is no reason to despair, however; this isn't bad luck, simply destiny collecting her due.

The deity *Tojil*, which means sacred fire, is like a regent for this sign. For *Toj*, therefore, communication with Fire as one of the four basic elements of nature is easy. Lighting candles is a good way to help their fellow man as well as themselves and avoid paying a physical price for the help they request. *Toj* are naturally drawn to candles and must learn about them within their own spiritual tradition, offering them to the Creator in their belief system. It is recommended that *Toj* make personal offerings at least every twenty days. If not, they will have personal, health, and family problems.

POSITIVE ASPECTS   *Toj* are people of great virtue. Possessing a fertile energy, they make good farmers. They are impressionable, strong, and respectful. They show fortitude in the face of any situation and have the capacity to increase this strength over time. They obtain energy from Father Sun.

NEGATIVE ASPECTS   *Toj* are ill-tempered and shortsighted. They are possessive, destructive, proud, and vain. They are restless and tend to be unfaithful. They are mentally unstable, sickly, and accident-prone, and they have a short life span. They face many problems and obstacles and could even destroy their own home.

ENERGY   This is the day to atone for our lives, for all the benefits we have received so as not to be given more obstacles along the way. It is a day to make payment or to ask that we be free of any negativity.

PROFESSIONS   Mathematician, social scientist, spiritual guide, researcher

GOVERNING BODY PARTS   Ears, semen

NAWAL   Fire, earth, mushrooms

ENERGY PLACES   Beaches, big rocks

COLORS   Red, white

COMPLEMENTARY SIGNS   *Toj, I'x, Kawoq,* and *K'at*

THE MAYAN CROSS

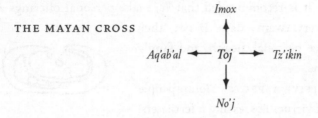

Imox

Aq'ab'al ← *Toj* → *Tz'ikin*

No'j

Toj as a birth sign will provide strength and warmth throughout life. Those born under this sign have a series of energy combinations that give them special power to easily develop their inner strength, which protects them at all times, saving them from danger. Their mission is to help others because the Creator listens and attends to their requests. Their vocation should therefore also be aimed at community service. *Toj* is payment as a result of their positive and negative actions, so they should lead a good life. Feeding hate or rancor will only slow their progress, both materially and spiritually, because such energy seeks revenge. They must be careful not to speak or think ill of others, because such thoughts will gain strength and affect other people. It is best to use this power for positive purposes.

Imox as the conception sign brings a good deal of sensitivity, and day by day *Toj* will see their intuition and revelations grow. Their left hand and mind work together to provide great strength and to develop their mental powers. They can cure illnesses and relieve pain with their left hand. *Imox* is responsible for their eccentricities and the unusual things Toj do that others may think are crazy. *Imox* also provides *Toj* with a good relationship with water. Being near this element in rivers, lakes, or oceans will favor their well-being and help maintain their energy.

Aq'ab'al in the right hemisphere will make *Toj* appear physically younger than they really are. It also brings good ideas and is a great builder and executor. It has to do with anything novel—new technology, new fashion, new art in any form. It provides a futuristic outlook. *Aq'ab'al* also brings many opportunities; the difficult part for *Toj* will be choosing the most appropriate. They shouldn't make hasty decisions, but neither should they let chances pass them by.

Tz'ikin in the left hemisphere is renewal. It provides extra energy that will make *Toj* seem tireless. They are protected in love, although they could become involved in passions that make life difficult. They could become obsessive and suffer a great deal unless they learn to control their jealousy. Since this energy could manifest itself as sensuality, it may cause them to desire several amorous relationships at once.

No'j as the destiny sign is the symbol of knowledge and wisdom as the goal, which *Toj* achieve by means of the experiences they have throughout life. *No'j* will make them undertake great crusades in favor of the dispossessed and will nourish their inner nobility. It will make their life a marvelous, honorable experience.

FAMOUS PEOPLE BORN UNDER *TOJ*   Ernesto "Che" Guevara, John Lennon, Mick Jagger, Madonna, Hugo Chávez, Oprah Winfrey, Indira Gandhi, Julia Roberts, Carolina Herrera, John Travolta, Zinedine Zidane.

Tz'i'

ENGLISH	*Law, Authority*
KAQCHIKEL	*Tz'i'*
YUCATEC	*Ok*
NAHUATL	*Itzcuintle*
DIRECTION	*South*
ELEMENT	*Water*
KEY	*Law and authority*
GROWTH	*Eliminating authoritarianism and drastic actions, cultivating love*

SIGNIFICANCE OF THE KAB'AWIL   This glyph signifies the staff used by indigenous authorities, as well as a dog's tail. It is spiritual law that cannot be bought or sold.

MEANING   *Tz'i'* is spiritual law and the law of man. It is the guardian of material and spiritual law. It is justice and material and spiritual life from beginning to end. It represents those who govern on a local or national level. It represents spiritual authorities and the straight path. It is the sign of both earthly and cosmic law and authority. It is justice and the day that brings the truth to light. It symbolizes fidelity, order, and precision and is represented by the cosmic authorities whose energy is on the Earth, whether in the form of people or places.

Great pyramids and natural altars are dedicated to these sacred authorities.

The first Fathers gave us the laws known as the Natural Order that governed the Classic Mayan world. These are practical, uncomplicated rules based on the harmony that reigns in nature.

Tz'i' is a day to be at peace and to correct our mistakes, desires, and sexual pleasures. It is a day to avoid *Wuqub' Qak'ix* (the Seven Sins—pride, ambition, envy, lies, crime, ingratitude, and ignorance) and to be balanced in every spiritual and material sense.

Tz'i' also means dog, which acts as secretary, assistant, and adviser. This is the Creator's representative on Earth who is in charge of applying and enforcing justice. *Tz'i'* means Jun Ajpu Wuch', Possum Hunter, and Jun Ajpu Utiw, Coyote Hunter. It is the guardian of hills, mountains, paths, and gullies. It is the *nawal* of sexuality. It is the thunderstone, created when lightning strikes, and a ceremony to free us from poverty and vice. This energy is related to writing, particularly sacred writing. It is the symbol of great scribes.

CHARACTERISTICS People born on this day have the conception sign *Iq'*, and their destiny sign is *Tijax*.

Tz'i' make good *Ajq'ijab'* (Mayan priests). They possess the necessary virtue to use divine laws to intercede with, correct, and pardon those who have fallen into the Seven Sins. They are balanced individuals, and they can grow a great deal spiritually. They are very good at eliminating negative energy and bringing benefit and prosperity to the community, but they must learn to value themselves.

They are faithful, kind, just, strong, frail, long-suffering, agile, and strategic. Nothing escapes *Tz'i'*. A good sense of hearing, sight, and smell allows them to maintain control. They are categorical and rarely turn back once they've made a decision. They have an adventurous spirit. They apply justice, but their own type of justice. They believe they are here by divine order and can impose their own laws.

Tz'i' are great writers and communicate with ease. Idealists, they do best in community work. Although they are responsible employees and excellent administrators, their entitled sense of justice often gets them into trouble.

They are desired in love and may be very tender and romantic. They have many brief affairs and are very good lovers but end up alone in later years. If they marry young, they usually separate in middle age. They continually seek the ancestral, and family matters most to them. They need to know their past in order to understand their current situation in life. They are very fertile and will have many children. There will be many who depend on them throughout life.

POSITIVE ASPECTS *Tz'i'* are *Ajq'ijab'* (Mayan priests) who handle both material and spiritual laws. They believe in social justice, peace, and spiritual faith. They are kind and cheerful. They are detectives and discoverers of great secrets. They worship divinity and are good, just, and balanced.

NEGATIVE ASPECTS *Tz'i'* want to be their own authority with their own rules. They only look out for themselves and don't care about betraying or overlooking others as long as they achieve their objective. They are manipulative and like to gossip and spy. They tend to be unfaithful, alcoholic, and adulterous. They are vicious and create enmities and discord between people. They are vengeful and destructive and may commit criminal acts. They are pleasure-seekers and don't like to be criticized. If born on an uneven day, they are disliked by others.

ENERGY This is the day to ask about legal problems and to request divine intervention to solve any type of problem.

PROFESSIONS Mathematician, educator, doctor, lawyer, spiritual leader, inventor, researcher, magistrate, auditor

GOVERNING BODY PARTS Brain, intuition

NAWAL Dog, coyote

ENERGY PLACES Mountains, beaches, nature

COLORS Yellow, white, beige

COMPLEMENTARY SIGNS *Tz'i, Tz'ikin, Ajpu,* and *Kan*

HARMONIOUS SIGNS *Tz'i, I'x, Tijax, Kame,* and *Iq'*

THE MAYAN CROSS

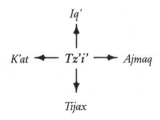

Iq'

K'at ← *Tz'i'* → *Ajmaq*

Tijax

Because *Tz'i'* is a sign of law, justice, and respect, it is easy for those born under this sign to stand out and attain prestige. The law will govern their lives, though it is their own law and they will try to impose it on family and friends. This energy makes them a good companion and excellent adviser. As a representative of the law, their life must be framed by it or they will be persecuted and even jailed. This sign tends to be idealistic, and their idealism will be at the center of everything they do. Never stopping to consider impossibilities, they almost always achieve their goals. Working for the community will bring respect and prestige. They work more than is required and do well in whatever job they have. Many successful politicians known for their good administration are born under this sign. They will be lucky in love and are romantic and sensitive; they will have many relationships if they so choose. They may become easily bored if their partner is submissive; they need someone to balance and control them. This is an unfaithful sign that craves variety and tends to have affairs. This only gets them into trouble and is a waste of their energy. Love relationships should be based on clarity and honesty.

Iq' as the conception sign provides *Tz'i'* with a great imagination, so much so that at times they lose touch with reality; this gets them into trouble. Their imagination could be profitable if they focus it on the arts. They are good with their hands and enjoy sensual pleasures. *Iq'* gives *Tz'i'* volatility, which they will have to learn to control, as well as a tendency to become too involved in others' lives and to criticize or attempt to govern others. The moon has a strong influence, and it is a good idea to study the different lunar phases in order to know which lift their spirits and which cause depression.

K'at in the right hemisphere brings entanglements. If *Tz'i'* learn, however, not to interfere with or attempt to govern others, this net can be used to catch what they most desire. They will achieve this through patience, a virtue they must cultivate as much as possible. This sign will bring many good experiences and relationships with important people.

Ajmaq in the left hemisphere is a sign of luck, placing *Tz'i'* in an enviable position and getting them out of trouble. It brings a good financial and social position as well as fame and prestige. It provides protection and caring friends. If trust is maintained, there will always be people willing to help them. *Ajmaq* also draws *Tz'i'* closer to spirituality and develops their vision and intuition, offering the gift of divination. As *Tz'i'* get older, they will have more and more positive aspects.

Tijax as the destiny sign is a categorical energy that helps *Tz'i'* dispel shadows on their path or anything that could harm them. *Tijax* cuts through veils and enables *Tz'i'* to obtain secrets or knowledge. *Tijax* will open doors they never dreamed of. It is a strength that gives them the power to eliminate negative energy simply by the power of thought.

FAMOUS PEOPLE BORN UNDER *TZ'I'* Sammy Davis Jr., Bob Marley, Steven Spielberg, Vladimir Putin, Nelson Mandela, David Copperfield, Sammy Sosa, J. K. Rowling, Mahatma Gandhi, Adolf Hitler, Gustave Eiffel

DETERMINING YOUR MAYAN SIGN

An Energy Table containing all 260 energies can be found immediately after this introduction on finding your Mayan sign. Each row contains one of the 20 days, from *B'atz'* to *Tz'i'*, and each of the columns contains the 13 forces, 1 through 13. Thus, all 20 signs with their 13 forces are represented (20 × 13 = 260).

Following the Energy Table is a Calendar Table that begins in the year 1900 and ends on December 21, 2012, the date that marks the end of the Mayan Long Count calendar, a period of 5,200 years. Dates are provided using the Mayan cycle of 13 days for the simple reason that it would be too much to include every single day. Find the year you were born and then look down to find the preceding date closest to your birthday. On the right is the corresponding Mayan date. Write this down. Now turn back to the Energy Table and find the name of the sign on the left and the corresponding number along that row in the cells to the right.

For example, if you were born on September 23, 1956, find the year 1956 in the Calendar Table. As you can see, September 23 appears in that table with the Mayan date 1 *No'j* beside it. Turning back to the Energy Table, 1 *No'j* is found in the seventh row, second column, and 1 *No'j* would be your sign.

Now, if you were born on December 28, 1951, the closest preceding date in the Calendar Table for 1951 is December 17, or 1 *Tz'ikin* according to the Mayan calendar. Turning to the Energy Table, 1 *Tz'ikin* is found in the fifth row, sixth column. Since there are 12 days from December 17 to December 28, count down 12 cells, starting from 1 *Tz'ikin*, to reach 12 *Kame*. This is your sign.

As another example, if you were born on July 9, 1933, you would find the year 1933 in the Calendar Table, and the closest preceding date would be June 27, which corresponds to 1 *Q'anil* in the Mayan calendar. In the Energy Table, 1 *Q'anil* is in the eighteenth row, sixth column. Since there are 13 days from June 27 to July 9, you would count down 13 cells from 1 *Q'anil*. Now, because this row ends just three cells down, you would continue to count from the top of the next column to the right. This takes you to 13 *Ajpu*, which is your sign.

ENERGY TABLE

B'ATZ'	1	8	2	9	3	10	4	11	5	12	6	13	7
E	2	9	3	10	4	11	5	12	6	13	7	1	8
AJ	3	10	4	11	5	12	6	13	7	1	8	2	9
I'X	4	11	5	12	6	13	7	1	8	2	9	3	10
TZ'IKIN	5	12	6	13	7	1	8	2	9	3	10	4	11
AJMAQ	6	13	7	1	8	2	9	3	10	4	11	5	12
NO'J	7	1	8	2	9	3	10	4	11	5	12	6	13
TIJAX	8	2	9	3	10	4	11	5	12	6	13	7	1
KAWOQ	9	3	10	4	11	5	12	6	13	7	1	8	2
AJPU	10	4	11	5	12	6	13	7	1	8	2	9	3
IMOX	11	5	12	6	13	7	1	8	2	9	3	10	4
IQ'	12	6	13	7	1	8	2	9	3	10	4	11	5
AQ'AB'AL	13	7	1	8	2	9	3	10	4	11	5	12	6
K'AT	1	8	2	9	3	10	4	11	5	12	6	13	7
KAN	2	9	3	10	4	11	5	12	6	13	7	1	8
KAME	3	10	4	11	5	12	6	13	7	1	8	2	9
KEJ	4	11	5	12	6	13	7	1	8	2	9	3	10
Q'ANIL	5	12	6	13	7	1	8	2	9	3	10	4	11
TOJ	6	13	7	1	8	2	9	3	10	4	11	5	12
TZ'I'	7	1	8	2	9	3	10	4	11	5	12	6	13

CALENDAR TABLE

Gregorian Date	Mayan Date	Gregorian Date	Mayan Date	Gregorian Date	Mayan Date
1900		**1901**		**1902**	
January 11	1 Q'anil	January 10	1 E	January 9	1 Ajmaq
January 24	1 Imox	January 23	1 Kan	January 22	1 Toj
February 6	1 I'x	February 5	1 Tijax	February 4	1 Iq'
February 19	1 Kej	February 18	1 B'atz'	February 17	1 Tz'ikin
March 4	1 Ajpu	March 3	1 K'at	March 2	1 Q'anil
March 17	1 Aj	March 16	1 No'j	March 15	1 Imox
March 30	1 Kame	March 29	1 Tz'i'	March 28	1 I'x
April 12	1 Kawoq	April 11	1 Aq'ab'al	April 10	1 Kej
April 25	1 E	April 24	1 Ajmaq	April 23	1 Ajpu
May 8	1 Kan	May 7	1 Toj	May 6	1 Aj
May 21	1 Tijax	May 20	1 Iq'	May 19	1 Kame
June 3	1 B'atz'	June 2	1 Tz'ikin	June 1	1 Kawoq
June 16	1 K'at	June 15	1 Q'anil	June 14	1 E
June 29	1 No'j	June 28	1 Imox	June 27	1 Kan
July 12	1 Tz'i'	July 11	1 I'x	July 10	1 Tijax
July 25	1 Aq'ab'al	July 24	1 Kej	July 23	1 B'atz'
August 7	1 Ajmaq	August 6	1 Ajpu	August 5	1 K'at
August 20	1 Toj	August 19	1 Aj	August 18	1 No'j
September 2	1 Iq'	September 1	1 Kame	August 31	1 Tz'i'
September 15	1 Tz'ikin	September 14	1 Kawoq	September 13	1 Aq'ab'al
September 28	1 Q'anil	September 27	1 E	September 26	1 Ajmaq
October 11	1 Imox	October 10	1 Kan	October 9	1 Toj
October 24	1 I'x	October 23	1 Tijax	October 22	1 Iq'
November 6	1 Kej	November 5	1 B'atz'	November 4	1 Tz'ikin
November 19	1 Ajpu	November 18	1 K'at	November 17	1 Q'anil
December 2	1 Aj	December 1	1 No'j	November 30	1 Imox
December 15	1 Kame	December 14	1 Tz'i'	December 13	1 I'x
December 28	1 Kawoq	December 27	1 Aq'ab'al	December 26	1 Kej

Gregorian Date	Mayan Date	Gregorian Date	Mayan Date	Gregorian Date	Mayan Date
1903		**1904**		**1905**	
January 8	1 Ajpu	January 7	1 K'at	January 5	1 Q'anil
January 21	1 Aj	January 20	1 No'j	January 18	1 Imox
February 3	1 Kame	February 2	1 Tz'i'	January 31	1 I'x
February 16	1 Kawoq	February 15	1 Aq'ab'al	February 13	1 Kej
March 1	1 E	February 28	1 Ajmaq	February 26	1 Ajpu
March 14	1 Kan	March 12	1 Toj	March 11	1 Aj
March 27	1 Tijax	March 25	1 Iq'	March 24	1 Kame
April 9	1 B'atz'	April 7	1 Tz'ikin	April 6	1 Kawoq
April 22	1 K'at	April 20	1 Q'anil	April 19	1 E
May 5	1 No'j	May 3	1 Imox	May 2	1 Kan
May 18	1 Tz'i'	May 16	1 I'x	May 15	1 Tijax
May 31	1 Aq'ab'al	May 29	1 Kej	May 28	1 B'atz'
June 13	1 Ajmaq	June 11	1 Ajpu	June 10	1 K'at
June 26	1 Toj	June 24	1 Aj	June 23	1 No'j
July 9	1 Iq'	July 7	1 Kame	July 6	1 Tz'i'
July 22	1 Tz'ikin	July 20	1 Kawoq	July 19	1 Aq'ab'al
August 4	1 Q'anil	August 2	1 E	August 1	1 Ajmaq
August 17	1 Imox	August 15	1 Kan	August 14	1 Toj
August 30	1 I'x	August 28	1 Tijax	August 27	1 Iq'
September 12	1 Kej	September 10	1 B'atz'	September 9	1 Tz'ikin
September 25	1 Ajpu	September 23	1 K'at	September 22	1 Q'anil
October 8	1 Aj	October 6	1 No'j	October 5	1 Imox
October 21	1 Kame	October 19	1 Tz'i'	October 18	1 I'x
November 3	1 Kawoq	November 1	1 Aq'ab'al	October 31	1 Kej
November 16	1 E	November 14	1 Ajmaq	November 13	1 Ajpu
November 29	1 Kan	November 27	1 Toj	November 26	1 Aj
December 12	1 Tijax	December 10	1 Iq'	December 9	1 Kame
December 25	1 B'atz'	December 23	1 Tz'ikin	December 22	1 Kawoq

Gregorian Date	Mayan Date	Gregorian Date	Mayan Date	Gregorian Date	Mayan Date
1906		**1907**		**1908**	
January 4	1 E	January 3	1 Ajmaq	January 2	1 Ajpu
January 17	1 Kan	January 16	1 Toj	January 15	1 Aj
January 30	1 Tijax	January 29	1 Iq'	January 28	1 Kame
February 12	1 B'atz'	February 11	1 Tz'ikin	February 10	1 Kawoq
February 25	1 K'at	February 24	1 Q'anil	February 23	1 E
March 10	1 No'j	March 9	1 Imox	March 7	1 Kan
March 23	1 Tz'i'	March 22	1 I'x	March 20	1 Tijax
April 5	1 Aq'ab'al	April 4	1 Kej	April 2	1 B'atz'
April 18	1 Ajmaq	April 17	1 Ajpu	April 15	1 K'at
May 1	1 Toj	April 30	1 Aj	April 28	1 No'j
May 14	1 Iq'	May 13	1 Kame	May 11	1 Tz'i'
May 27	1 Tz'ikin	May 26	1 Kawoq	May 24	1 Aq'ab'al
June 9	1 Q'anil	June 8	1 E	June 6	1 Ajmaq
June 22	1 Imox	June 21	1 Kan	June 19	1 Toj
July 5	1 I'x	July 4	1 Tijax	July 2	1 Iq'
July 18	1 Kej	July 17	1 B'atz'	July 15	1 Tz'ikin
July 31	1 Ajpu	July 30	1 K'at	July 28	1 Q'anil
August 13	1 Aj	August 12	1 No'j	August 10	1 Imox
August 26	1 Kame	August 25	1 Tz'i'	August 23	1 I'x
September 8	1 Kawoq	September 7	1 Aq'ab'al	September 5	1 Kej
September 21	1 E	September 20	1 Ajmaq	September 18	1 Ajpu
October 4	1 Kan	October 3	1 Toj	October 1	1 Aj
October 17	1 Tijax	October 16	1 Iq'	October 14	1 Kame
October 30	1 B'atz'	October 29	1 Tz'ikin	October 27	1 Kawoq
November 12	1 K'at	November 11	1 Q'anil	November 9	1 E
November 25	1 No'j	November 24	1 Imox	November 22	1 Kan
December 8	1 Tz'i'	December 7	1 I'x	December 5	1 Tijax
December 21	1 Aq'ab'al	December 20	1 Kej	December 18	1 B'atz'
				December 31	1 K'at

Gregorian Date	Mayan Date	Gregorian Date	Mayan Date	Gregorian Date	Mayan Date
1909		**1910**		**1911**	
January 13	1 No'j	January 12	1 Imox	January 11	1 Kan
January 26	1 Tz'i'	January 25	1 I'x	January 24	1 Tijax
February 8	1 Aq'ab'al	February 7	1 Kej	February 6	1 B'atz'
February 21	1 Ajmaq	February 20	1 Ajpu	February 19	1 K'at
March 6	1 Toj	March 5	1 Aj	March 4	1 No'j
March 19	1 Iq'	March 18	1 Kame	March 17	1 Tz'i'
April 1	1 Tz'ikin	March 31	1 Kawoq	March 30	1 Aq'ab'al
April 14	1 Q'anil	April 13	1 E	April 12	1 Ajmaq
April 27	1 Imox	April 26	1 Kan	April 25	1 Toj
May 10	1 I'x	May 9	1 Tijax	May 8	1 Iq'
May 23	1 Kej	May 22	1 B'atz'	May 21	1 Tz'ikin
June 5	1 Ajpu	June 4	1 K'at	June 3	1 Q'anil
June 18	1 Aj	June 17	1 No'j	June 16	1 Imox
July 1	1 Kame	June 30	1 Tz'i'	June 29	1 I'x
July 14	1 Kawoq	July 13	1 Aq'ab'al	July 12	1 Kej
July 27	1 E	July 26	1 Ajmaq	July 25	1 Ajpu
August 9	1 Kan	August 8	1 Toj	August 7	1 Aj
August 22	1 Tijax	August 21	1 Iq'	August 20	1 Kame
September 4	1 B'atz'	September 3	1 Tz'ikin	September 2	1 Kawoq
September 17	1 K'at	September 16	1 Q'anil	September 15	1 E
September 30	1 No'j	September 29	1 Imox	September 28	1 Kan
October 13	1 Tz'i'	October 12	1 I'x	October 11	1 Tijax
October 26	1 Aq'ab'al	October 25	1 Kej	October 24	1 B'atz'
November 8	1 Ajmaq	November 7	1 Ajpu	November 6	1 K'at
November 21	1 Toj	November 20	1 Aj	November 19	1 No'j
December 4	1 Iq'	December 3	1 Kame	December 2	1 Tz'i'
December 17	1 Tz'ikin	December 16	1 Kawoq	December 15	1 Aq'ab'al
December 30	1 Q'anil	December 29	1 E	December 28	1 Ajmaq

Gregorian Date	Mayan Date	Gregorian Date	Mayan Date	Gregorian Date	Mayan Date
1912		**1913**		**1914**	
January 10	1 Toj	January 8	1 Aj	January 7	1 No'j
January 23	1 Iq'	January 21	1 Kame	January 20	1 Tz'i'
February 5	1 Tz'ikin	February 3	1 Kawoq	February 2	1 Aq'ab'al
February 18	1 Q'anil	February 16	1 E	February 15	1 Ajmaq
March 2	1 Imox	March 1	1 Kan	February 28	1 Toj
March 15	1 I'x	March 14	1 Tijax	March 13	1 Iq'
March 28	1 Kej	March 27	1 B'atz'	March 26	1 Tz'ikin
April 10	1 Ajpu	April 9	1 K'at	April 8	1 Q'anil
April 23	1 Aj	April 22	1 No'j	April 21	1 Imox
May 6	1 Kame	May 5	1 Tz'i'	May 4	1 I'x
May 19	1 Kawoq	May 18	1 Aq'ab'al	May 17	1 Kej
June 1	1 E	May 31	1 Ajmaq	May 30	1 Ajpu
June 14	1 Kan	June 13	1 Toj	June 12	1 Aj
June 27	1 Tijax	June 26	1 Iq'	June 25	1 Kame
July 10	1 B'atz'	July 9	1 Tz'ikin	July 8	1 Kawoq
July 23	1 K'at	July 22	1 Q'anil	July 21	1 E
August 5	1 No'j	August 4	1 Imox	August 3	1 Kan
August 18	1 Tz'i'	August 17	1 I'x	August 16	1 Tijax
August 31	1 Aq'ab'al	August 30	1 Kej	August 29	1 B'atz'
September 13	1 Ajmaq	September 12	1 Ajpu	September 11	1 K'at
September 26	1 Toj	September 25	1 Aj	September 24	1 No'j
October 9	1 Iq'	October 8	1 Kame	October 7	1 Tz'i'
October 22	1 Tz'ikin	October 21	1 Kawoq	October 20	1 Aq'ab'al
November 4	1 Q'anil	November 3	1 E	November 2	1 Ajmaq
November 17	1 Imox	November 16	1 Kan	November 15	1 Toj
November 30	1 I'x	November 29	1 Tijax	November 28	1 Iq'
December 13	1 Kej	December 12	1 B'atz'	December 11	1 Tz'ikin
December 26	1 Ajpu	December 25	1 K'at	December 24	1 Q'anil

Gregorian Date	Mayan Date	Gregorian Date	Mayan Date	Gregorian Date	Mayan Date
1915		**1916**		**1917**	
January 6	1 Imox	January 5	1 Kan	January 3	1 Toj
January 19	1 I'x	January 18	1 Tijax	January 16	1 Iq'
February 1	1 Kej	January 31	1 B'atz'	January 29	1 Tz'ikin
February 14	1 Ajpu	February 13	1 K'at	February 11	1 Q'anil
February 27	1 Aj	February 26	1 No'j	February 24	1 Imox
March 12	1 Kame	March 10	1 Tz'i'	March 9	1 I'x
March 25	1 Kawoq	March 23	1 Aq'ab'al	March 22	1 Kej
April 7	1 E	April 5	1 Ajmaq	April 4	1 Ajpu
April 20	1 Kan	April 18	1 Toj	April 17	1 Aj
May 3	1 Tijax	May 1	1 Iq'	April 30	1 Kame
May 16	1 B'atz'	May 14	1 Tz'ikin	May 13	1 Kawoq
May 29	1 K'at	May 27	1 Q'anil	May 26	1 E
June 11	1 No'j	June 9	1 Imox	June 8	1 Kan
June 24	1 Tz'i'	June 22	1 I'x	June 21	1 Tijax
July 7	1 Aq'ab'al	July 5	1 Kej	July 4	1 B'atz'
July 20	1 Ajmaq	July 18	1 Ajpu	July 17	1 K'at
August 2	1 Toj	July 31	1 Aj	July 30	1 No'j
August 15	1 Iq'	August 13	1 Kame	August 12	1 Tz'i'
August 28	1 Tz'ikin	August 26	1 Kawoq	August 25	1 Aq'ab'al
September 10	1 Q'anil	September 8	1 E	September 7	1 Ajmaq
September 23	1 Imox	September 21	1 Kan	September 20	1 Toj
October 6	1 I'x	October 4	1 Tijax	October 3	1 Iq'
October 19	1 Kej	October 17	1 B'atz'	October 16	1 Tz'ikin
November 1	1 Ajpu	October 30	1 K'at	October 29	1 Q'anil
November 14	1 Aj	November 12	1 No'j	November 11	1 Imox
November 27	1 Kame	November 25	1 Tz'i'	November 24	1 I'x
December 10	1 Kawoq	December 8	1 Aq'ab'al	December 7	1 Kej
December 23	1 E	December 21	1 Ajmaq	December 20	1 Ajpu

Gregorian Date	Mayan Date	Gregorian Date	Mayan Date	Gregorian Date	Mayan Date
1918		**1919**		**1920**	
January 2	1 Aj	January 1	1 No'j	January 13	1 I'x
January 15	1 Kame	January 14	1 Tz'i'	January 26	1 Kej
January 28	1 Kawoq	January 27	1 Aq'ab'al	February 8	1 Ajpu
February 10	1 E	February 9	1 Ajmaq	February 21	1 Aj
February 23	1 Kan	February 22	1 Toj	March 5	1 Kame
March 8	1 Tijax	March 7	1 Iq'	March 18	1 Kawoq
March 21	1 B'atz'	March 20	1 Tz'ikin	March 31	1 E
April 3	1 K'at	April 2	1 Q'anil	April 13	1 Kan
April 16	1 No'j	April 15	1 Imox	April 26	1 Tijax
April 29	1 Tz'i'	April 28	1 I'x	May 9	1 B'atz'
May 12	1 Aq'ab'al	May 11	1 Kej	May 22	1 K'at
May 25	1 Ajmaq	May 24	1 Ajpu	June 4	1 No'j
June 7	1 Toj	June 6	1 Aj	June 17	1 Tz'i'
June 20	1 Iq'	June 19	1 Kame	June 30	1 Aq'ab'al
July 3	1 Tz'ikin	July 2	1 Kawoq	July 13	1 Ajmaq
July 16	1 Q'anil	July 15	1 E	July 26	1 Toj
July 29	1 Imox	July 28	1 Kan	August 8	1 Iq'
August 11	1 I'x	August 10	1 Tijax	August 21	1 Tz'ikin
August 24	1 Kej	August 23	1 B'atz'	September 3	1 Q'anil
September 6	1 Ajpu	September 5	1 K'at	September 16	1 Imox
September 19	1 Aj	September 18	1 No'j	September 29	1 I'x
October 2	1 Kame	October 1	1 Tz'i'	October 12	1 Kej
October 15	1 Kawoq	October 14	1 Aq'ab'al	October 25	1 Ajpu
October 28	1 E	October 27	1 Ajmaq	November 7	1 Aj
November 10	1 Kan	November 9	1 Toj	November 20	1 Kame
November 23	1 Tijax	November 22	1 Iq'	December 3	1 Kawoq
December 6	1 B'atz'	December 5	1 Tz'ikin	December 16	1 E
December 19	1 K'at	December 18	1 Q'anil	December 29	1 Kan
		December 31	1 Imox		

Gregorian Date	Mayan Date	Gregorian Date	Mayan Date	Gregorian Date	Mayan Date
1921		**1922**		**1923**	
January 11	1 Tijax	January 10	1 Iq'	January 9	1 Kame
January 24	1 B'atz'	January 23	1 Tz'ikin	January 22	1 Kawoq
February 6	1 K'at	February 5	1 Q'anil	February 4	1 E
February 19	1 No'j	February 18	1 Imox	February 17	1 Kan
March 4	1 Tz'i'	March 3	1 I'x	March 2	1 Tijax
March 17	1 Aq'ab'al	March 16	1 Kej	March 15	1 B'atz'
March 30	1 Ajmaq	March 29	1 Ajpu	March 28	1 K'at
April 12	1 Toj	April 11	1 Aj	April 10	1 No'j
April 25	1 Iq'	April 24	1 Kame	April 23	1 Tz'i'
May 8	1 Tz'ikin	May 7	1 Kawoq	May 6	1 Aq'ab'al
May 21	1 Q'anil	May 20	1 E	May 19	1 Ajmaq
June 3	1 Imox	June 2	1 Kan	June 1	1 Toj
June 16	1 I'x	June 15	1 Tijax	June 14	1 Iq'
June 29	1 Kej	June 28	1 B'atz'	June 27	1 Tz'ikin
July 12	1 Ajpu	July 11	1 K'at	July 10	1 Q'anil
July 25	1 Aj	July 24	1 No'j	July 23	1 Imox
August 7	1 Kame	August 6	1 Tz'i'	August 5	1 I'x
August 20	1 Kawoq	August 19	1 Aq'ab'al	August 18	1 Kej
September 2	1 E	September 1	1 Ajmaq	August 31	1 Ajpu
September 15	1 Kan	September 14	1 Toj	September 13	1 Aj
September 28	1 Tijax	September 27	1 Iq'	September 26	1 Kame
October 11	1 B'atz'	October 10	1 Tz'ikin	October 9	1 Kawoq
October 24	1 K'at	October 23	1 Q'anil	October 22	1 E
November 6	1 No'j	November 5	1 Imox	November 4	1 Kan
November 19	1 Tz'i'	November 18	1 I'x	November 17	1 Tijax
December 2	1 Aq'ab'al	December 1	1 Kej	November 30	1 B'atz'
December 15	1 Ajmaq	December 14	1 Ajpu	December 13	1 K'at
December 28	1 Toj	December 27	1 Aj	December 26	1 No'j

Gregorian Date	Mayan Date	Gregorian Date	Mayan Date	Gregorian Date	Mayan Date
1924		**1925**		**1926**	
January 8	1 Tz'i'	January 6	1 I'x	January 5	1 Tijax
January 21	1 Aq'ab'al	January 19	1 Kej	January 18	1 B'atz'
February 3	1 Ajmaq	February 1	1 Ajpu	January 31	1 K'at
February 16	1 Toj	February 14	1 Aj	February 13	1 No'j
February 29	1 Iq'	February 27	1 Kame	February 26	1 Tz'i'
March 13	1 Tz'ikin	March 12	1 Kawoq	March 11	1 Aq'ab'al
March 26	1 Q'anil	March 25	1 E	March 24	1 Ajmaq
April 8	1 Imox	April 7	1 Kan	April 6	1 Toj
April 21	1 I'x	April 20	1 Tijax	April 19	1 Iq'
May 4	1 Kej	May 3	1 B'atz'	May 2	1 Tz'ikin
May 17	1 Ajpu	May 16	1 K'at	May 15	1 Q'anil
May 30	1 Aj	May 29	1 No'j	May 28	1 Imox
June 12	1 Kame	June 11	1 Tz'i'	June 10	1 I'x
June 25	1 Kawoq	June 24	1 Aq'ab'al	June 23	1 Kej
July 8	1 E	July 7	1 Ajmaq	July 6	1 Ajpu
July 21	1 Kan	July 20	1 Toj	July 19	1 Aj
August 3	1 Tijax	August 2	1 Iq'	August 1	1 Kame
August 16	1 B'atz'	August 15	1 Tz'ikin	August 14	1 Kawoq
August 29	1 K'at	August 28	1 Q'anil	August 27	1 E
September 11	1 No'j	September 10	1 Imox	September 9	1 Kan
September 24	1 Tz'i'	September 23	1 I'x	September 22	1 Tijax
October 7	1 Aq'ab'al	October 6	1 Kej	October 5	1 B'atz'
October 20	1 Ajmaq	October 19	1 Ajpu	October 18	1 K'at
November 2	1 Toj	November 1	1 Aj	October 31	1 No'j
November 15	1 Iq'	November 14	1 Kame	November 13	1 Tz'i'
November 28	1 Tz'ikin	November 27	1 Kawoq	November 26	1 Aq'ab'al
December 11	1 Q'anil	December 10	1 E	December 9	1 Ajmaq
December 24	1 Imox	December 23	1 Kan	December 22	1 Toj

Gregorian Date	Mayan Date	Gregorian Date	Mayan Date	Gregorian Date	Mayan Date
1927		**1928**		**1929**	
January 4	1 Iq'	January 3	1 Kame	January 1	1 Tz'i'
January 17	1 Tz'ikin	January 16	1 Kawoq	January 14	1 Aq'ab'al
January 30	1 Q'anil	January 29	1 E	January 27	1 Ajmaq
February 12	1 Imox	February 11	1 Kan	February 9	1 Toj
February 25	1 I'x	February 24	1 Tijax	February 22	1 Iq'
March 10	1 Kej	March 8	1 B'atz'	March 7	1 Tz'ikin
March 23	1 Ajpu	March 21	1 K'at	March 20	1 Q'anil
April 5	1 Aj	April 3	1 No'j	April 2	1 Imox
April 18	1 Kame	April 16	1 Tz'i'	April 15	1 I'x
May 1	1 Kawoq	April 29	1 Aq'ab'al	April 28	1 Kej
May 14	1 E	May 12	1 Ajmaq	May 11	1 Ajpu
May 27	1 Kan	May 25	1 Toj	May 24	1 Aj
June 9	1 Tijax	June 7	1 Iq'	June 6	1 Kame
June 22	1 B'atz'	June 20	1 Tz'ikin	June 19	1 Kawoq
July 5	1 K'at	July 3	1 Q'anil	July 2	1 E
July 18	1 No'j	July 16	1 Imox	July 15	1 Kan
July 31	1 Tz'i'	July 29	1 I'x	July 28	1 Tijax
August 13	1 Aq'ab'al	August 11	1 Kej	August 10	1 B'atz'
August 26	1 Ajmaq	August 24	1 Ajpu	August 23	1 K'at
September 8	1 Toj	September 6	1 Aj	September 5	1 No'j
September 21	1 Iq'	September 19	1 Kame	September 18	1 Tz'i'
October 4	1 Tz'ikin	October 2	1 Kawoq	October 1	1 Aq'ab'al
October 17	1 Q'anil	October 15	1 E	October 14	1 Ajmaq
October 30	1 Imox	October 28	1 Kan	October 27	1 Toj
November 12	1 I'x	November 10	1 Tijax	November 9	1 Iq'
November 25	1 Kej	November 23	1 B'atz'	November 22	1 Tz'ikin
December 8	1 Ajpu	December 6	1 K'at	December 5	1 Q'anil
December 21	1 Aj	December 19	1 No'j	December 18	1 Imox
				December 31	1 I'x

Gregorian Date	Mayan Date	Gregorian Date	Mayan Date	Gregorian Date	Mayan Date
1930		**1931**		**1932**	
January 13	1 Kej	January 12	1 B'atz'	January 11	1 Tz'ikin
January 26	1 Ajpu	January 25	1 K'at	January 24	1 Q'anil
February 8	1 Aj	February 7	1 No'j	February 6	1 Imox
February 21	1 Kame	February 20	1 Tz'i'	February 19	1 I'x
March 6	1 Kawoq	March 5	1 Aq'ab'al	March 3	1 Kej
March 19	1 E	March 18	1 Ajmaq	March 16	1 Ajpu
April 1	1 Kan	March 31	1 Toj	March 29	1 Aj
April 14	1 Tijax	April 13	1 Iq'	April 11	1 Kame
April 27	1 B'atz'	April 26	1 Tz'ikin	April 24	1 Kawoq
May 10	1 K'at	May 9	1 Q'anil	May 7	1 E
May 23	1 No'j	May 22	1 Imox	May 20	1 Kan
June 5	1 Tz'i'	June 4	1 I'x	June 2	1 Tijax
June 18	1 Aq'ab'al	June 17	1 Kej	June 15	1 B'atz'
July 1	1 Ajmaq	June 30	1 Ajpu	June 28	1 K'at
July 14	1 Toj	July 13	1 Aj	July 11	1 No'j
July 27	1 Iq'	July 26	1 Kame	July 24	1 Tz'i'
August 9	1 Tz'ikin	August 8	1 Kawoq	August 6	1 Aq'ab'al
August 22	1 Q'anil	August 21	1 E	August 19	1 Ajmaq
September 4	1 Imox	September 3	1 Kan	September 1	1 Toj
September 17	1 I'x	September 16	1 Tijax	September 14	1 Iq'
September 30	1 Kej	September 29	1 B'atz'	September 27	1 Tz'ikin
October 13	1 Ajpu	October 12	1 K'at	October 10	1 Q'anil
October 26	1 Aj	October 25	1 No'j	October 23	1 Imox
November 8	1 Kame	November 7	1 Tz'i'	November 5	1 I'x
November 21	1 Kawoq	November 20	1 Aq'ab'al	November 18	1 Kej
December 4	1 E	December 3	1 Ajmaq	December 1	1 Ajpu
December 17	1 Kan	December 16	1 Toj	December 14	1 Aj
December 30	1 Tijax	December 29	1 Iq'	December 27	1 Kame

Gregorian Date	Mayan Date	Gregorian Date	Mayan Date	Gregorian Date	Mayan Date
1933		**1934**		**1935**	
January 9	1 Kawoq	January 8	1 Aq'ab'al	January 7	1 Kej
January 22	1 E	January 21	1 Ajmaq	January 20	1 Ajpu
February 4	1 Kan	February 3	1 Toj	February 2	1 Aj
February 17	1 Tijax	February 16	1 Iq'	February 15	1 Kame
March 2	1 B'atz'	March 1	1 Tz'ikin	February 28	1 Kawoq
March 15	1 K'at	March 14	1 Q'anil	March 13	1 E
March 28	1 No'j	March 27	1 Imox	March 26	1 Kan
April 10	1 Tz'i'	April 9	1 I'x	April 8	1 Tijax
April 23	1 Aq'ab'al	April 22	1 Kej	April 21	1 B'atz'
May 6	1 Ajmaq	May 5	1 Ajpu	May 4	1 K'at
May 19	1 Toj	May 18	1 Aj	May 17	1 No'j
June 1	1 Iq'	May 31	1 Kame	May 30	1 Tz'i'
June 14	1 Tz'ikin	June 13	1 Kawoq	June 12	1 Aq'ab'al
June 27	1 Q'anil	June 26	1 E	June 25	1 Ajmaq
July 10	1 Imox	July 9	1 Kan	July 8	1 Toj
July 23	1 I'x	July 22	1 Tijax	July 21	1 Iq'
August 5	1 Kej	August 4	1 B'atz'	August 3	1 Tz'ikin
August 18	1 Ajpu	August 17	1 K'at	August 16	1 Q'anil
August 31	1 Aj	August 30	1 No'j	August 29	1 Imox
September 13	1 Kame	September 12	1 Tz'i'	September 11	1 I'x
September 26	1 Kawoq	September 25	1 Aq'ab'al	September 24	1 Kej
October 9	1 E	October 8	1 Ajmaq	October 7	1 Ajpu
October 22	1 Kan	October 21	1 Toj	October 20	1 Aj
November 4	1 Tijax	November 3	1 Iq'	November 2	1 Kame
November 17	1 B'atz'	November 16	1 Tz'ikin	November 15	1 Kawoq
November 30	1 K'at	November 29	1 Q'anil	November 28	1 E
December 13	1 No'j	December 12	1 Imox	December 11	1 Kan
December 26	1 Tz'i'	December 25	1 I'x	December 24	1 Tijax

Gregorian Date	Mayan Date	Gregorian Date	Mayan Date	Gregorian Date	Mayan Date
1936		**1937**		**1938**	
January 6	1 B'atz'	January 4	1 Tz'ikin	January 3	1 Kawoq
January 19	1 K'at	January 17	1 Q'anil	January 16	1 E
February 1	1 No'j	January 30	1 Imox	January 29	1 Kan
February 14	1 Tz'i'	February 12	1 I'x	February 11	1 Tijax
February 27	1 Aq'ab'al	February 25	1 Kej	February 24	1 B'atz'
March 11	1 Ajmaq	March 10	1 Ajpu	March 9	1 K'at
March 24	1 Toj	March 23	1 Aj	March 22	1 No'j
April 6	1 Iq'	April 5	1 Kame	April 4	1 Tz'i'
April 19	1 Tz'ikin	April 18	1 Kawoq	April 17	1 Aq'ab'al
May 2	1 Q'anil	May 1	1 E	April 30	1 Ajmaq
May 15	1 Imox	May 14	1 Kan	May 13	1 Toj
May 28	1 I'x	May 27	1 Tijax	May 26	1 Iq'
June 10	1 Kej	June 9	1 B'atz'	June 8	1 Tz'ikin
June 23	1 Ajpu	June 22	1 K'at	June 21	1 Q'anil
July 6	1 Aj	July 5	1 No'j	July 4	1 Imox
July 19	1 Kame	July 18	1 Tz'i'	July 17	1 I'x
August 1	1 Kawoq	July 31	1 Aq'ab'al	July 30	1 Kej
August 14	1 E	August 13	1 Ajmaq	August 12	1 Ajpu
August 27	1 Kan	August 26	1 Toj	August 25	1 Aj
September 9	1 Tijax	September 8	1 Iq'	September 7	1 Kame
September 22	1 B'atz'	September 21	1 Tz'ikin	September 20	1 Kawoq
October 5	1 K'at	October 4	1 Q'anil	October 3	1 E
October 18	1 No'j	October 17	1 Imox	October 16	1 Kan
October 31	1 Tz'i'	October 30	1 I'x	October 29	1 Tijax
November 13	1 Aq'ab'al	November 12	1 Kej	November 11	1 B'atz'
November 26	1 Ajmaq	November 25	1 Ajpu	November 24	1 K'at
December 9	1 Toj	December 8	1 Aj	December 7	1 No'j
December 22	1 Iq'	December 21	1 Kame	December 20	1 Tz'i'

Gregorian Date	Mayan Date	Gregorian Date	Mayan Date	Gregorian Date	Mayan Date
1939		**1940**		**1941**	
January 1	1 Aq'ab'al	January 1	1 Kej	January 12	1 K'at
January 15	1 Ajmaq	January 14	1 Ajpu	January 25	1 No'j
January 28	1 Toj	January 27	1 Aj	February 7	1 Tz'i'
February 10	1 Iq'	February 9	1 Kame	February 20	1 Aq'ab'al
February 23	1 Tz'ikin	February 22	1 Kawoq	March 5	1 Ajmaq
March 8	1 Q'anil	March 6	1 E	March 18	1 Toj
March 21	1 Imox	March 19	1 Kan	March 31	1 Iq'
April 3	1 I'x	April 1	1 Tijax	April 13	1 Tz'ikin
April 16	1 Kej	April 14	1 B'atz'	April 26	1 Q'anil
April 29	1 Ajpu	April 27	1 K'at	May 9	1 Imox
May 12	1 Aj	May 10	1 No'j	May 22	1 I'x
May 25	1 Kame	May 23	1 Tz'i'	June 4	1 Kej
June 7	1 Kawoq	June 5	1 Aq'ab'al	June 17	1 Ajpu
June 20	1 E	June 18	1 Ajmaq	June 30	1 Aj
July 3	1 Kan	July 1	1 Toj	July 13	1 Kame
July 16	1 Tijax	July 14	1 Iq'	July 26	1 Kawoq
July 29	1 B'atz'	July 27	1 Tz'ikin	August 8	1 E
August 11	1 K'at	August 9	1 Q'anil	August 21	1 Kan
August 24	1 No'j	August 22	1 Imox	September 3	1 Tijax
September 6	1 Tz'i'	September 4	1 I'x	September 16	1 B'atz'
September 19	1 Aq'ab'al	September 17	1 Kej	September 29	1 K'at
October 2	1 Ajmaq	September 30	1 Ajpu	October 12	1 No'j
October 15	1 Toj	October 13	1 Aj	October 25	1 Tz'i'
October 28	1 Iq'	October 26	1 Kame	November 7	1 Aq'ab'al
November 10	1 Tz'ikin	November 8	1 Kawoq	November 20	1 Ajmaq
November 23	1 Q'anil	November 21	1 E	December 3	1 Toj
December 6	1 Imox	December 4	1 Kan	December 16	1 Iq'
December 19	1 I'x	December 17	1 Tijax	December 29	1 Tz'ikin
		December 30	1 B'atz'		

Gregorian Date	Mayan Date	Gregorian Date	Mayan Date	Gregorian Date	Mayan Date
1942		**1943**		**1944**	
January 11	1 Q'anil	January 10	1 E	January 9	1 Ajmaq
January 24	1 Imox	January 23	1 Kan	January 22	1 Toj
February 6	1 I'x	February 5	1 Tijax	February 4	1 Iq'
February 19	1 Kej	February 18	1 B'atz'	February 17	1 Tz'ikin
March 4	1 Ajpu	March 3	1 K'at	March 1	1 Q'anil
March 17	1 Aj	March 16	1 No'j	March 14	1 Imox
March 30	1 Kame	March 29	1 Tz'i'	March 27	1 I'x
April 12	1 Kawoq	April 11	1 Aq'ab'al	April 9	1 Kej
April 25	1 E	April 24	1 Ajmaq	April 22	1 Ajpu
May 8	1 Kan	May 7	1 Toj	May 5	1 Aj
May 21	1 Tijax	May 20	1 Iq'	May 18	1 Kame
June 3	1 B'atz'	June 2	1 Tz'ikin	May 31	1 Kawoq
June 16	1 K'at	June 15	1 Q'anil	June 13	1 E
June 29	1 No'j	June 28	1 Imox	June 26	1 Kan
July 12	1 Tz'i'	July 11	1 I'x	July 9	1 Tijax
July 25	1 Aq'ab'al	July 24	1 Kej	July 22	1 B'atz'
August 7	1 Ajmaq	August 6	1 Ajpu	August 4	1 K'at
August 20	1 Toj	August 19	1 Aj	August 17	1 No'j
September 2	1 Iq'	September 1	1 Kame	August 30	1 Tz'i'
September 15	1 Tz'ikin	September 14	1 Kawoq	September 12	1 Aq'ab'al
September 28	1 Q'anil	September 27	1 E	September 25	1 Ajmaq
October 11	1 Imox	October 10	1 Kan	October 8	1 Toj
October 24	1 I'x	October 23	1 Tijax	October 21	1 Iq'
November 6	1 Kej	November 5	1 B'atz'	November 3	1 Tz'ikin
November 19	1 Ajpu	November 18	1 K'at	November 16	1 Q'anil
December 2	1 Aj	December 1	1 No'j	November 29	1 Imox
December 15	1 Kame	December 14	1 Tz'i'	December 12	1 I'x
December 28	1 Kawoq	December 27	1 Aq'ab'al	December 25	1 Kej

Gregorian Date	Mayan Date	Gregorian Date	Mayan Date	Gregorian Date	Mayan Date
1945		**1946**		**1947**	
January 7	1 Ajpu	January 6	1 K'at	January 5	1 Q'anil
January 20	1 Aj	January 19	1 No'j	January 18	1 Imox
February 2	1 Kame	February 1	1 Tz'i'	January 31	1 I'x
February 15	1 Kawoq	February 14	1 Aq'ab'al	February 13	1 Kej
February 28	1 E	February 27	1 Ajmaq	February 26	1 Ajpu
March 13	1 Kan	March 12	1 Toj	March 11	1 Aj
March 26	1 Tijax	March 25	1 Iq'	March 24	1 Kame
April 8	1 B'atz'	April 7	1 Tz'ikin	April 6	1 Kawoq
April 21	1 K'at	April 20	1 Q'anil	April 19	1 E
May 4	1 No'j	May 3	1 Imox	May 2	1 Kan
May 17	1 Tz'i'	May 16	1 I'x	May 15	1 Tijax
May 30	1 Aq'ab'al	May 29	1 Kej	May 28	1 B'atz'
June 12	1 Ajmaq	June 11	1 Ajpu	June 10	1 K'at
June 25	1 Toj	June 24	1 Aj	June 23	1 No'j
July 8	1 Iq'	July 7	1 Kame	July 6	1 Tz'i'
July 21	1 Tz'ikin	July 20	1 Kawoq	July 19	1 Aq'ab'al
August 3	1 Q'anil	August 2	1 E	August 1	1 Ajmaq
August 16	1 Imox	August 15	1 Kan	August 14	1 Toj
August 29	1 I'x	August 28	1 Tijax	August 27	1 Iq'
September 11	1 Kej	September 10	1 B'atz'	September 9	1 Tz'ikin
September 24	1 Ajpu	September 23	1 K'at	September 22	1 Q'anil
October 7	1 Aj	October 6	1 No'j	October 5	1 Imox
October 20	1 Kame	October 19	1 Tz'i'	October 18	1 I'x
November 2	1 Kawoq	November 1	1 Aq'ab'al	October 31	1 Kej
November 15	1 E	November 14	1 Ajmaq	November 13	1 Ajpu
November 28	1 Kan	November 27	1 Toj	November 26	1 Aj
December 11	1 Tijax	December 10	1 Iq'	December 9	1 Kame
December 24	1 B'atz'	December 23	1 Tz'ikin	December 22	1 Kawoq

Gregorian Date	Mayan Date	Gregorian Date	Mayan Date	Gregorian Date	Mayan Date
1948		**1949**		**1950**	
January 4	1 E	January 2	1 Ajmaq	January 1	1 Ajpu
January 17	1 Kan	January 15	1 Toj	January 14	1 Aj
January 30	1 Tijax	January 28	1 Iq'	January 27	1 Kame
February 12	1 B'atz'	February 10	1 Tz'ikin	February 9	1 Kawoq
February 25	1 K'at	February 23	1 Q'anil	February 22	1 E
March 9	1 No'j	March 8	1 Imox	March 7	1 Kan
March 22	1 Tz'i'	March 21	1 I'x	March 20	1 Tijax
April 4	1 Aq'ab'al	April 3	1 Kej	April 2	1 B'atz'
April 17	1 Ajmaq	April 16	1 Ajpu	April 15	1 K'at
April 30	1 Toj	April 29	1 Aj	April 28	1 No'j
May 13	1 Iq'	May 12	1 Kame	May 11	1 Tz'i'
May 26	1 Tz'ikin	May 25	1 Kawoq	May 24	1 Aq'ab'al
June 8	1 Q'anil	June 7	1 E	June 6	1 Ajmaq
June 21	1 Imox	June 20	1 Kan	June 19	1 Toj
July 4	1 I'x	July 3	1 Tijax	July 2	1 Iq'
July 17	1 Kej	July 16	1 B'atz'	July 15	1 Tz'ikin
July 30	1 Ajpu	July 29	1 K'at	July 28	1 Q'anil
August 12	1 Aj	August 11	1 No'j	August 10	1 Imox
August 25	1 Kame	August 24	1 Tz'i'	August 23	1 I'x
September 7	1 Kawoq	September 6	1 Aq'ab'al	September 5	1 Kej
September 20	1 E	September 19	1 Ajmaq	September 18	1 Ajpu
October 3	1 Kan	October 2	1 Toj	October 1	1 Aj
October 16	1 Tijax	October 15	1 Iq'	October 14	1 Kame
October 29	1 B'atz'	October 28	1 Tz'ikin	October 27	1 Kawoq
November 11	1 K'at	November 10	1 Q'anil	November 9	1 E
November 24	1 No'j	November 23	1 Imox	November 22	1 Kan
December 7	1 Tz'i'	December 6	1 I'x	December 5	1 Tijax
December 20	1 Aq'ab'al	December 19	1 Kej	December 18	1 B'atz'
				December 31	1 K'at

Gregorian Date	Mayan Date	Gregorian Date	Mayan Date	Gregorian Date	Mayan Date
1951		**1952**		**1953**	
January 13	1 No'j	January 12	1 Imox	January 10	1 Kan
January 26	1 Tz'i'	January 25	1 I'x	January 23	1 Tijax
February 8	1 Aq'ab'al	February 7	1 Kej	February 5	1 B'atz'
February 21	1 Ajmaq	February 20	1 Ajpu	February 18	1 K'at
March 6	1 Toj	March 4	1 Aj	March 3	1 No'j
March 19	1 Iq'	March 17	1 Kame	March 16	1 Tz'i'
April 1	1 Tz'ikin	March 30	1 Kawoq	March 29	1 Aq'ab'al
April 14	1 Q'anil	April 12	1 E	April 11	1 Ajmaq
April 27	1 Imox	April 25	1 Kan	April 24	1 Toj
May 10	1 I'x	May 8	1 Tijax	May 7	1 Iq'
May 23	1 Kej	May 21	1 B'atz'	May 20	1 Tz'ikin
June 5	1 Ajpu	June 3	1 K'at	June 2	1 Q'anil
June 18	1 Aj	June 16	1 No'j	June 15	1 Imox
July 1	1 Kame	June 29	1 Tz'i'	June 28	1 I'x
July 14	1 Kawoq	July 12	1 Aq'ab'al	July 11	1 Kej
July 27	1 E	July 25	1 Ajmaq	July 24	1 Ajpu
August 9	1 Kan	August 7	1 Toj	August 6	1 Aj
August 22	1 Tijax	August 20	1 Iq'	August 19	1 Kame
September 4	1 B'atz'	September 2	1 Tz'ikin	September 1	1 Kawoq
September 17	1 K'at	September 15	1 Q'anil	September 14	1 E
September 30	1 No'j	September 28	1 Imox	September 27	1 Kan
October 13	1 Tz'i'	October 11	1 I'x	October 10	1 Tijax
October 26	1 Aq'ab'al	October 24	1 Kej	October 23	1 B'atz'
November 8	1 Ajmaq	November 6	1 Ajpu	November 5	1 K'at
November 21	1 Toj	November 19	1 Aj	November 18	1 No'j
December 4	1 Iq'	December 2	1 Kame	December 1	1 Tz'i'
December 17	1 Tz'ikin	December 15	1 Kawoq	December 14	1 Aq'ab'al
December 30	1 Q'anil	December 28	1 E	December 27	1 Ajmaq

Gregorian Date	Mayan Date	Gregorian Date	Mayan Date	Gregorian Date	Mayan Date
1954		**1955**		**1956**	
January 9	1 Toj	January 8	1 Aj	January 7	1 No'j
January 22	1 Iq'	January 21	1 Kame	January 20	1 Tz'i'
February 4	1 Tz'ikin	February 3	1 Kawoq	February 2	1 Aq'ab'al
February 17	1 Q'anil	February 16	1 E	February 15	1 Ajmaq
March 2	1 Imox	March 1	1 Kan	February 28	1 Toj
March 15	1 I'x	March 14	1 Tijax	March 12	1 Iq'
March 28	1 Kej	March 27	1 B'atz'	March 25	1 Tz'ikin
April 10	1 Ajpu	April 9	1 K'at	April 7	1 Q'anil
April 23	1 Aj	April 22	1 No'j	April 20	1 Imox
May 6	1 Kame	May 5	1 Tz'i'	May 3	1 I'x
May 19	1 Kawoq	May 18	1 Aq'ab'al	May 16	1 Kej
June 1	1 E	May 31	1 Ajmaq	May 29	1 Ajpu
June 14	1 Kan	June 13	1 Toj	June 11	1 Aj
June 27	1 Tijax	June 26	1 Iq'	June 24	1 Kame
July 10	1 B'atz'	July 9	1 Tz'ikin	July 7	1 Kawoq
July 23	1 K'at	July 22	1 Q'anil	July 20	1 E
August 5	1 No'j	August 4	1 Imox	August 2	1 Kan
August 18	1 Tz'i'	August 17	1 I'x	August 15	1 Tijax
August 31	1 Aq'ab'al	August 30	1 Kej	August 28	1 B'atz'
September 13	1 Ajmaq	September 12	1 Ajpu	September 10	1 K'at
September 26	1 Toj	September 25	1 Aj	September 23	1 No'j
October 9	1 Iq'	October 8	1 Kame	October 6	1 Tz'i'
October 22	1 Tz'ikin	October 21	1 Kawoq	October 19	1 Aq'ab'al
November 4	1 Q'anil	November 3	1 E	November 1	1 Ajmaq
November 17	1 Imox	November 16	1 Kan	November 14	1 Toj
November 30	1 I'x	November 29	1 Tijax	November 27	1 Iq'
December 13	1 Kej	December 12	1 B'atz'	December 10	1 Tz'ikin
December 26	1 Ajpu	December 25	1 K'at	December 23	1 Q'anil

Gregorian Date	Mayan Date	Gregorian Date	Mayan Date	Gregorian Date	Mayan Date
1957		**1958**		**1959**	
January 5	1 Imox	January 4	1 Kan	January 3	1 Toj
January 18	1 I'x	January 17	1 Tijax	January 16	1 Iq'
January 31	1 Kej	January 30	1 B'atz'	January 29	1 Tz'ikin
February 13	1 Ajpu	February 12	1 K'at	February 11	1 Q'anil
February 26	1 Aj	February 25	1 No'j	February 24	1 Imox
March 11	1 Kame	March 10	1 Tz'i'	March 9	1 I'x
March 24	1 Kawoq	March 23	1 Aq'ab'al	March 22	1 Kej
April 6	1 E	April 5	1 Ajmaq	April 4	1 Ajpu
April 19	1 Kan	April 18	1 Toj	April 17	1 Aj
May 2	1 Tijax	May 1	1 Iq'	April 30	1 Kame
May 15	1 B'atz'	May 14	1 Tz'ikin	May 13	1 Kawoq
May 28	1 K'at	May 27	1 Q'anil	May 26	1 E
June 10	1 No'j	June 9	1 Imox	June 8	1 Kan
June 23	1 Tz'i'	June 22	1 I'x	June 21	1 Tijax
July 6	1 Aq'ab'al	July 5	1 Kej	July 4	1 B'atz'
July 19	1 Ajmaq	July 18	1 Ajpu	July 17	1 K'at
August 1	1 Toj	July 31	1 Aj	July 30	1 No'j
August 14	1 Iq'	August 13	1 Kame	August 12	1 Tz'i'
August 27	1 Tz'ikin	August 26	1 Kawoq	August 25	1 Aq'ab'al
September 9	1 Q'anil	September 8	1 E	September 7	1 Ajmaq
September 22	1 Imox	September 21	1 Kan	September 20	1 Toj
October 5	1 I'x	October 4	1 Tijax	October 3	1 Iq'
October 18	1 Kej	October 17	1 B'atz'	October 16	1 Tz'ikin
October 31	1 Ajpu	October 30	1 K'at	October 29	1 Q'anil
November 13	1 Aj	November 12	1 No'j	November 11	1 Imox
November 26	1 Kame	November 25	1 Tz'i'	November 24	1 I'x
December 9	1 Kawoq	December 8	1 Aq'ab'al	December 7	1 Kej
December 22	1 E	December 21	1 Ajmaq	December 20	1 Ajpu

Gregorian Date	Mayan Date	Gregorian Date	Mayan Date	Gregorian Date	Mayan Date
1960		**1961**		**1962**	
January 2	1 Aj	January 13	1 Tz'i'	January 12	1 I'x
January 15	1 Kame	January 26	1 Aq'ab'al	January 25	1 Kej
January 28	1 Kawoq	February 8	1 Ajmaq	February 7	1 Ajpu
February 10	1 E	February 21	1 Toj	February 20	1 Aj
February 23	1 Kan	March 6	1 Iq'	March 5	1 Kame
March 7	1 Tijax	March 19	1 Tz'ikin	March 18	1 Kawoq
March 20	1 B'atz'	April 1	1 Q'anil	March 31	1 E
April 2	1 K'at	April 14	1 Imox	April 13	1 Kan
April 15	1 No'j	April 27	1 I'x	April 26	1 Tijax
April 28	1 Tz'i'	May 10	1 Kej	May 9	1 B'atz'
May 11	1 Aq'ab'al	May 23	1 Ajpu	May 22	1 K'at
May 24	1 Ajmaq	June 5	1 Aj	June 4	1 No'j
June 6	1 Toj	June 18	1 Kame	June 17	1 Tz'i'
June 19	1 Iq'	July 1	1 Kawoq	June 30	1 Aq'ab'al
July 2	1 Tz'ikin	July 14	1 E	July 13	1 Ajmaq
July 15	1 Q'anil	July 27	1 Kan	July 26	1 Toj
July 28	1 Imox	August 9	1 Tijax	August 8	1 Iq'
August 10	1 I'x	August 22	1 B'atz'	August 21	1 Tz'ikin
August 23	1 Kej	September 4	1 K'at	September 3	1 Q'anil
September 5	1 Ajpu	September 17	1 No'j	September 16	1 Imox
September 18	1 Aj	September 30	1 Tz'i'	September 29	1 I'x
October 1	1 Kame	October 13	1 Aq'ab'al	October 12	1 Kej
October 14	1 Kawoq	October 26	1 Ajmaq	October 25	1 Ajpu
October 27	1 E	November 8	1 Toj	November 7	1 Aj
November 9	1 Kan	November 21	1 Iq'	November 20	1 Kame
November 22	1 Tijax	December 4	1 Tz'ikin	December 3	1 Kawoq
December 5	1 B'atz'	December 17	1 Q'anil	December 16	1 E
December 18	1 K'at	December 30	1 Imox	December 29	1 Kan
December 31	1 No'j				

Gregorian Date	Mayan Date	Gregorian Date	Mayan Date	Gregorian Date	Mayan Date
1963		**1964**		**1965**	
January 11	1 Tijax	January 10	1 Iq'	January 8	1 Kame
January 24	1 B'atz'	January 23	1 Tz'ikin	January 21	1 Kawoq
February 6	1 K'at	February 5	1 Q'anil	February 3	1 E
February 19	1 No'j	February 18	1 Imox	February 16	1 Kan
March 4	1 Tz'i'	March 2	1 I'x	March 1	1 Tijax
March 17	1 Aq'ab'al	March 15	1 Kej	March 14	1 B'atz'
March 30	1 Ajmaq	March 28	1 Ajpu	March 27	1 K'at
April 12	1 Toj	April 10	1 Aj	April 9	1 No'j
April 25	1 Iq'	April 23	1 Kame	April 22	1 Tz'i'
May 8	1 Tz'ikin	May 6	1 Kawoq	May 5	1 Aq'ab'al
May 21	1 Q'anil	May 19	1 E	May 18	1 Ajmaq
June 3	1 Imox	June 1	1 Kan	May 31	1 Toj
June 16	1 I'x	June 14	1 Tijax	June 13	1 Iq'
June 29	1 Kej	June 27	1 B'atz'	June 26	1 Tz'ikin
July 12	1 Ajpu	July 10	1 K'at	July 9	1 Q'anil
July 25	1 Aj	July 23	1 No'j	July 22	1 Imox
August 7	1 Kame	August 5	1 Tz'i'	August 4	1 I'x
August 20	1 Kawoq	August 18	1 Aq'ab'al	August 17	1 Kej
September 2	1 E	August 31	1 Ajmaq	August 30	1 Ajpu
September 15	1 Kan	September 13	1 Toj	September 12	1 Aj
September 28	1 Tijax	September 26	1 Iq'	September 25	1 Kame
October 11	1 B'atz'	October 9	1 Tz'ikin	October 8	1 Kawoq
October 24	1 K'at	October 22	1 Q'anil	October 21	1 E
November 6	1 No'j	November 4	1 Imox	November 3	1 Kan
November 19	1 Tz'i'	November 17	1 I'x	November 16	1 Tijax
December 2	1 Aq'ab'al	November 30	1 Kej	November 29	1 B'atz'
December 15	1 Ajmaq	December 13	1 Ajpu	December 12	1 K'at
December 28	1 Toj	December 26	1 Aj	December 25	1 No'j

Gregorian Date	Mayan Date	Gregorian Date	Mayan Date	Gregorian Date	Mayan Date
1966		**1967**		**1968**	
January 7	1 Tz'i'	January 6	1 I'x	January 5	1 Tijax
January 20	1 Aq'ab'al	January 19	1 Kej	January 18	1 B'atz'
February 2	1 Ajmaq	February 1	1 Ajpu	January 31	1 K'at
February 15	1 Toj	February 14	1 Aj	February 13	1 No'j
February 28	1 Iq'	February 27	1 Kame	February 26	1 Tz'i'
March 13	1 Tz'ikin	March 12	1 Kawoq	March 10	1 Aq'ab'al
March 26	1 Q'anil	March 25	1 E	March 23	1 Ajmaq
April 8	1 Imox	April 7	1 Kan	April 5	1 Toj
April 21	1 I'x	April 20	1 Tijax	April 18	1 Iq'
May 4	1 Kej	May 3	1 B'atz'	May 1	1 Tz'ikin
May 17	1 Ajpu	May 16	1 K'at	May 14	1 Q'anil
May 30	1 Aj	May 29	1 No'j	May 27	1 Imox
June 12	1 Kame	June 11	1 Tz'i'	June 9	1 I'x
June 25	1 Kawoq	June 24	1 Aq'ab'al	June 22	1 Kej
July 8	1 E	July 7	1 Ajmaq	July 5	1 Ajpu
July 21	1 Kan	July 20	1 Toj	July 18	1 Aj
August 3	1 Tijax	August 2	1 Iq'	July 31	1 Kame
August 16	1 B'atz'	August 15	1 Tz'ikin	August 13	1 Kawoq
August 29	1 K'at	August 28	1 Q'anil	August 26	1 E
September 11	1 No'j	September 10	1 Imox	September 8	1 Kan
September 24	1 Tz'i'	September 23	1 I'x	September 21	1 Tijax
October 7	1 Aq'ab'al	October 6	1 Kej	October 4	1 B'atz'
October 20	1 Ajmaq	October 19	1 Ajpu	October 17	1 K'at
November 2	1 Toj	November 1	1 Aj	October 30	1 No'j
November 15	1 Iq'	November 14	1 Kame	November 12	1 Tz'i'
November 28	1 Tz'ikin	November 27	1 Kawoq	November 25	1 Aq'ab'al
December 11	1 Q'anil	December 10	1 E	December 8	1 Ajmaq
December 24	1 Imox	December 23	1 Kan	December 21	1 Toj

Gregorian Date	Mayan Date	Gregorian Date	Mayan Date	Gregorian Date	Mayan Date
1969		**1970**		**1971**	
January 3	1 Iq'	January 2	1 Kame	January 1	1 Tz'i'
January 16	1 Tz'ikin	January 15	1 Kawoq	January 14	1 Aq'ab'al
January 29	1 Q'anil	January 28	1 E	January 27	1 Ajmaq
February 11	1 Imox	February 10	1 Kan	February 9	1 Toj
February 24	1 I'x	February 23	1 Tijax	February 22	1 Iq'
March 9	1 Kej	March 8	1 B'atz'	March 7	1 Tz'ikin
March 22	1 Ajpu	March 21	1 K'at	March 20	1 Q'anil
April 4	1 Aj	April 3	1 No'j	April 2	1 Imox
April 17	1 Kame	April 16	1 Tz'i'	April 15	1 I'x
April 30	1 Kawoq	April 29	1 Aq'ab'al	April 28	1 Kej
May 13	1 E	May 12	1 Ajmaq	May 11	1 Ajpu
May 26	1 Kan	May 25	1 Toj	May 24	1 Aj
June 8	1 Tijax	June 7	1 Iq'	June 6	1 Kame
June 21	1 B'atz'	June 20	1 Tz'ikin	June 19	1 Kawoq
July 4	1 K'at	July 3	1 Q'anil	July 2	1 E
July 17	1 No'j	July 16	1 Imox	July 15	1 Kan
July 30	1 Tz'i'	July 29	1 I'x	July 28	1 Tijax
August 12	1 Aq'ab'al	August 11	1 Kej	August 10	1 B'atz'
August 25	1 Ajmaq	August 24	1 Ajpu	August 23	1 K'at
September 7	1 Toj	September 6	1 Aj	September 5	1 No'j
September 20	1 Iq'	September 19	1 Kame	September 18	1 Tz'i'
October 3	1 Tz'ikin	October 2	1 Kawoq	October 1	1 Aq'ab'al
October 16	1 Q'anil	October 15	1 E	October 14	1 Ajmaq
October 29	1 Imox	October 28	1 Kan	October 27	1 Toj
November 11	1 I'x	November 10	1 Tijax	November 9	1 Iq'
November 24	1 Kej	November 23	1 B'atz'	November 22	1 Tz'ikin
December 7	1 Ajpu	December 6	1 K'at	December 5	1 Q'anil
December 20	1 Aj	December 19	1 No'j	December 18	1 Imox
				December 31	1 I'x

Gregorian Date	Mayan Date	Gregorian Date	Mayan Date	Gregorian Date	Mayan Date
1972		**1973**		**1974**	
January 13	1 Kej	January 11	1 B'atz'	January 10	1 Tz'ikin
January 26	1 Ajpu	January 24	1 K'at	January 23	1 Q'anil
February 8	1 Aj	February 6	1 No'j	February 5	1 Imox
February 21	1 Kame	February 19	1 Tz'i'	February 18	1 I'x
March 5	1 Kawoq	March 4	1 Aq'ab'al	March 3	1 Kej
March 18	1 E	March 17	1 Ajmaq	March 16	1 Ajpu
March 31	1 Kan	March 30	1 Toj	March 29	1 Aj
April 13	1 Tijax	April 12	1 Iq'	April 11	1 Kame
April 26	1 B'atz'	April 25	1 Tz'ikin	April 24	1 Kawoq
May 9	1 K'at	May 8	1 Q'anil	May 7	1 E
May 22	1 No'j	May 21	1 Imox	May 20	1 Kan
June 4	1 Tz'i'	June 3	1 I'x	June 2	1 Tijax
June 17	1 Aq'ab'al	June 16	1 Kej	June 15	1 B'atz'
June 30	1 Ajmaq	June 29	1 Ajpu	June 28	1 K'at
July 13	1 Toj	July 12	1 Aj	July 11	1 No'j
July 26	1 Iq'	July 25	1 Kame	July 24	1 Tz'i'
August 8	1 Tz'ikin	August 7	1 Kawoq	August 6	1 Aq'ab'al
August 21	1 Q'anil	August 20	1 E	August 19	1 Ajmaq
September 3	1 Imox	September 2	1 Kan	September 1	1 Toj
September 16	1 I'x	September 15	1 Tijax	September 14	1 Iq'
September 29	1 Kej	September 28	1 B'atz'	September 27	1 Tz'ikin
October 12	1 Ajpu	October 11	1 K'at	October 10	1 Q'anil
October 25	1 Aj	October 24	1 No'j	October 23	1 Imox
November 7	1 Kame	November 6	1 Tz'i'	November 5	1 I'x
November 20	1 Kawoq	November 19	1 Aq'ab'al	November 18	1 Kej
December 3	1 E	December 2	1 Ajmaq	December 1	1 Ajpu
December 16	1 Kan	December 15	1 Toj	December 14	1 Aj
December 29	1 Tijax	December 28	1 Iq'	December 27	1 Kame

Gregorian Date	Mayan Date	Gregorian Date	Mayan Date	Gregorian Date	Mayan Date
1975		**1976**		**1977**	
January 9	1 Kawoq	January 8	1 Aq'ab'al	January 6	1 Kej
January 22	1 E	January 21	1 Ajmaq	January 19	1 Ajpu
February 4	1 Kan	February 3	1 Toj	February 1	1 Aj
February 17	1 Tijax	February 16	1 Iq'	February 14	1 Kame
March 2	1 B'atz'	February 29	1 Tz'ikin	February 27	1 Kawoq
March 15	1 K'at	March 13	1 Q'anil	March 12	1 E
March 28	1 No'j	March 26	1 Imox	March 25	1 Kan
April 10	1 Tz'i'	April 8	1 I'x	April 7	1 Tijax
April 23	1 Aq'ab'al	April 21	1 Kej	March 20	1 B'atz'
May 6	1 Ajmaq	May 4	1 Ajpu	May 3	1 K'at
May 19	1 Toj	May 17	1 Aj	May 16	1 No'j
June 1	1 Iq'	May 30	1 Kame	May 29	1 Tz'i'
June 14	1 Tz'ikin	June 12	1 Kawoq	June 11	1 Aq'ab'al
June 27	1 Q'anil	June 25	1 E	June 24	1 Ajmaq
July 10	1 Imox	July 8	1 Kan	July 7	1 Toj
July 23	1 I'x	July 21	1 Tijax	July 20	1 Iq'
August 5	1 Kej	August 3	1 B'atz'	August 2	1 Tz'ikin
August 18	1 Ajpu	August 16	1 K'at	August 15	1 Q'anil
August 31	1 Aj	August 29	1 No'j	August 28	1 Imox
September 13	1 Kame	September 11	1 Tz'i'	September 10	1 I'x
September 26	1 Kawoq	September 24	1 Aq'ab'al	September 23	1 Kej
October 9	1 E	October 7	1 Ajmaq	October 6	1 Ajpu
October 22	1 Kan	October 20	1 Toj	October 19	1 Aj
November 4	1 Tijax	November 2	1 Iq'	November 1	1 Kame
November 17	1 B'atz'	November 15	1 Tz'ikin	November 14	1 Kawoq
November 30	1 K'at	November 28	1 Q'anil	November 27	1 E
December 13	1 No'j	December 11	1 Imox	December 10	1 Kan
December 26	1 Tz'i'	December 24	1 I'x	December 23	1 Tijax

Gregorian Date	Mayan Date	Gregorian Date	Mayan Date	Gregorian Date	Mayan Date
1978		**1979**		**1980**	
January 5	1 B'atz'	January 4	1 Tz'ikin	January 3	1 Kawoq
January 18	1 K'at	January 17	1 Q'anil	January 16	1 E
January 31	1 No'j	January 30	1 Imox	January 29	1 Kan
February 13	1 Tz'i'	February 12	1 I'x	February 11	1 Tijax
February 26	1 Aq'ab'al	February 25	1 Kej	February 24	1 B'atz'
March 11	1 Ajmaq	March 10	1 Ajpu	March 8	1 K'at
March 24	1 Toj	March 23	1 Aj	March 21	1 No'j
April 6	1 Iq'	April 5	1 Kame	April 3	1 Tz'i'
April 19	1 Tz'ikin	April 18	1 Kawoq	April 16	1 Aq'ab'al
May 2	1 Q'anil	May 1	1 E	April 29	1 Ajmaq
May 15	1 Imox	May 14	1 Kan	May 12	1 Toj
May 28	1 I'x	May 27	1 Tijax	May 25	1 Iq'
June 10	1 Kej	June 9	1 B'atz'	June 7	1 Tz'ikin
June 23	1 Ajpu	June 22	1 K'at	June 20	1 Q'anil
July 6	1 Aj	July 5	1 No'j	July 3	1 Imox
July 19	1 Kame	July 18	1 Tz'i'	July 16	1 I'x
August 1	1 Kawoq	July 31	1 Aq'ab'al	July 29	1 Kej
August 14	1 E	August 13	1 Ajmaq	August 11	1 Ajpu
August 27	1 Kan	August 26	1 Toj	August 24	1 Aj
September 9	1 Tijax	September 8	1 Iq'	September 6	1 Kame
September 22	1 B'atz'	September 21	1 Tz'ikin	September 19	1 Kawoq
October 5	1 K'at	October 4	1 Q'anil	October 2	1 E
October 18	1 No'j	October 17	1 Imox	October 15	1 Kan
October 31	1 Tz'i'	October 30	1 I'x	October 28	1 Tijax
November 13	1 Aq'ab'al	November 12	1 Kej	November 10	1 B'atz'
November 26	1 Ajmaq	November 25	1 Ajpu	November 23	1 K'at
December 9	1 Toj	December 8	1 Aj	December 6	1 No'j
December 22	1 Iq'	December 21	1 Kame	December 19	1 Tz'i'

Gregorian Date	Mayan Date	Gregorian Date	Mayan Date	Gregorian Date	Mayan Date
1981		**1982**		**1983**	
January 1	1 Aq'ab'al	January 13	1 Ajpu	January 12	1 K'at
January 14	1 Ajmaq	January 26	1 Aj	January 25	1 No'j
January 27	1 Toj	February 8	1 Kame	February 7	1 Tz'i'
February 9	1 Iq'	February 21	1 Kawoq	February 20	1 Aq'ab'al
February 22	1 Tz'ikin	March 6	1 E	March 5	1 Ajmaq
March 7	1 Q'anil	March 19	1 Kan	March 18	1 Toj
March 20	1 Imox	April 1	1 Tijax	March 31	1 Iq'
April 2	1 I'x	April 14	1 B'atz'	April 13	1 Tz'ikin
April 15	1 Kej	April 27	1 K'at	April 26	1 Q'anil
April 28	1 Ajpu	May 10	1 No'j	May 9	1 Imox
May 11	1 Aj	May 23	1 Tz'i'	May 22	1 I'x
May 24	1 Kame	June 5	1 Aq'ab'al	June 4	1 Kej
June 6	1 Kawoq	June 18	1 Ajmaq	June 17	1 Ajpu
June 19	1 E	July 1	1 Toj	June 30	1 Aj
July 2	1 Kan	July 14	1 Iq'	July 13	1 Kame
July 15	1 Tijax	July 27	1 Tz'ikin	July 26	1 Kawoq
July 28	1 B'atz'	August 9	1 Q'anil	August 8	1 E
August 10	1 K'at	August 22	1 Imox	August 21	1 Kan
August 23	1 No'j	September 4	1 I'x	September 3	1 Tijax
September 5	1 Tz'i'	September 17	1 Kej	September 16	1 B'atz'
September 18	1 Aq'ab'al	September 30	1 Ajpu	September 29	1 K'at
October 1	1 Ajmaq	October 13	1 Aj	October 12	1 No'j
October 14	1 Toj	October 26	1 Kame	October 25	1 Tz'i'
October 27	1 Iq'	November 8	1 Kawoq	November 7	1 Aq'ab'al
November 9	1 Tz'ikin	November 21	1 E	November 20	1 Ajmaq
November 22	1 Q'anil	December 4	1 Kan	December 3	1 Toj
December 5	1 Imox	December 17	1 Tijax	December 16	1 Iq'
December 18	1 I'x	December 30	1 B'atz'	December 29	1 Tz'ikin
December 31	1 Kej				

Gregorian Date	Mayan Date	Gregorian Date	Mayan Date	Gregorian Date	Mayan Date
1984		**1985**		**1986**	
January 11	1 Q'anil	January 9	1 E	January 8	1 Ajmaq
January 24	1 Imox	January 22	1 Kan	January 21	1 Toj
February 6	1 I'x	February 4	1 Tijax	February 3	1 Iq'
February 19	1 Kej	February 17	1 B'atz'	February 16	1 Tz'ikin
March 3	1 Ajpu	March 2	1 K'at	March 1	1 Q'anil
March 16	1 Aj	March 15	1 No'j	March 14	1 Imox
March 29	1 Kame	March 28	1 Tz'i'	March 27	1 I'x
April 11	1 Kawoq	April 10	1 Aq'ab'al	April 9	1 Kej
April 24	1 E	April 23	1 Ajmaq	April 22	1 Ajpu
May 7	1 Kan	May 6	1 Toj	May 5	1 Aj
May 20	1 Tijax	May 19	1 Iq'	May 18	1 Kame
June 2	1 B'atz'	June 1	1 Tz'ikin	May 31	1 Kawoq
June 15	1 K'at	June 14	1 Q'anil	June 13	1 E
June 28	1 No'j	June 27	1 Imox	June 26	1 Kan
July 11	1 Tz'i'	July 10	1 I'x	July 9	1 Tijax
July 24	1 Aq'ab'al	July 23	1 Kej	July 22	1 B'atz'
August 6	1 Ajmaq	August 5	1 Ajpu	August 4	1 K'at
August 19	1 Toj	August 18	1 Aj	August 17	1 No'j
September 1	1 Iq'	August 31	1 Kame	August 30	1 Tz'i'
September 14	1 Tz'ikin	September 13	1 Kawoq	September 12	1 Aq'ab'al
September 27	1 Q'anil	September 26	1 E	September 25	1 Ajmaq
October 10	1 Imox	October 9	1 Kan	October 8	1 Toj
October 23	1 I'x	October 22	1 Tijax	October 21	1 Iq'
November 5	1 Kej	November 4	1 B'atz'	November 3	1 Tz'ikin
November 18	1 Ajpu	November 17	1 K'at	November 16	1 Q'anil
December 1	1 Aj	November 30	1 No'j	November 29	1 Imox
December 14	1 Kame	December 13	1 Tz'i'	December 12	1 I'x
December 27	1 Kawoq	December 26	1 Aq'ab'al	December 25	1 Kej

Gregorian Date	Mayan Date	Gregorian Date	Mayan Date	Gregorian Date	Mayan Date
1987		**1988**		**1989**	
January 7	1 Ajpu	January 6	1 K'at	January 4	1 Q'anil
January 20	1 Aj	January 19	1 No'j	January 17	1 Imox
February 2	1 Kame	February 1	1 Tz'i'	January 30	1 I'x
February 15	1 Kawoq	February 14	1 Aq'ab'al	February 12	1 Kej
February 28	1 E	February 27	1 Ajmaq	February 25	1 Ajpu
March 13	1 Kan	March 11	1 Toj	March 10	1 Aj
March 26	1 Tijax	March 24	1 Iq'	March 23	1 Kame
April 8	1 B'atz'	April 6	1 Tz'ikin	April 5	1 Kawoq
April 21	1 K'at	April 19	1 Q'anil	April 18	1 E
May 4	1 No'j	May 2	1 Imox	May 1	1 Kan
May 17	1 Tz'i'	May 15	1 I'x	May 14	1 Tijax
May 30	1 Aq'ab'al	May 28	1 Kej	May 27	1 B'atz'
June 12	1 Ajmaq	June 10	1 Ajpu	June 9	1 K'at
June 25	1 Toj	June 23	1 Aj	June 22	1 No'j
July 8	1 Iq'	July 6	1 Kame	July 5	1 Tz'i'
July 21	1 Tz'ikin	July 19	1 Kawoq	July 18	1 Aq'ab'al
August 3	1 Q'anil	August 1	1 E	July 31	1 Ajmaq
August 16	1 Imox	August 14	1 Kan	August 13	1 Toj
August 29	1 I'x	August 27	1 Tijax	August 26	1 Iq'
September 11	1 Kej	September 9	1 B'atz'	September 8	1 Tz'ikin
September 24	1 Ajpu	September 22	1 K'at	September 21	1 Q'anil
October 7	1 Aj	October 5	1 No'j	October 4	1 Imox
October 20	1 Kame	October 18	1 Tz'i'	October 17	1 I'x
November 2	1 Kawoq	October 31	1 Aq'ab'al	October 30	1 Kej
November 15	1 E	November 13	1 Ajmaq	November 12	1 Ajpu
November 28	1 Kan	November 26	1 Toj	November 25	1 Aj
December 11	1 Tijax	December 9	1 Iq'	December 8	1 Kame
December 24	1 B'atz'	December 22	1 Tz'ikin	December 21	1 Kawoq

Gregorian Date	Mayan Date	Gregorian Date	Mayan Date	Gregorian Date	Mayan Date
1990		**1991**		**1992**	
January 3	1 E	January 2	1 Ajmaq	January 1	1 Ajpu
January 16	1 Kan	January 15	1 Toj	January 14	1 Aj
January 29	1 Tijax	January 28	1 Iq'	January 27	1 Kame
February 11	1 B'atz'	February 10	1 Tz'ikin	February 9	1 Kawoq
February 24	1 K'at	February 23	1 Q'anil	February 22	1 E
March 9	1 No'j	March 8	1 Imox	March 6	1 Kan
March 22	1 Tz'i'	March 21	1 I'x	March 19	1 Tijax
April 4	1 Aq'ab'al	April 3	1 Kej	April 1	1 B'atz'
April 17	1 Ajmaq	April 16	1 Ajpu	April 14	1 K'at
April 30	1 Toj	April 29	1 Aj	April 27	1 No'j
May 13	1 Iq'	May 12	1 Kame	May 10	1 Tz'i'
May 26	1 Tz'ikin	May 25	1 Kawoq	May 23	1 Aq'ab'al
June 8	1 Q'anil	June 7	1 E	June 5	1 Ajmaq
June 21	1 Imox	June 20	1 Kan	June 18	1 Toj
July 4	1 I'x	July 3	1 Tijax	July 1	1 Iq'
July 17	1 Kej	July 16	1 B'atz'	July 14	1 Tz'ikin
July 30	1 Ajpu	July 29	1 K'at	July 27	1 Q'anil
August 12	1 Aj	August 11	1 No'j	August 9	1 Imox
August 25	1 Kame	August 24	1 Tz'i'	August 22	1 I'x
September 7	1 Kawoq	September 6	1 Aq'ab'al	September 4	1 Kej
September 20	1 E	September 19	1 Ajmaq	September 17	1 Ajpu
October 3	1 Kan	October 2	1 Toj	September 30	1 Aj
October 16	1 Tijax	October 15	1 Iq'	October 13	1 Kame
October 29	1 B'atz'	October 28	1 Tz'ikin	October 26	1 Kawoq
November 11	1 K'at	November 10	1 Q'anil	November 8	1 E
November 24	1 No'j	November 23	1 Imox	November 21	1 Kan
December 7	1 Tz'i'	December 6	1 I'x	December 4	1 Tijax
December 20	1 Aq'ab'al	December 19	1 Kej	December 17	1 B'atz'
				December 30	1 K'at

Gregorian Date	Mayan Date	Gregorian Date	Mayan Date	Gregorian Date	Mayan Date
1993		**1994**		**1995**	
January 12	1 No'j	January 11	1 Imox	January 10	1 Kan
January 25	1 Tz'i'	January 24	1 I'x	January 23	1 Tijax
February 7	1 Aq'ab'al	February 6	1 Kej	February 5	1 B'atz'
February 20	1 Ajmaq	February 19	1 Ajpu	February 18	1 K'at
March 5	1 Toj	March 4	1 Aj	March 3	1 No'j
March 18	1 Iq'	March 17	1 Kame	March 16	1 Tz'i'
March 31	1 Tz'ikin	March 30	1 Kawoq	March 29	1 Aq'ab'al
April 13	1 Q'anil	April 12	1 E	April 11	1 Ajmaq
April 26	1 Imox	April 25	1 Kan	April 24	1 Toj
May 9	1 I'x	May 8	1 Tijax	May 7	1 Iq'
May 22	1 Kej	May 21	1 B'atz'	May 20	1 Tz'ikin
June 4	1 Ajpu	June 3	1 K'at	June 2	1 Q'anil
June 17	1 Aj	June 16	1 No'j	June 15	1 Imox
June 30	1 Kame	June 29	1 Tz'i'	June 28	1 I'x
July 13	1 Kawoq	July 12	1 Aq'ab'al	July 11	1 Kej
July 26	1 E	July 25	1 Ajmaq	July 24	1 Ajpu
August 8	1 Kan	August 7	1 Toj	August 6	1 Aj
August 21	1 Tijax	August 20	1 Iq'	August 19	1 Kame
September 3	1 B'atz'	September 2	1 Tz'ikin	September 1	1 Kawoq
September 16	1 K'at	September 15	1 Q'anil	September 14	1 E
September 29	1 No'j	September 28	1 Imox	September 27	1 Kan
October 12	1 Tz'i'	October 11	1 I'x	October 10	1 Tijax
October 25	1 Aq'ab'al	October 24	1 Kej	October 23	1 B'atz'
November 7	1 Ajmaq	November 6	1 Ajpu	November 5	1 K'at
November 20	1 Toj	November 19	1 Aj	November 18	1 No'j
December 3	1 Iq'	December 2	1 Kame	December 1	1 Tz'i'
December 16	1 Tz'ikin	December 15	1 Kawoq	December 14	1 Aq'ab'al
December 29	1 Q'anil	December 28	1 E	December 27	1 Ajmaq

Gregorian Date	Mayan Date	Gregorian Date	Mayan Date	Gregorian Date	Mayan Date
1996		**1997**		**1998**	
January 9	1 Toj	January 7	1 Aj	January 6	1 No'j
January 22	1 Iq'	January 20	1 Kame	January 19	1 Tz'i'
February 4	1 Tz'ikin	February 2	1 Kawoq	February 1	1 Aq'ab'al
February 17	1 Q'anil	February 15	1 E	February 14	1 Ajmaq
March 1	1 Imox	February 28	1 Kan	February 27	1 Toj
March 14	1 I'x	March 13	1 Tijax	March 12	1 Iq'
March 27	1 Kej	March 26	1 B'atz'	March 25	1 Tz'ikin
April 9	1 Ajpu	April 8	1 K'at	April 7	1 Q'anil
April 22	1 Aj	April 21	1 No'j	April 20	1 Imox
May 5	1 Kame	May 4	1 Tz'i'	May 3	1 I'x
May 18	1 Kawoq	May 17	1 Aq'ab'al	May 16	1 Kej
May 31	1 E	May 30	1 Ajmaq	May 29	1 Ajpu
June 13	1 Kan	June 12	1 Toj	June 11	1 Aj
June 26	1 Tijax	June 25	1 Iq'	June 24	1 Kame
July 9	1 B'atz'	July 8	1 Tz'ikin	July 7	1 Kawoq
July 22	1 K'at	July 21	1 Q'anil	July 20	1 E
August 4	1 No'j	August 3	1 Imox	August 2	1 Kan
August 17	1 Tz'i'	August 16	1 I'x	August 15	1 Tijax
August 30	1 Aq'ab'al	August 29	1 Kej	August 28	1 B'atz'
September 12	1 Ajmaq	September 11	1 Ajpu	September 10	1 K'at
September 25	1 Toj	September 24	1 Aj	September 23	1 No'j
October 8	1 Iq'	October 7	1 Kame	October 6	1 Tz'i'
October 21	1 Tz'ikin	October 20	1 Kawoq	October 19	1 Aq'ab'al
November 3	1 Q'anil	November 2	1 E	November 1	1 Ajmaq
November 16	1 Imox	November 15	1 Kan	November 14	1 Toj
November 29	1 I'x	November 28	1 Tijax	November 27	1 Iq'
December 12	1 Kej	December 11	1 B'atz'	December 10	1 Tz'ikin
December 25	1 Ajpu	December 24	1 K'at	December 23	1 Q'anil

Gregorian Date	Mayan Date	Gregorian Date	Mayan Date	Gregorian Date	Mayan Date
1999		**2000**		**2001**	
January 5	1 Imox	January 4	1 Kan	January 2	1 Toj
January 18	1 I'x	January 17	1 Tijax	January 15	1 Iq'
January 31	1 Kej	January 30	1 B'atz'	January 28	1 Tz'ikin
February 13	1 Ajpu	February 12	1 K'at	February 10	1 Q'anil
February 26	1 Aj	February 25	1 No'j	February 23	1 Imox
March 11	1 Kame	March 9	1 Tz'i'	March 8	1 I'x
March 24	1 Kawoq	March 22	1 Aq'ab'al	March 21	1 Kej
April 6	1 E	April 4	1 Ajmaq	April 3	1 Ajpu
April 19	1 Kan	April 17	1 Toj	April 16	1 Aj
May 2	1 Tijax	April 30	1 Iq'	April 29	1 Kame
May 15	1 B'atz'	May 13	1 Tz'ikin	May 12	1 Kawoq
May 28	1 K'at	May 26	1 Q'anil	May 25	1 E
June 10	1 No'j	June 8	1 Imox	June 7	1 Kan
June 23	1 Tz'i'	June 21	1 I'x	June 20	1 Tijax
July 6	1 Aq'ab'al	July 4	1 Kej	July 3	1 B'atz'
July 19	1 Ajmaq	July 17	1 Ajpu	July 16	1 K'at
August 1	1 Toj	July 30	1 Aj	July 29	1 No'j
August 14	1 Iq'	August 12	1 Kame	August 11	1 Tz'i'
August 27	1 Tz'ikin	August 25	1 Kawoq	August 25	1 Aq'ab'al
September 9	1 Q'anil	September 7	1 E	September 6	1 Ajmaq
September 22	1 Imox	September 20	1 Kan	September 19	1 Toj
October 5	1 I'x	October 3	1 Tijax	October 2	1 Iq'
October 18	1 Kej	October 16	1 B'atz'	October 15	1 Tz'ikin
October 31	1 Ajpu	October 29	1 K'at	October 28	1 Q'anil
November 13	1 Aj	November 11	1 No'j	November 10	1 Imox
November 26	1 Kame	November 24	1 Tz'i'	November 23	1 I'x
December 9	1 Kawoq	December 7	1 Aq'ab'al	December 6	1 Kej
December 22	1 E	December 20	1 Ajmaq	December 19	1 Ajpu

Gregorian Date	Mayan Date	Gregorian Date	Mayan Date	Gregorian Date	Mayan Date
2002		**2003**		**2004**	
January 1	1 Aj	January 13	1 Tz'i'	January 12	1 I'x
January 14	1 Kame	January 26	1 Aq'ab'al	January 25	1 Kej
January 27	1 Kawoq	February 8	1 Ajmaq	February 7	1 Ajpu
February 9	1 E	February 21	1 Toj	February 20	1 Aj
February 22	1 Kan	March 6	1 Iq'	March 4	1 Kame
March 7	1 Tijax	March 19	1 Tz'ikin	March 17	1 Kawoq
March 20	1 B'atz'	April 1	1 Q'anil	March 30	1 E
April 2	1 K'at	April 14	1 Imox	April 12	1 Kan
April 15	1 No'j	April 27	1 I'x	April 25	1 Tijax
April 28	1 Tz'i'	May 10	1 Kej	May 8	1 B'atz'
May 11	1 Aq'ab'al	May 23	1 Ajpu	May 21	1 K'at
May 24	1 Ajmaq	June 5	1 Aj	June 3	1 No'j
June 6	1 Toj	June 18	1 Kame	June 16	1 Tz'i'
June 19	1 Iq'	July 1	1 Kawoq	June 29	1 Aq'ab'al
July 2	1 Tz'ikin	July 14	1 E	July 12	1 Ajmaq
July 15	1 Q'anil	July 27	1 Kan	July 25	1 Toj
July 28	1 Imox	August 9	1 Tijax	August 7	1 Iq'
August 10	1 I'x	August 22	1 B'atz'	August 20	1 Tz'ikin
August 23	1 Kej	September 4	1 K'at	September 2	1 Q'anil
September 5	1 Ajpu	September 17	1 No'j	September 15	1 Imox
September 18	1 Aj	September 30	1 Tz'i'	September 28	1 I'x
October 1	1 Kame	October 13	1 Aq'ab'al	October 11	1 Kej
October 14	1 Kawoq	October 26	1 Ajmaq	October 24	1 Ajpu
October 27	1 E	November 8	1 Toj	November 6	1 Aj
November 9	1 Kan	November 21	1 Iq'	November 19	1 Kame
November 22	1 Tijax	December 4	1 Tz'ikin	December 2	1 Kawoq
December 5	1 B'atz'	December 17	1 Q'anil	December 15	1 E
December 18	1 K'at	December 30	1 Imox	December 28	1 Kan
December 31	1 No'j				

Gregorian Date	Mayan Date	Gregorian Date	Mayan Date	Gregorian Date	Mayan Date
2005		**2006**		**2007**	
January 10	1 Tijax	January 9	1 Iq'	January 8	1 Kame
January 23	1 B'atz'	January 22	1 Tz'ikin	January 21	1 Kawoq
February 5	1 K'at	February 4	1 Q'anil	February 3	1 E
February 18	1 No'j	February 17	1 Imox	February 16	1 Kan
March 3	1 Tz'i'	March 2	1 I'x	March 1	1 Tijax
March 16	1 Aq'ab'al	March 15	1 Kej	March 14	1 B'atz'
March 29	1 Ajmaq	March 28	1 Ajpu	March 27	1 K'at
April 11	1 Toj	April 10	1 Aj	April 9	1 No'j
April 24	1 Iq'	April 23	1 Kame	April 22	1 Tz'i'
May 7	1 Tz'ikin	May 6	1 Kawoq	May 5	1 Aq'ab'al
May 20	1 Q'anil	May 19	1 E	May 18	1 Ajmaq
June 2	1 Imox	June 1	1 Kan	May 31	1 Toj
June 15	1 I'x	June 14	1 Tijax	June 13	1 Iq'
June 28	1 Kej	June 27	1 B'atz'	June 26	1 Tz'ikin
July 11	1 Ajpu	July 10	1 K'at	July 9	1 Q'anil
July 24	1 Aj	July 23	1 No'j	July 22	1 Imox
August 6	1 Kame	August 5	1 Tz'i'	August 4	1 I'x
August 19	1 Kawoq	August 18	1 Aq'ab'al	August 17	1 Kej
September 1	1 E	August 31	1 Ajmaq	August 30	1 Ajpu
September 14	1 Kan	September 13	1 Toj	September 12	1 Aj
September 27	1 Tijax	September 26	1 Iq'	September 25	1 Kame
October 10	1 B'atz'	October 9	1 Tz'ikin	October 8	1 Kawoq
October 23	1 K'at	October 22	1 Q'anil	October 21	1 E
November 5	1 No'j	November 4	1 Imox	November 3	1 Kan
November 18	1 Tz'i'	November 17	1 I'x	November 16	1 Tijax
December 1	1 Aq'ab'al	November 30	1 Kej	November 29	1 B'atz'
December 14	1 Ajmaq	December 13	1 Ajpu	December 12	1 K'at
December 27	1 Toj	December 26	1 Aj	December 25	1 No'j

Gregorian Date	Mayan Date	Gregorian Date	Mayan Date	Gregorian Date	Mayan Date
2008		**2009**		**2010**	
January 7	1 Tz'i'	January 5	1 I'x	January 4	1 Tijax
January 20	1 Aq'ab'al	January 18	1 Kej	January 17	1 B'atz'
February 2	1 Ajmaq	January 31	1 Ajpu	January 30	1 K'at
February 15	1 Toj	February 13	1 Aj	February 12	1 No'j
February 28	1 Iq'	February 26	1 Kame	February 25	1 Tz'i'
March 12	1 Tz'ikin	March 11	1 Kawoq	March 10	1 Aq'ab'al
March 25	1 Q'anil	March 24	1 E	March 23	1 Ajmaq
April 7	1 Imox	April 6	1 Kan	April 5	1 Toj
April 20	1 I'x	April 19	1 Tijax	April 18	1 Iq'
May 3	1 Kej	May 2	1 B'atz'	May 1	1 Tz'ikin
May 16	1 Ajpu	May 15	1 K'at	May 14	1 Q'anil
May 29	1 Aj	May 28	1 No'j	May 27	1 Imox
June 11	1 Kame	June 10	1 Tz'i'	June 9	1 I'x
June 24	1 Kawoq	June 23	1 Aq'ab'al	June 22	1 Kej
July 7	1 E	July 6	1 Ajmaq	July 5	1 Ajpu
July 20	1 Kan	July 19	1 Toj	July 18	1 Aj
August 2	1 Tijax	August 1	1 Iq'	July 31	1 Kame
August 15	1 B'atz'	August 14	1 Tz'ikin	August 13	1 Kawoq
August 28	1 K'at	August 27	1 Q'anil	August 26	1 E
September 10	1 No'j	September 9	1 Imox	September 8	1 Kan
September 23	1 Tz'i'	September 22	1 I'x	September 21	1 Tijax
October 6	1 Aq'ab'al	October 5	1 Kej	October 4	1 B'atz'
October 19	1 Ajmaq	October 18	1 Ajpu	October 17	1 K'at
November 1	1 Toj	October 31	1 Aj	October 30	1 No'j
November 14	1 Iq'	November 13	1 Kame	November 12	1 Tz'i'
November 27	1 Tz'ikin	November 26	1 Kawoq	November 25	1 Aq'ab'al
December 10	1 Q'anil	December 9	1 E	December 8	1 Ajmaq
December 23	1 Imox	December 22	1 Kan	December 21	1 Toj

Gregorian Date	Mayan Date	Gregorian Date	Mayan Date
2011		**2012**	
January 3	1 Iq'	January 2	1 Kame
January 16	1 Tz'ikin	January 15	1 Kawoq
January 29	1 Q'anil	January 28	1 E
February 11	1 Imox	February 10	1 Kan
February 24	1 I'x	February 23	1 Tijax
March 9	1 Kej	March 7	1 B'atz'
March 22	1 Ajpu	March 20	1 K'at
April 4	1 Aj	April 2	1 No'j
April 17	1 Kame	April 15	1 Tz'i'
April 30	1 Kawoq	April 28	1 Aq'ab'al
May 13	1 E	May 11	1 Ajmaq
May 26	1 Kan	May 24	1 Toj
June 8	1 Tijax	June 6	1 Iq'
June 21	1 B'atz'	June 19	1 Tz'ikin
July 4	1 K'at	July 2	1 Q'anil
July 17	1 No'j	July 15	1 Imox
July 30	1 Tz'i'	July 28	1 I'x
August 12	1 Aq'ab'al	August 10	1 Kej
August 25	1 Ajmaq	August 23	1 Ajpu
September 7	1 Toj	September 5	1 Aj
September 20	1 Iq'	September 18	1 Kame
October 3	1 Tz'ikin	October 1	1 Kawoq
October 16	1 Q'anil	October 14	1 E
October 29	1 Imox	October 27	1 Kan
November 11	1 I'x	November 9	1 Tijax
November 24	1 Kej	November 22	1 B'atz'
December 7	1 Ajpu	December 5	1 K'at
December 20	1 Aj	December 18	1 No'j
		December 21	4 Ajpu

GLOSSARY

Aj Zotz' Tz'i' Kan See *Chilam Balam.*

Ajaw The best-known name for the Great Father or Supreme Being.

Ajpop Literally, Lord of the Mat. Used in reference to gods and great lords or chiefs, since only they were allowed to sit on the mat.

Ajpop Katuja A king in Mayan mythology who went down to the underworld.

Ajpu The blowgun hunter, and one of the twenty days in the sacred *Cholq'ij* calendar. In some regions, *Ajpu* is the name for the Sun.

Ajq'ij' A Mayan priest who worships the Sun. The day keeper who keeps count of the days and performs the required rituals. Known as *Chi-Mam* in more traditional locations. Also known as *H-Men.*

Ajq'ijab' Plural of *Ajq'ij.*

Alaneb Cycle known as *gestation*, which forms part of the cycles of the Tiku.

Alautun Numerical value for the ninth position in the vigesimal system, equal to a period of 64 million years of 360 days each.

Alom The incomprehensible force, the omnipotent emanation, the seed and whole of the wise word of God that no language can express. With *K'ajolom*, *B'itol*, and *Tz'aquol*, one of the four creation deities in the *Popol Vuh*. *K'ajolom* and *Alom* are the makers and givers of life.

Aq'ab' Tz'ib' Nocturnal writing that is seen during the day and understood in dreams at night. A sacred form of writing practiced by the Itzaj.

Aq'omanela' Mayan healers.

Atija To manipulate water. Meditation.

Atitlán   Both a lake and a town in the Guatemalan highlands. Considered one of the most sacred lakes. The town of Santiago Atitlán is the cradle of the Tzutujil people, one of the most traditional tribes. The tradition of Ri Laj Mam, or Maximón, is maintained there.

Aztec   Central Mexican empire also known as the Mexica, descended from the Toltec tradition.

baktun   Numerical value for the fifth position in the vigesimal system, equal to a period of 400 years of 360 days each.

B'alam   Literally, jaguar. The name used to refer to the first four Men-Gods in the *Popol Vuh* who taught the fourth (and current) humanity: B'alam K'itze', B'alam Aq'ab', Majukutaj, and Ik'i' B'alam.

B'alam   Aq'ab'   The second *B'alameb'*. He reigns in the West and is guardian of the night.

B'alam K'itze'   The first *B'alameb'*. He reigns in the East and was the first to offer copal incense to welcome Father Sun.

B'alameb'   Men-Gods (plural of *B'alam*).

B'itol   The part of divine will that acts in creating the universe and all things. Known in some places as the regent of the sky. With *K'ajolom*, *Alom*, and *Tz'aqol*, one of the four creation deities in the *Popol Vuh*. *Tz'aqol* and *B'itol* are the Creator and Maker.

B'olom   Tiku'   Prophetic period consisting of nine cycles of fifty-two years each. Known as the Nine Underworlds, or the Nine Hells.

bujil   Literally, pyramid or pyramidal temple. Buildings found in Mesoamerica. According to the *Books of Chilam Balam*, more than 52,000 pyramids were built. Some are over 295 feet high.

Cabrakan   One of the deities in the *Popol Vuh*. Son of Vukuk Kakix and brother of Zipakna, he was a giant who would stamp his feet and make the earth tremble. Overly proud of his abilities, he was defeated by the divine twins Jun Ajpu and Ixb'alamke.

Cahabón   Town in the department of Baja Verapaz, Guatemala. Home to the Rab'inaleb' tribe and to Don Isidro Akabal.

Cakchiquel   See *Kaqchikel*.

Chac Ahau   Literally, Lord Red. One of the titles used to refer to the Sun, represented by Kolop.

Chamula   A Mayan tribe. One of the original settlements, and still one of the most traditional. Located in the highlands of Chiapas, Mexico, they are neighbors to the Mam and Q'anjob'al tribes of Huehuetenango, Guatemala.

chay The sacred stone obsidian used for visions, as well as to make arrowheads. It is also the representation of lightning, and the word used to mean glass.

Chichén Itzá City and ceremonial center located in the state of Yucatán in southern Mexico. Famous for the Temple of Kukulkan. The cradle of the Mopán people (Chichén Moján) and then the Itzaj.

Chilam Balam The greatest Mayan prophet and sorcerer-priest, whose real name was Aj Zotz' Tz'i' Kan. Little else is known about him with any certainty. The *Books of Chilam Balam* is the name given to a collection of various Mayan texts found in different towns that narrate the prophecies. Found by Catholic priests and friars during the conquest, these were transcribed into Latin script by Mayan scribes.

Chi-Mam Name for the Mayan priests in the most traditional areas of the Mayan highlands, particularly in the Cuchumatanes Mountains in Guatemala, where this great civilization began. Known in other areas as *Ajq'ij* or *H-Men*.

Chol Mayan tribe located in northern Chiapas, Mexico. The Chortí and Chol languages are considered the imperial Mayan language (as Sanskrit is to the Hindu).

Cholq'ij The sacred calendar consisting of 260 days with the cosmic and telluric energies that affect each day. Also known as the *Tzolkin* calendar, it forms the basis for the *Ch'umilal Wuj*, or *Book of Destiny*. Mayans take on the name, or *nawal*, that governs the day of their birth.

Chortí Mayan tribe located in western Guatemala. The Chortí and Chol languages are considered the imperial Mayan language (as Sanskrit is to the Hindu).

Ch'umilal Wuj The *Book of Destiny* or *Book of Fate*. One of the most important Mayan texts, it is preserved in absolute secrecy and is still used today. Based on the sacred *Cholq'ij* calendar, it is a way to use the information contained there.

codices Mayan books written using hieroglyphs. Spanish priests, seeing these books as pagan, destroyed most of them during the conquest. Written on deerskin or paper made from the *amatle* tree that was folded into an accordion-style book, they contain a wealth of information. Four known to have survived were found in Europe and Mexico. According to the Elders, more remain hidden in Guatemala and are going to be revealed soon. See *Dresden Codex, Grolier Codex, Madrid Codex*, and *Paris Codex*.

Copán   City and ceremonial center in northwestern Honduras. It was the most important scientific center of the Mayan world, as well as the greatest astronomical observatory, and the Mayan calendars were investigated there. Famous for its extraordinary sculptures and sophisticated refinement known as Mayan baroque.

Cuchumatanes   Mountain range in the department of Huehuetenango in northwestern Guatemala. This is where the Mayan culture arose.

Cuello   Ancient Mayan city in Belize where archaeologists discovered the earliest known human burials. These appeared to date to three thousand years before the present—nearly one thousand years before those excavated previously.

Cuicuilco   Located in the Valley of Mexico and potentially one of the oldest Mayan sites. Best known for the circular pyramid that rises up in four tiers.

Dresden Codex   Ancient Mayan hieroglyphic text containing exceptionally accurate astronomical calculations. Found in 1739 and donated to the Dresden Royal Library in 1744, where it remains housed.

Dzensal   Mayan tribe in the highlands of Chiapas, Mexico. Along with the Lacandón, Chamula, and Tzotzil, they are the most traditional people in this region.

El Mayab   The Mayan homeland or territory stretching from central Mexico to northern Honduras.

El Mirador   Massive, ancient Mayan city and ceremonial center in the extreme northern part of Petén. One of the earliest Mayan settlements and the site where one of the crystal skulls was found.

Four Hundred Boys   In the *Popol Vuh*, the Four Hundred Boys were killed by the deity Zipakna and rose up into the sky to become the Pleiades. For the Maya, "four hundred" is an indeterminate number, similar to the Western world's use of the words "hundreds" and "thousands."

Grolier Codex   Ancient Mayan hieroglyphic text containing astronomical observations regarding Venus. Found in 1965 in Mexico and shown in 1971 at the Grolier Club in New York City, it was subsequently donated to the Mexican government.

Hacavitz   Mountain in the *Popol Vuh*, also known as Mount Waq'xaqi Aq'ab'al, where the first four Men-Gods were when the sun dawned. Also a mountain in the department of El Quiché in Guatemala.

Halach-Winic The true man; the Elder male whose family inheritance entitles him to sit on the throne. Ruler of all Mayan nations and thus, in a theocracy, the highest spiritual and political authority. Don Isidro Akabal, descended from Q'eqchi royalty, was one of the last.

H-Men See *Chi-Mam.*

H-Menob' Plural of *H-men.*

Hun Itzam Na Mayan deity, son of the supreme Jun Ab Ku and husband of Ixchel or Ix Chebel Yax. Perhaps the most important Mayan god, he gave humankind writing and the calendar. He was also the patron of medicine.

Ik'i' B'alam The fourth *B'alameb'* (Man-God), and the last to join them. He reigns in the South and is the energy of Water. He left no descendants, and now is when his power will reign. He is the key to accessing the fourth dimension.

Itzaj Mayan tribe. See *Petén Itzá* and *Tayasal.*

Itzam Na Literally, House of Iguanas. Refers to certain pyramids built in honor of the deity Hun Itzam Na that contain many figures of iguanas, his reigning animal.

Ixb'alamke One of the divine twins, the first demigods, like their older half-brothers Jun B'atz' and Jun Chowen. In the *Popol Vuh*, Ixb'alamke and his twin Jun Ajpu descended to Xib'alb'ay (the underworld) and passed the tests given to them. They then rose up into the sky, and Ixb'alamke became the Moon.

Ixchel or **Ix Chebel Yax** Mayan deity, wife of Hun Itzam Na. She was the moon goddess and patron of womanly crafts.

Ixil A Mayan tribe found in the highland departments of Quiché and Huehuetenango, Guatemala.

ixim Sacred corn. Originating in the Americas, corn is now grown and used around the world as food for humans and livestock and as a raw material. According to the *Popol Vuh*, corn was brought from Paxil and Kayala, then used to make the four *B'alameb'*, or fathers of this humanity. It was so important to the Maya that calendars were made based on its agricultural cycle, and it is used for divining purposes. The four colors of corn—red, black, white, and yellow—represent the races of humanity.

Ixmukane According to the *Popol Vuh*, Ixmukane and Ixpiyakok, the first two grandparents, divined using the *tz'ite* (coral tree) seeds to confirm how to make this humanity.

Ixpiyakok See *Ixmukane.*

Izamal Ancient Mayan city and ceremonial site located in the state of Yucatán, Mexico. Dedicated to the deity Itzam Na.

Jakawitz Deity who, along with Avilix, forms one of the couples of creation. Idol that Majukutaj brought from Tulán.

Jolom Konob' A town located in the department of Huehuetenango in northwestern Guatemala. Currently the purest and most traditional population.

Jun Ab Ku Supreme deity, the Heart of Hearts, the one, the unnameable. The only god that is manifest in everything.

Jun Ajpu One of the divine twins, the first demigods, like their older half-brothers Jun B'atz' and Jun Chowen. In the *Popol Vuh*, Jun Ajpu and his twin Ixb'alamke descended to Xib'alb'ay (the underworld) and passed the tests given to them. They then rose up into the sky and Jun Ajpu became Father Sun.

Jun Ajpu Utiw Coyote Hunter.

Jun Ajpu Wuch' Possum Hunter.

Jun B'atz' and Jun Chowen According to the *Popol Vuh*, the first two demigods, and Ixpiyakok's grandchildren. The allegory is that those of this first generation of humanity were great wizards and possessed awesome powers. Owing to their egoism and arrogance, they were turned into monkeys.

kab'awil Physical representation of any of the Mayan deities, whether in clay, wood, stone, jade, or metal (gold or silver). These representations are believed to have extraordinary powers. Some have a glyph. "The first to be carried out was the idol Tojil, in the care of B'alam K'itze'" (*Popol Vuh*).

Kaib'il B'alam Wise ruler who governed Zaculeu and fought off the conquistadors.

K'ajolom Infinite space consisting of the generating matrix that created and made the universe. One of the four creation deities in the *Popol Vuh*. *Alom* and *K'ajolom* are the makers and givers of life.

kalab'tun Numerical value for the seventh position in the vigesimal system, equal to a period of 160,000 years of 360 days each.

Kaminal Juyu' Ancient Mayan city and ceremonial center located in what is now Guatemala City. One of the first Mayan cities, according to our Grandfathers' tradition, called Tulan Zu. It is part of the Pocomam people's domain.

K'amol B'ey Community guides.

kan The macrospiral in which reality is manifest, within the spiral of *najt* (space-time). The energy where all of material reality is manifest.

Kanek Itzaj The last Mayan king of Tayasal in the department of Petén in northern Guatemala. He resisted Spanish domination, and his people remained true to Mayan traditions until 1780.

Kaqchikel One of the Mayan tribes. Along with the K'iche, they were the most organized at the time of the conquest.

Kaqulja' Literally, lightning. Deity that has various manifestations: *Rax Kaqulja'*, Green Lightning, is the manifestation of nature; *Chip Kaqulja'*, Micro or Small Lightning, is the divine spark; and *Nim Kaqulja'*, Great Lightning, is the strength or power of the Sky, Thunder.

kaxlan Literally, the white race of men. This originally referred to the Spanish conquistadors and came to refer to anyone who is not indigenous.

Kayala See *Paxil*.

k'exelon Midwife.

K'iche Currently the largest Mayan tribe, living in the departments of Quiché, Totonicapán, and Quetzaltenango, Guatemala. Like the other traditional tribes, they have preserved the majority of their traditions.

Kin Literally, the Sun. It represents the Father and has many manifestations.

Kin Chac Ahau Literally, Lord Red of the Sun. One of the titles used to refer to the Sun, represented by Kolop. Also spelled "Kinich Ahau." The reference to "red sun" is dusk, which struggles in the darkness and brings the light again.

Kinich Ahau See *Kin Chac Ahau*.

Kinich Kakmo One representation of Kin, the Sun.

kinichiltun Numerical value for the eighth position in the vigesimal system, equal to a period of 3.2 million years of 360 days each.

Kolop Literally, the rope or knot; that which binds or ties existence. One representation of Kin, the Sun. Also known by the titles Chac Ahau and Kin Chac Ahau.

Kukulkan The Plumed Serpent, also known as Quetzalcóatl and Q'uq'umatz. According to tradition, he was a spiritual guide who renewed the Aztecs' vision, forbade human sacrifice, and traveled south to spread his doctrine. He is recognized as one of the greatest avatars of humankind.

Kumarkaj Capital of the K'iche nation in the highlands of northwestern Guatemala. The name was changed to Utatlán and then to Santa Cruz del Quiché, as it is known today.

Lacandón Mayan tribe along the Mexico-Guatemala border and the Belize-Guatemala border. Along with the Dzensal, Chamula, and Tzotzil, the Lacandón are one of the most traditional people.

Laj Mam See *Maximón*.

Lubaantun Ancient Mayan city and ceremonial center located in southern Belize. The daughter of F. A. Mitchell-Hedges, a British adventurer, is said to have found the most famous of the crystal skulls here in 1926.

Madrid Codex Ancient Mayan hieroglyphic text that contains astrological and divinatory information. Split into two parts, they were reunited in 1888 and are now in the Museum of America in Madrid.

Majukutaj The third *B'alameb'* (Man-God), guardian of the North and the element Air.

Mam Literally, grandfather. Mam are the eldest, the Grandfathers, the original Maya. This tribe—located in the Guatemalan departments of Huehuetenango and San Marcos—and the Q'anjob'al are the oldest Mayan people. Mam spirituality is one of the purest and most traditional.

maq'uq' See *quetzal*.

Maximón An indigenous saint who originated with the Tzutujil tribe in Santiago Atitlán, Guatemala, and is now known throughout the world.

Mayan Cross A five-point cross consisting of five signs. The center is the day of birth, which defines the energy each person comes into the world with. Above is the conception sign, the energy under which a person is conceived. Father, mother, everything the person brings from previous lives, and his or her family genes are all imprinted at the moment of conception. Below is the destiny sign, or where a person must aim his or her life in order to grow. The right side speaks of the physical and material side of a person, while the left side determines the spiritual and emotional side. The combination of all five signs outlines a person's strengths and weaknesses.

Mayapán Ancient Mayan city and ceremonial center southeast of what is now Mérida, in the state of Yucatán, Mexico.

Mexica See *Aztec*.

Mopán Mayan tribe that was originally from Chichén Itzá, then inhabited central Belize and Petén in Guatemala, and now lives in southern Belize.

nahual   See *nawal*.

nahualism   See *nawalism*.

Nahuatl   The language of the Aztec and Toltec civilizations. Still spoken in central and western Mexico.

najt   Also known as *naj*, this is the Mayan concept used to determine space-time. In the Mayan way of thinking, there is no difference between time and space; one does not exist without the other. *Najt* is where so-called reality exists.

nawal   Spirit or energy; the power that animates the various days in the sacred *Cholq'ij* calendar. Because it is usually related to a reigning animal, *nawal* has been connected to the spirit of the animal that governs a sign.

nawalism   The ability of some people with extreme spiritual power to physically become the animal that governs their sign.

Nim Kaqulja'   One of the manifestations of the Lightning deity. *Nim* means "great" and *Kaqulja'* "breath of life." Thus, *Nim Kaqulja'* is the great breath of life, the power of nature, that which opens a portal to the next dimension.

nimaja   Literally, great house. This is where the Grandfathers' spiritual tradition is maintained. The *nimaja* is now what the *bujil* (Mayan pyramid) used to be: a place where ceremonies are held and *Chi-Mam* are consulted. Though they do not now possess the same splendor as in the Classic period, in the most traditional places the *nimaja* continue to function as they did in the past.

Oxlajuj Tiku'   Prophetic period consisting of 13 cycles of 52 years of 360 days each. Known as the Thirteen Heavens, or the Thirteen Lights. It is a period of abundance, peace, harmony, and spiritual development.

Pakal Botan   Known as Pakal the Great, Pakal Botan governed the Mayan city and ceremonial center of Palenque in Mexico. Literally, *pakal* means shield.

Palenque   One of the most important cities and ceremonial centers in the Mayan world. Made famous by archaeologist Alberto Ruz L'Huillier's discovery of the tomb of Pakal Botan, which offered a new perspective on the study of the Maya. Three more tombs of equal importance have recently been discovered and will shed new light on the age of the Mayan world.

Paris Codex   Ancient Mayan hieroglyphic text containing Mayan ritual and ceremonial information. Found in 1859 at the Bibliothèque Nationale in Paris and now housed at the Newberry Library of Chicago.

Paxil According to the Elders' oral tradition and stories in the *Popol Vuh*, Paxil, or Kayala, is a place of peace, harmony, and wisdom in the next dimension that exists in this reality. The great Elders have access to it through dimensional portals. According to the *Popol Vuh*, this is where the *ixim* (kernels of corn) were obtained to make this humanity. Paxil is similar to the lost paradise in the Judeo-Christian tradition.

Petén Vast department in northern Guatemala. Most of this territory is a forest that, sadly, is being destroyed out of greed for natural resources. This is where the early Mayan people, after leaving the Cuchumatanes Mountains, settled and founded various city-states, Tikal being the largest.

Petén Itzá A lake in the middle of the department of Petén in northern Guatemala. Also known as Petén Itzaj. Cradle of the Itzaj people, who founded the city of Tayasal, the last to be abandoned by the Maya.

piktun Numerical value for the sixth position in the vigesimal system, equal to a period of 8,000 years of 360 days each.

Pixom Q'aq'al The Sacred Pouch worn by *Chi-Mam* that identifies them as such. It contains the sacred seeds from the *tz'ite* (coral tree) that are used to cast a fortune or to divine and answer a person's questions. Perhaps the oldest divinatory art known to mankind, it is spoken of in the *Popol Vuh*.

Pocomam Mayan tribe in the highlands of eastern Guatemala.

pom Mayan incense known as copal, made from the resin of various aromatic trees. The *B'alameb'* (Men-Gods) offered *pom* to Father Sun so that he would shine again.

pop Mat that was used only by the highest dignitaries and was a symbol of power. *Popol* is the newer form of the word. Both are accepted by the Guatemalan Academy of Mayan Languages.

Popol Vuh Sacred book of the Maya K'iche. Known as the Mayan bible, it was also once called the *Pop Vuh*. It was transcribed into Latin script by the first indigenous people who learned that writing system after the Spanish conquest, copying from the original written in Mayan characters or glyphs. It tells the story of how the Maya arose, from the time they were made by the Creator and Maker right up until the time of the conquest. It is an epic tale of their coming to Mesoamerica, their god-heroes, and their sacred tradition.

pulsista Pulse-taker. A divinatory technique used by highly skilled *Chi-Mam*. It consists of taking a person's pulse at the wrist and thereby obtaining information about him or her. It includes a vision of the past, present, and future, particularly the most important moments in that person's life. Don Pascual Mendoza was one of the best-known practitioners of this technique.

Q'anjob'al Currently one of the most traditional Mayan tribes, having preserved all of their ancestors' knowledge. They are located in the department of Huehuetenango, northwestern Guatemala, cradle of this great civilization and the Mam tribe.

Q'eqchi' One of the most traditional Mayan tribes, living in the department of Alta Verapaz, Guatemala.

q'ij, or kin Numerical value for the first position in the vigesimal system, equal to a period of one day.

Q'uq'umatz See *Kukulkan*.

quetzal Bird that symbolizes freedom. Called the Plumed Serpent owing to its long, beautiful tail that undulates during flight, similar to the way a snake moves. It is associated with Kukulkan. The quetzal is the national bird of Guatemala.

Quetzalcóatl See *Kukulkan*.

Quiché See *K'iche*.

Quiriguá Ancient Mayan city and ceremonial center, located in the department of Izabal, Guatemala. Famous for its gigantic stelae, this is where Stela C is found.

Rajtz'uk Kaq'iq' The path of wind or air; the North.

Rajtz'uk Ya' The path of Water; the South.

Releb'al Q'ij Sunrise; the East.

Ri Laj Mam See *Maximón*.

Ruqajib'al Q'ij Sunset; the West.

Saq B'e Literally, the White Road. This is the sacred road that runs between one ceremonial center and another; the road used by *Chi-Mam* to take their knowledge elsewhere; and the road that followers must take with their guides. It is also the name used to refer to the Milky Way.

Saq Kan Tiku' Ceremonial site located in the department of Petén, Guatemala.

Saqtekaw According to the *Annals of the Kaqchikeles*, Saqtekaw was one of the first Fathers and Grandfathers who parted the waters and led the people across the sea from Tulán.

Stela C An enormous stone slab found in Quiriguá that mentions the *Ajaw* cycles, periods of 5,200 years, and records the Mayan date of creation, or year 0, as 13.0.0.0.0 4 *Ajaw* 8 *Kumku*, which corresponds to approximately August 12, 3113 BCE on the Gregorian calendar.

stelae The huge stones, carved with Mayan characters or glyphs, that were erected every *k'atun* (twenty years) and told of the most important events during this period. Some are as much as fifty feet high and three feet wide. They are found in every Mayan city or ceremonial center.

tab'al *Chi-Mam's* altar, the table where they place their *kab'awil* (idols and objects of power). Also refers to natural altars, usually places where there are large rocks that concentrate cosmic and telluric energy.

Tayasal Ancient Mayan city-state, cradle of the Itzaj tribe, and the last Mayan city to be abandoned according to the prophecy. Mythical kingdom of Kanek, the last Mayan king. Located on the shores of Lake Petén Itzá, in the department of Petén in northern Guatemala.

Tecpán Ancient Mayan city and ceremonial center located in El Salvador. Cradle of the Pipil tribe.

teos The universe.

Teotihuacán Ancient city northeast of what is now Mexico City. Perhaps the largest, most important Mayan site, it covers approximately eight square miles and had a population that made it one of the largest cities in the world at the time. Its Pyramid of the Sun is one of the largest structures of its type in the Western Hemisphere.

tetun Literally, stela. See *stelae*.

Tikal The largest and most majestic of the ancient Mayan cities, Tikal's magnificent buildings cover several square miles. It was the major center and is located in the department of Petén in northern Guatemala.

Tiku' See *B'olom Tiku'* and *Oxlajuj Tiku'*.

Tikutz'i' Divine law.

tixjob' Mayan planting stick used to make a hole in the soil where a seed can then be dropped.

Tlaxcaltec A nation of people in Mexico who allied themselves with the conquistador Hernán Cortés.

Tojil Idol in the *Popol Vuh* that possessed fire and gave it to humankind, but then the four *B'alameb'* (Men-Gods) put it out. It is the sacred ceremonial fire.

Toltec Civilization from northern Mexico that originated in the Guatemalan highlands.

Tonalamatl Aztec or Mexica calendar used in central Mexico and structured exactly like the sacred *Cholq'ij* calendar.

Tula or Tulán Literally, breast or mother's breast. Tula is the mythical place where the first Maya came from, to the east on the other side of the sea; according to the Elders, it was destroyed by a great cataclysm. In the Mayan tradition, various groups were sent to found the five Tulas. Those known of today are Tula of the North in the state of Hidalgo, Mexico, and Tulán Ziu, or Tulan Zu, in what is now Guatemala City.

Tula, Mexico Ancient city located near the contemporary town of Tula in the state of Hidalgo, Mexico. The Atlantes statues—four colossal warriors, some sixteen feet high—were found on top of a pyramid in Tula.

Tulum Ancient Mayan city and ceremonial center located on the seashore in the state of Quintana Roo, Mexico. The conquistadors found the first remains of the Mayan civilization in Tulum. The famous pyramid that overlooks the ocean is the only building of its kind on a beach. It is said that it was built there to remind the Maya of the land their ancestors came from across the ocean, the mythical Tula.

tun Numerical value for the third position in the vigesimal system, equal to a period of 360 days, or one Mayan year.

Tz'aqol The divine will that is manifest in nature, making it awake into action. With *K'ajolom*, *Alom*, and *B'itol*, one of the four creation deities in the *Popol Vuh*. *Tz'aqol* and *B'itol* are the Creator and Maker.

tz'ite The divine coral tree, the seeds of which are used to fill the *Pixom Q'aq'al* (Sacred Pouch) that *Chi-Mam* use for the divinatory arts. In some places, the *Pixom Q'aq'al* itself is called *tz'ite*. The trunk of this tree was also used to make the effigy of Maximón.

Tzob' Uxe' Ch'umil Name for the Pleiades, a cluster of stars that figures prominently in Mayan mythology and life. It is said that the four *B'alameb'* (Men-Gods) came from the Pleiades and that everything that exists originated there. The Four Hundred Boys who were killed by the deity Zipakna in the *Popol Vuh* rose up to form this constellation. There is a calendar based on the cycle of Pleiades.

Tzolkin See *Cholq'ij*.

Tzotzil Mayan tribe of central Chiapas, Mexico. Along with the Dzensal, Chamula, and Lacandón, they are the most traditional people in this region.

Tzutujil Mayan tribe located on the shores of Lake Atitlán in the highlands of Guatemala. Once warriors and very traditional. The worship of Maximón began with this tribe.

Uaxactun Ancient Mayan city and scientific center. The first Mayan observatory was built here. One of the oldest settlements, Uaxactun is located a few miles from Tikal in the department of Petén in northern Guatemala.

Uxmal Ancient Mayan site in the state of Yucatán, Mexico, west-southwest of Chichén Itzá and southwest of Mayapán.

vigesimal system Numeral system used by the Maya based on the number twenty. Also known as the base-twenty system.

Vukuk Kakix Deity representing Venus, father of the deities Cabrakan and Zipakna. According to the *Popol Vuh*, Vukuk Kakix thought it was as great as Heart of Sky and tricked people into believing it was the sun and the moon. Its punishment was to be made into the star that heralds their coming.

walking trees Humans are considered to have the same properties as trees and are thus poetically known as "walking trees."

Waq'xaqi Aq'ab'al Mythical mountain in the *Popol Vuh*, also known as Hacavitz, where the *B'alameb'* (Men-Gods) made offerings to ask Father Sun to come out.

Wayeb Five-day period at the end of a 360-day year when people looked inward and made offerings to Ajaw, the Great Father.

Wayeb Tiku' A period of nine years after one *Tiku'* cycle ends and another begins. Known as the gestation period.

winal Numerical value for the second position in the vigesimal system, equal to a period of twenty days, known as the Mayan month. Also refers to a human being—in other words, he who completed the twenty energies, or days.

Wuqub' Ajpu Another name in the *Popol Vuh* for one of the twin demigods, Ixb'alamke. See *Jun Ajpu* and *Ixb'alamke*.

Wuqub' Qak'ix The worst demon in the *Popol Vuh*; a symbol of arrogance. Also known as the Seven Sins because he is filled with pride, ambition, envy, lies, crimes, ingratitude, and ignorance.

Xahil A tribe within the Kaqchikel people that came with the others from

Tula. The Xahil were the ones who parted the sea with their magic staff in order to reach these lands.

Xib'alb'ay Literally, the underworld. Inhabited by beings who took refuge underground as a result of the cataclysms during the last Ice Age. The twin demigods Jun Ajpu and Ixb'alamke went down to Xib'alb'ay to pass the tests set by the lords who governed in darkness. After dying and being resuscitated, they rose up to the sky to become the Sun and the Moon, respectively. Influenced by the first Catholic priests who came with the conquistadors, some have mistakenly confused Xib'alb'ay with the Christian concept of hell.

Xukulem Mayan ceremony to be at peace with Ajaw, nature, and the cosmos.

Xukulem Chuwach Ri Qajaw Mayan ceremony to ask for good luck.

year bearer Reigning energy. There are five groups that contain four year bearers each, and these are the guardian regents for each year or cycle, no matter how big or small. That is, there is a year bearer for the *tun*, *k'atun*, *choltun*, *baktun*, and so on. The bearer is the reigning energy, the guardian, and the key to how a cycle will unfold. In the case of a Mayan sign, it is the pro-tector, guardian, and energy responsible for how a person, entity, country, and so on, grows and evolves.

Yucatec Language spoken in the Yucatán Peninsula in Mexico, Belize, and northern Guatemala.

Zaculeu Literally, White Land. Also known as Zakulew. An ancient Mayan city and ceremonial center, it is the cradle of the Mam kingdom in the state of Huehuetenango, northwestern Guatemala.

Zipakna One of the deities in the *Popol Vuh*. Son of Vukuk Kakix and brother of Cabrakan, he was very strong and would create mountains in a single night. Overly proud of his abilities, he was defeated by the divine twins Jun Ajpu and Ixb'alamke.

BIBLIOGRAPHY

Akabal, Don Isidro. N.d. "Fragments of a Lost Teaching." Unpublished.

Anales de los Xahiles (Annals of the Xahil). 1946. Translation and notes by Georges Raynaud, Miguel A. Asturias, and González Bolio. Ediciones de la Universidad Nacional Autónoma, Mexico.

The Annals of the Cakchiquels. 1967. Translated from the Cakchiquel Maya by Adrián Recinos and Delia Goetz. University of Oklahoma Press, Norman, OK.

Araujo, Rolando, and Hugo Solís. 1965. *I Chol Kin.* Universidad de Yucatán, Mérida, Mexico.

Barrios, Carlos. N.d. Oral stories from the Chi-Mam Elders Don Pascual Mendoza and Don Isidro Akabal. Notes compiled over more than twenty years.

Estrada Monroy, Agustín. 1973. *Popol Vuh: Empiezan las Historias del Origen de los Indios de esta Provincia de Guatemala.* Editorial José de Pineda Ibarra, Guatemala.

———. 2002. *Popol Vuh: Versión Actualizada, Basada en los Textos Quiché, Castellano y Anotaciones al Manuscrito de Fray Francisco Ximénez, o.p.* Editores Mexicanos Unidos, Mexico.

Girard, Rafael. 1982. *Los Mayas Eternos.* Biblioteca Maya Ojer Tzij, Guatemala.

———. 1996. *El Calendario Maya-Mexica.* Biblioteca Maya Ojer Tzij, Guatemala.

———. 1998. *Esoterismo en el Popol Vuh.* Biblioteca Maya Ojer Tzij, Guatemala.

Libro de Chilam Balam. 1955. Translated by Antonio Mediz Bolio. EDUCA, Costa Rica.

Libro de Chilam Balam de Chumayel. 1985. Prologue, introduction, and notes by Mercedes de la Garza. Translation from Mayan into Spanish by Antonio Mediz Bolio. Secretaría de Educación Pública, Mexico, D.F.

Popol Vuh: The Definitive Edition of the Mayan Book of the Dawn of Life and the Glories of Gods and Kings. 1996. Translated by Dennis Tedlock. Simon & Schuster, New York.

Squirru, Ludovica. 1998, 1999. *Horóscopo Chino.* Editorial Atlántida, Buenos Aires.

Title of the Lords of Totonicapán. 1967. Translated from the Quiché text into Spanish by Dionisio José Chonay. English version by Delia Goetz. University of Oklahoma Press, Norman, OK.

Xitumul, Mariano, and Gerardo Barrios. 1999. *Libro del Destino, El Efemérides.* Mayas Rabinal Achi, Guatemala.

SOURCES FOR ILLUSTRATIONS, DRAWINGS, AND MAPS

Freidel, David, Linda Schele, and Joy Parker. 1993. *Maya Cosmos: Three Thousand Years on the Shaman's Path*. William Morrow, New York.

Schele, Linda, and Mary Ellen Miller. 1986. *The Blood of Kings: Dynasty and Ritual in Maya Art*. George Braziller, New York.

Schmidt, Peter, Mercedes de la Garza, and Enrique Nalda. 1998. *Maya*. Rizzoli International.

Thompson, J. Erick. 1978. *Maya Hieroglyphic Writing*. University of Oklahoma Press, Norman, OK.